The UK Trader's Bible

The Complete Guide to Trading the UK Stock Market

by Dominic Connolly

HARRIMAN HOUSE LTD

3A Penns Road
Petersfield
Hampshire
GU32 2EW
GREAT BRITAIN

Tel: +44 (0)1730 233870
Fax: +44 (0)1730 233880
Email: enquiries@harriman-house.com
Website: www.harriman-house.com

First published in Great Britain in 2005
Reprinted 2007, 2010 and 2011

Copyright © Harriman House Ltd

The right of Dominic Connolly to be identified as author has been asserted
in accordance with the Copyright, Design and Patents Act 1988.

ISBN 978-1897597-392

British Library Cataloguing in Publication Data
A CIP catalogue record for this book can be obtained from the British Library.

Printed and bound by CPI, Antony Rowe.

Contents

Appendices   **293**

Index   **341**

Index of figures

Section 1

Section 2

Index of tables

Section 1

Section 2

About the author

During his career in the City, Dominic Connolly has worked for some of the most prestigious trading institutions in London. In 1990, he joined the index arbitrage, derivatives and program trading desk at Smith New Court, London's top market-maker, which pioneered the application of the equity contract for difference (CFD) product in the UK. He joined Bankers Trust in 1993, one of the powerhouses of the equity derivatives revolution, where he established the European equity arbitrage desk. In 1999, he joined GNI and was instrumental in establishing them as one of the premier providers of equity CFDs to both institutional and retail users.

During the period 1999 to 2003, the author's trading account returned a net return after all costs of over 1200%, predominantly through utilising CFDs to trade the UK market both long and short with leverage.

The author is currently director and head of CFDs at ING, the Dutch bank, insurer and financial services provider and remains an active investor.

Acknowledgements

This book would not have been possible without contributions from the following, all experts in their own individual field: Dr. Sally Bennett, Jonathan Cantouris, Robin Cave, Heather Connolly, Heath Dacre, Piers Dibben, Sam di Francesco, Eddie, Mark Freeman, Steve Gladstone, Algernon Hall, James Hoare, Ian Holden, Ed Laver, Lawrence Lever, James Lewis, Angus McCrone, Peter Minihan, Tim Nutter, Lee Oliver, Peter Osler, Nicola Paine, James Quinn, RAW, Paul Scott, Patrick Sherwen, Nick Slater, Simon 'Smudger' Smith, Nick Wardle, Leonard White, Andy Yates, and Stephen Eckett, whose idea the book originally was.

Screenshots reproduced with the permission of Bloomberg L.P.

Preface

What the book covers

The UK Trader's Bible aims to be an invaluable resource for all traders of the UK stock market. The book explains in detail:

- exactly how the various London Stock Exchange trading platforms operate;
- how to choose the best platform for a specific style of trading;
- who the major players are in the market;
- secrets from the dealing room;
- which are the best trading instruments to use;
- how to interpret Level 2 screens;
- how to interpret reported trades information;
- what traders should be doing at specific times throughout the trading day;
- how to interpret regulatory news announcements;
- the secrets behind market neutral, and arbitrage strategies;
- a definitive account of takeover procedures and regulations; plus
- many other trading opportunities including auction imbalances, seasonal effects, stock buybacks, dividend payments, directors' dealings, brokers' upgrades and downgrades and many more.

Who the book is for

The book has been written for UK stock traders of all levels. Having said that, the book does assume some basic knowledge of how markets work, and so some parts may not be immediately accessible to absolute beginners.

How the book is structured

The book is comprised of two main sections:

1. **How The UK Stock Market Works**

   This explains how the major trading platforms in the UK operate. This covers: SEAQ, SETS, SETSmm and SEATS Plus. The book stresses the importance of understanding how stocks trade, and why certain traders need direct market access. The section then goes on to explain how traders can use contracts for difference, spread betting and other instruments. Finally, there is an explanation of portfolio (basket) trading, and how this can affect the market.

2. **Trading Notes & Strategies**

   This starts with a detailed description of the trading day: what happens, and when. This is followed by an explanation of trading on margin. The rest of the section goes through the many market opportunities for an active trader, and describes how they can be exploited.

Supporting website

The website supporting this book can be found at:

www.harriman-house.com/tradersbible

Introduction

My introduction to the financial markets came about almost by chance. Although I graduated in Electronic Engineering in 1988, my first job was as a systems analyst at the London Stock Exchange – a decision influenced mainly by the fact that the London Stock Exchange paid a salary of £500 more than the going rate for graduates. In 1990, I responded to an advert in the *Financial Times* for trainee dealers at Smith New Court, the premier market maker later taken over by Merrill Lynch. I was offered an opportunity to work on the index arbitrage and derivatives desk with Gerald Freedman – widely acknowledged as the pioneer of equity CFDs in the UK.

From the moment I walked into Smith's dealing room for the first time, and experienced the rush of the stock market, I was hooked. Three years later, an opportunity arose to establish a European equity arbitrage desk at the derivatives powerhouse Bankers Trust. After that, in 1999, I joined GNI, an exchange-traded derivatives broker, which became one of London's foremost CFD providers.

My experience at a UK market maker, as a proprietary trader, and more recently at GNI, enabled me to learn at first hand how the market really works. I witnessed some incredible success stories – trading accounts that were opened with just a few thousand pounds and then turned into seven figure sums – and also the slow decimation of many novice traders.

I saw that the consistent winners were ex-market traders, especially those who were able to combine trading discipline with knowledge of the trading characteristics of certain stocks. A good fundamental knowledge didn't seem terribly important to trading profitability. The other successful individuals were those who brought a competitive advantage to the market. Almost without exception they would restrict their trading to a certain sector, or group of stocks that they understood. Often they had a professional background relevant to the stocks they were trading.

Those who lost money seemed to have no clear strategy and no clear competitive advantage. They approached the market as though it owed them a living. Demise was sometimes gradual – through a steady erosion of capital and conversion of equity into commission – or sudden, through an irrecoverable loss sustained from too large a leveraged position or poor trading discipline. There is a certain truth to the oft cited mantra at training courses that novice traders overwhelmingly lose their capital while learning their apprenticeship. Market professionals meanwhile have usually already served their apprenticeship risking an investments bank's capital rather than their own.

The combination of electronic trading, increased market accessibility through direct access, visibility and cost effective trading instruments such as contracts for difference, mean that it is now possible to trade for a living in the UK as many of my friends successfully do. The internet also allows the active trader to research situations 24/7, as well as in real time during the trading day, offering a competitive advantage. Not all price sensitive information reaches the market through the regulatory news services!

My own trading strategy has been to focus on market inefficiencies and special situations, often involving takeovers, which can be loosely categorised under the term *arbitrage*. Keeping a close eye on stake building, particularly by established savvy investors with a proven track record, can be rewarding and often results in later corporate activity.

There has been a quiet revolution in the financial markets in the UK over the last few years. This has been driven by the introduction of electronic trading and the growth of the internet. Despite this transformation making the stock market more accessible to a much wider audience, it became clear to me, during my time as Chief Strategist at GNI, that no clear reference work existed on the modern stock market. There was a great deal of information out there, but it didn't seem available in one place.

Thus, many people, while drawn to the market by this new accessibility and with a natural interest in trading and investing, are coming to the market without the benefit of the knowledge of the workings of the market taken for granted by market professionals.

The UK Trader's Bible aims to fill that gap and provide a basic explanation of the marketplace that all traders (and investors) need to know.

This book is not primarily about either of the two traditional methodologies for trading: fundamentals or technically-driven analysis. Its primary aim is to give the reader an insight into the workings of the modern UK stock market and what makes share prices move, as well as the opportunities the marketplace offers. Anyone who subscribes to the theory that a stock price reflects all the information currently in the public domain, simply doesn't understand how the market works.

I believe the book will be of interest not only to those who wish to trade the market full time, but also to anyone with a desire to interpret the nuances of the modern market and achieve a deeper understanding – both essential to mastering the financial markets.

Section 1

How The UK Stock Market Works

The Modern Stock Market

The markets

Main Market

More than 2000 companies are quoted on the Main Market of the London Stock Exchange known as the *UKLA Official List*. Joining is a two-stage process of having the company's securities:

1. admitted to the Official List by the UK Listing Authority, and also
2. admitted to trading by the Exchange.

Suspension of shares

Stocks can have their quote suspended for a number of reasons including:

- a breaking of the Listing Rules, such as failing to report financial results or failing to file accounts on time, or
- pending an announcement clarifying the company's financial position.

Generally a company must finalise its annual results within 120 days (four months) after the period to which it relates: for example, 29th April for companies with a year-end of 31st December in the preceding year.

Listing Rules do not stipulate a maximum time that a company's shares can remain suspended (AIM companies are de-listed automatically after six months), although the regulator can apply some discretion.

Effects of suspension on traders

Suspended stocks can be bad news, not just for traders who have capital locked into an unproductive position, but also for margin traders who are unable to release funds to deploy elsewhere.

CFD providers also have the right to mark CFD positions on suspended stocks to market based on their evaluation of what the stock is actually worth. So if a CFD provider believes a stock is worthless, the position may be marked down to zero, even if some residual value is later recouped and refunded to the client. In addition, the provider may mark long and short positions at different prices to provide some credit protection. This is what happened when Railtrack was suspended in September 2001 – long positions were arbitrarily marked-to-market at a lower price than short positions.

Stock Exchange rules do allow for occasional trading in suspended shares, for instance to allow a market maker to cover entitlements associated with a short-sold share.

Case study – Baltimore Technologies

During the battle for Baltimore between the incumbent management and shareholder activist Acquisitor Holdings (Bermuda) in 2004, there was a brief period at the end of April when there appeared a risk that Baltimore would be suspended and possibly de-listed. This was because Acquisitor had made a clerical error in filing its resolutions to appoint a new board and there was a risk that it would succeed in removing the existing board but fail in getting its own candidates appointed. This would leave Baltimore without any acting directors, resulting in an automatic suspension of the shares under UK Listing Rules.

In the end Acquisitor was forced to vote against one of its own resolutions to ensure an existing director remained as it would be difficult for a cash shell to regain its quote on the official market. Despite Baltimore being a cash shell with a cash balance equivalent to around 42p per share, the share sold off sharply as traders declined the opportunity to buy the stock cheaply because of the risk of committing capital to a position which they might be stuck in for some time.

Figure 1.1: Baltimore Technologies (BLM) – under threat of suspension

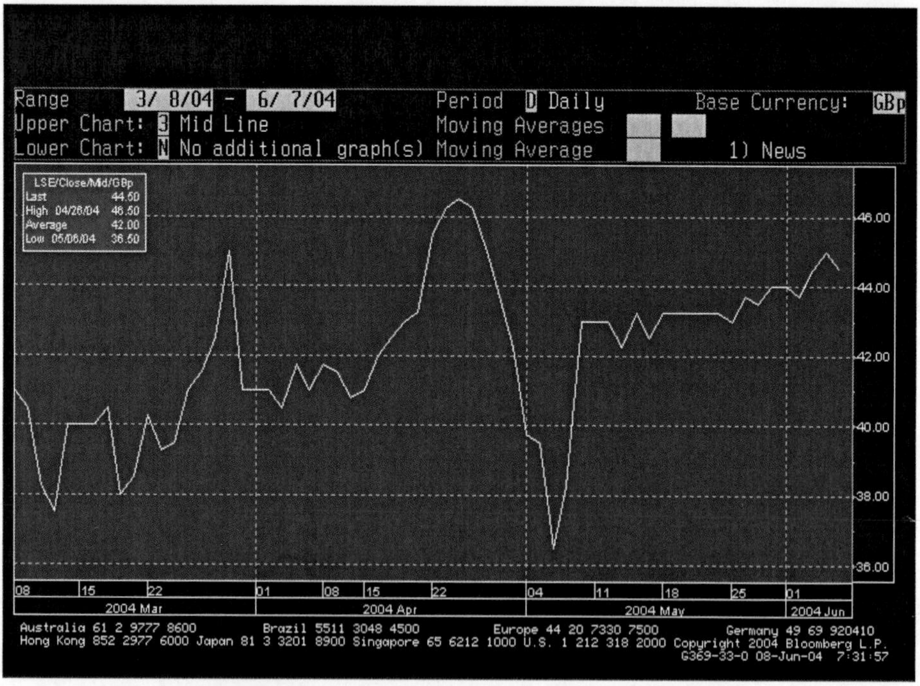

Used with permission from Bloomberg L.P.

Alternative Investment Market (AIM)

Over 1,400 companies (as of 31 January 2006) are currently traded on AIM and, since opening in 1995, more than 2,200 companies have been admitted.

It can be attractive for a new company to list on AIM rather than the Main Market, as the entry criteria are less rigorous. For example, there is no rule stipulating a minimum issue of shares to the public, or minimum market value for the company. But while listing may be quicker and easier, the disadvantage is that the stock may be priced at a discount to that which it might command on the Main Market.

Unlike the Official List there are no suitability criteria. All AIM companies must, however, retain a Nominated Adviser (*Nomad*, usually the company's broker). AIM is regulated and operated by the LSE rather than the FSA. Once a company has been on AIM for two years it can request admittance to the Main Market.

Admission from a Designated Market

If a company has had its securities traded on an AIM Designated Market for at least 18 months, it can apply to be admitted to AIM without having to publish an admission document. These Designated Markets are the main markets of:

- Australian Stock Exchange;
- Deutsche Borse;
- Euronext;
- Johannesburg Stock Exchange;
- NASDAQ;
- NYSE;
- Stockholmborsen;
- Swiss Exchange;
- Toronto Stock Exchange;
- UKLA Official List.

For example, in 2003 and 2004 many mining companies joined AIM by virtue of being listed on exchanges elsewhere.

Tax treatment of AIM stocks

Shares in AIM companies are treated as unquoted for tax purposes and capital gains tax can be reduced to as little as 10% after two years. However AIM stocks cannot be held in ISAs or PEPs, unless quoted elsewhere on the recognised exchange so there can occasionally be forced selling when a company moves down from the Main Market to AIM. Over 150 companies have moved down, mainly because of the lower costs associated with listing on AIM. AIM shares are classed as business assets, become free of inheritance tax after being held for two years and qualify for higher rates of CGT taper relief than main market stocks.

Reference

Further information on AIM can be found at:

London Stock Exchange: www.londonstockexchange.com

Aimquoted.com: www.aimquoted.com

One of the leading community websites for AIM information and news.

In addition to the London Stock Exchange, a number of junior alternative markets have started up.

Ofex

Plus Markets operates an equity market that trades more than 750 small and mid-cap stocks. Plus Markets' platform, the Plus service, now incorporates the 151 companies that were formerly quoted on Ofex, several hundred small and mid-cap companies quoted on the LSE and six AIM companies (due to be extended). Ofex was originally created in October 1995 and permitted LSE member firms to enter into matched bargains off-exchange in unquoted securities. Ofex itself floated on the AIM market in 2003, but in November 2004 shareholders backed a rescue plan that involved a refinancing and change of name to Plus Markets.

The Plus service is based on a competing market model (quote-driven system) in direct contrast to the LSE's drive towards electronic trading. There are currently four market makers in Ofex stocks: Hoodless Brennan, KBC Peel Hunt, Teather & Greenwood and Winterflood Securities. These four market makers, in addition to Cenkos Securities, also make markets in the other listed stocks on Plus.

Reference

Further information on Plus Markets and Ofex can be found at:

www.plusmarketsgroup.com

www.unquoted.co.uk

One of the leading websites for the discussion and exchange of information on Ofex st

ShareMark

Founded in June 2000, ShareMark is an internet-based facility for dealing in shares through regular auctions in around ten companies and is run by Aylesbury-based stockbroker, The Share Centre and its parent company, Share plc.

ShareMark allows dealings in shares also listed on AIM (such as Ringprop and Fountains) and Ofex. Listing costs are around £5,000 per year.

Reference

Sharemark: www.sharemark.com

535X

A new matched-bargain platform for unlisted PLCs, which takes its name from an old Stock Exchange rule that permitted off-Exchange trading. Five companies are currently signed up.

The market runs through 535X's website and allows FSA registered brokers to post best bids and offers, last traded price and market capitalisations. Investors may also view company news and announcements.

JP Jenkins Ltd

Established by JP Jenkins, the market-making firm that founded Ofex and launched in August 2003, potential investors need to instruct a stock broking firm to trade on their behalf. The website displays mid-price, share volume and last trade dates for over 90 unlisted public companies, including former listed refugees, with continuous trading on a matched bargain basis. The exchange is attractive for companies that have previously de-listed from AIM and the Official List.

Reference

JP Jenkins: www.jpjl.co.uk

London Stock Exchange trading platforms

The London Stock Exchange has recognised that because of issues such as liquidity, it is not appropriate to have the securities of both larger and smaller companies traded on the same platform.

Prior to 1997, UK companies were traded via a quote-driven, market making system, but since the introduction of electronic trading, the larger blue-chip companies have been traded electronically through an order book by price matching.

In all, there are five trading services for UK shares:

1. **SETS**
   An electronic limit order book for the top 205 UK stocks (as of March 2006), including the FTSE 100, UK FTSE Eurotop 300 stocks, those with traded options and FTSE reserve status.

2. **SEAQ**
   A quote display system used as the price reference point for telephone execution, between market makers and brokers for stocks with at least two registered market makers.

3. **SEAQ Crosses**
   Used infrequently but allows participants to match orders on the Exchange four times daily.

4. **SETSmm**
   A hybrid platform combining electronic order book trading with the support of market makers who provide continuous quotes to maintain liquidity at all times. This service was introduced in November 2003.

5. **SEATS Plus**

Used for less liquid UK stocks, with less than two UK market makers, known as *committed principals*.

A solid understanding of how the different platforms operate and the associated nuances of each are essential to trading the markets both efficiently and successfully.

Important listing rules

Until recently, companies on the Official List and AIM could simply de-list by serving their shareholders with twenty business days' notice, no vote was necessary. Now, however, AIM companies have to seek approval from 75% of shareholders before de-listing and the FSA is reviewing whether to adopt the same policy for companies listed on the Official List. Once a company has de-listed, the only option for shareholders is to approach the company secretary, register an intention to buy or sell, then wait for someone to match the indicated bid or offer. Institutions often get out before the companies go private. Once a stock has de-listed it must return within six months or face expulsion from the Official List.

Normally a free float of at least 25% is required for membership of the main market. If the free float falls below this level, the company is usually given six months grace before it is de-listed automatically, although the company can petition the FSA to be allowed to stay if it can demonstrate normal trading exists.

There are around 300 London Stock Exchange member firms, conducting over 100m bargains annually in the 2,700 companies currently quoted on the two markets supervised by the London Stock Exchange.

Retail Service Providers (RSPs)

There is also a *Retail Service Provider* (RSP) network, which allows member firms and in particular internet-based, execution-only stockbrokers to deal almost instantaneously with market makers while simultaneously achieving a price improvement.

Instant execution of small orders

BZW, Merrill Lynch and Winterflood originally developed the RSP system to release market makers from having to deal with multiple small orders. The RSP network allows automatic instantaneous execution of smaller orders, normally under the Normal Market Size (NMS), thus removing the manual process of phoning a market maker. Typically when you enter an order on an internet-based execution-only system like Comdirect or iDealing, you will receive a two-way quote valid for between 15 and 30 seconds. The broker will electronically poll the market makers with whom it has an existing relationship and the most competitive quote is reflected back to the client. Often there can be a further improvement on the quote when the trade is actually struck.

For example, if you see 1,000 shares trade at 428.73p with the SEAQ stock quoted at 420-430p on the screen, it will almost certainly be a retail buyer with the trade conducted through an RSP. The buyer has received an improvement on the displayed screen price by utilising an RSP while the broker has kept his overheads down by routing the trade electronically rather than manually processing the order. Although instantaneous dealing and a modest improvement on the screen price have been achieved, this still represents a wide bid-offer spread.

Brokers are very secretive about their RSP relationships but most have around 5-10 in place with RSP providers like:

- Credit Suisse First Boston;
- Dresdner Kleinwort Wasserstein;
- KBC Peel Hunt;
- Merrill Lynch;
- Shore Capital;
- Winterflood.

Comdirect currently claims seven and iDealing claims five, although they are all cagey about who they have signed up. More recently the London Stock Exchange has developed the RSP Gateway in an attempt to co-ordinate the matrix of RSPs. Beware that the RSP facility generally closes at 16.15.

Good for fast dealing in small quantities of SEAQ stocks

RSPs are excellent for fast dealing in small quantities of shares, particularly SEAQ stocks. For bigger orders, it is preferable to use the phone for SEAQ stocks and get your broker to talk directly to a market maker; also consider getting direct market access (DMA) for stocks traded on SETS and SETSmm if dealing at all frequently.

> *Note*: Even some of the execution-only brokers like iDealing have dealers who will approach the market makers directly by phone on your behalf. Use them.

RSPs do not offer the level of interaction that DMA does. It is excellent for instant dealing for those prepared to cross the bid-offer spread possibly because a stock is on the move or they want to buy it immediately and are not particularly price sensitive. But because it does not allow interaction with the SETS or SETSmm order books it is **difficult to place limit orders**.

The RSPs are cheap for the brokers to utilise as they are not manually intensive and, as automatic trades on SETS and SETSmm are for standard settlement only (T+3: trade date plus 3 business days) through CREST, they provide a means of execution when the client holds the stock in certificated form and therefore cannot trade it on the order book.

The RSP system handles around 96% of private investor trading (there are around 12 million retail transactions a year) by number of deals, although as the majority of them are of relatively small size, it represents a much smaller proportion of the overall turnover of the market.

The higher the percentage of the retail market that one particular broker can attract, the stronger his negotiating position with the market makers who want to see the flow of business, and the more likely the broker is to get improved prices from more market makers. Many execution-only brokers now advertise their strength on the number of relationships they have.

Institutional crossing

There are two main crossing networks for institutional investors and broker dealers:

1. POSIT (E-Crossnet was bought by and merged into POSIT in 2005);
2. LiquidNet.

Portfolio System for Institutional Trading (POSIT)

POSIT is operated by ITG Europe, which was established in 1998. ITG calls itself a *new generation agency stockbroker* using advanced technology to deliver enhanced trading performance to institutional investors and broker dealers. POSIT is effectively an *Electronic Communications Network* (ECN) bringing together buyers and sellers in an anonymous environment. Crossing always takes place at the middle price of the current bid and offer price displayed on the main market.

Although the system covers 8,000 listed stocks on the European markets, I use it mainly for UK stocks where there are eight daily matches. Around 200 European broker dealers, institutions and hedge funds use POSIT and orders can be submitted to ITG either by phone or via an electronic front end.

In the UK the crossings take place at 09.00, 09.30, 10.00, 11.00, 12.00, 14.00, 15.00 and 16.00.

How the crossing works

The example I give below is for a SEAQ stock where the process is more relevant and can offer an advantage – I trade SETS and SETSmm stocks via direct access.

Say a stock, Benchmark, is currently 244-247p in the underlying market and I have approached the market through my broker as a prospective buyer, but the stock is not currently available any cheaper than the screen offer of 247p. That in itself is disappointing as I usually expect to deal inside the spread. I phone my broker, who has a POSIT screen and ask him to submit an order to buy 10,000 Benchmark for the next crossing which happens to be at 11.00. POSIT is anonymous but also not transparent, so I cannot see if there are any other buyers or sellers in the system, you just place your order and wait and see. At the next uncrossing, between 11.00 and some random time before 11.04 (to avoid market manipulation of the quote), the uncrossing will run and match any orders at the current middle price, in this case 245.5p.

Some features of POSIT:

- It is **pointless submitting unrealistic limit orders** as they will always be executed at the uncrossing price if at all.
- POSIT **does not utilise the price discovery mechanism** used for the auctions on SETS that uncross at the price where most volume would be executed.
- There is **no time priority** so orders put in later than an earlier competing order are not disadvantaged.
- There is also **no price priority**, but there is size priority so if buyers and sellers are not equally weighted the order gets rationed out on a pro-rata basis.

A few minutes after the match has been run my broker calls to tell me whether my order has been filled. If it has not been, I can elect to leave my order in for all subsequent matches in the hope of a fill later in the day. The two sides to the transaction are charged 10 basis points (bps) each by POSIT, so in this case my buy order will go through at 245.75p and the seller will be filled at 245.26p.

Figure 1.2: Benchmark time (BMK) and sales printed on POSIT

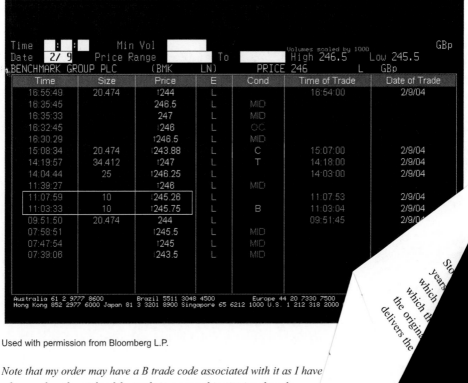

Used with permission from Bloomberg L.P.

Note that my order may have a B trade code associated with it as I have whereas the other side of the trade is a normal institutional trade.

I will then also pay my normal commission rate to my broker, but in this instance I did the trade as a CFD so there will be no further trade reporting or stamp duty payable. The broker simply holds the stock on his book and writes me a CFD.

> *Note*: Ask your broker if he has access to POSIT. If not, find one that does.

The London Stock Exchange operates a similar order-driven execution mechanism for SEAQ stocks called SEAQ Crosses (explained later).

Summary

To summarise, I have managed to complete a cost-effective trade in Benchmark, by dealing at the middle price, avoiding stamp duty and simultaneously establishing my long CFD position. POSIT is just another source of liquidity and although it is primarily for institutions there is no reason why the individual cannot get indirect access to it. I could also have done a short sell via a CFD so long as my broker can borrow the stock and deliver it on my behalf to the counter party that I have dealt with. The cost savings may sound modest but they really do add up for an active trader like myself.

Reference

ITG Europe: www.itgeurope.com

Stock lending and borrowing

The normal share trading market (often referred to as the *cash market*), CFD and stock lending markets all operate separately but are interrelated. The lending and borrowing of financial instruments is a well-established procedure, which operates within an organised framework, and is not limited to the equity markets. Most investment banks and CFD providers will have equity financing desks that take care of the requirements of the equity trading business.

Each day the financing desk will assess the firm's net position to maximise income.

- If the firm is **net short** in a stock and needs to deliver stock that it does not currently own, the stock borrowing desk will source the stock from a lender with whom it has an agreement, to deliver into the market on settlement day. All stock looks alike so the buyer will not see the difference between borrowed stock and ordinary stock.
- If the firm is **net long**, the bank may lend out that stock to attract a lending fee or to raise cash.

ck lending and borrowing is governed by standardised legal agreements that have evolved over the but the industry is moving towards the *Global Master Securities Lending Agreement* (GMSLA) standardises issues such as the treatment of corporate actions, defaults and non-delivery, under e signing parties are legally bound. Borrowing stock means the beneficial interest remains with l holder so the borrower does not have any economic risk until he actually shorts sells and borrowed stock to the buyer.

De-regulation led to an increased demand for borrowed stock

Stock lending facilitates liquidity and has evolved from the days when it simply allowed market makers to offer stock to the market when they were not in possession of it. Since the de-regulation of the market in 1997, and the introduction of electronic trading, there has been an increased demand for borrowed stock to satisfy short sales. When market makers lost their monopoly on stamp duty exemption and the borrowing of stock in 1997, other member firms were able to participate in the borrowing and lending of stock to satisfy the requirements of a CFD facility.

The rapid growth in the number of hedge funds adopting market neutral strategies (simultaneously buying one stock and short selling another) has also led to a big increase in the amount of stock lent.

Without an efficient borrowing and lending mechanism there would be a risk of market discontinuity. One could argue that decreased liquidity could put the index membership of some stocks at risk, particularly where the free float is limited, as index membership can be dependent on meeting certain liquidity criteria.

Beneficial rights on the stock remain with the lender

It is important to remember that when an institution lends stock to the market, subject to the terms of the agreement, legal title passes to the new owner of the stock and it is re-registered in their name. All beneficial rights relating to the stock, however, reside with the lender, including those associated with:

- corporate actions;
- dividends; and
- other rights pertaining to open offers.

Manufactured dividends are paid to the lender on the same day as the real dividend, and the lender retains the decision-making powers with regard to corporate actions. The stock will often be recalled at the time of EGMs or AGMs (which are subject to 21 days notice under UK law) and the borrower may need to find stock elsewhere to borrow to deliver. Therefore some stocks can be difficult to borrow around the time of corporate actions, takeovers, rights issues, tenders and important votes.

Stock is usually borrowed to satisfy existing sale obligations so it is rare for the borrower to retain the stock and to not sell it on. However, one week before British Land's AGM in 2002, the shareholder activist Laxey Partners borrowed 8% of the shares for the sole purpose of exercising the voting rights. This raises the issue of stock being borrowed not for the purposes that it was originally intended and the possibility of the votes being used against the wishes of the long-term holders. There is therefore a separation between the voting power of the shares and the economic risk, as borrowing stock does not expose the borrower to the performance of the shares, as his only obligation is to return the stock. This raises some corporate governance issues and with shareholder activism on the increase this may result in more frequent recalls of stock by the lender.

Settlement for borrowed stock

As settlement in the UK is T+3, the borrower will always have a minimum of three days to source stock before being *bought in* against. Quite often the borrower can procrastinate and there is sometimes a failure to deliver stock on settlement day. There is always strong demand for borrowed stock around corporate actions for this reason and a stock can become *tight*. The short position that developed in Room Service (see page 16) was complicated by the associated corporate action.

Stock lending

An institution lends stock to enhance income on its portfolio. The fee is expressed in terms of annual interest rates and the procedure is as follows:

The lender lends stock to the borrower and in return accepts collateral such as cash or government stock as security. The lender pays the borrower interest on his cash, but at a rate below base rates. So, if for instance current base rates are 4% and the borrowing fee is 0.5%, the stock lender will pay the borrower 3.5% on his cash. All figures are annualised interest rates. The higher the borrowing fee, the less interest the borrower receives on his cash. Blue chip UK stocks are cheap to borrow at below 25bps (annualised) but if a stock is in high demand, borrowing rates can climb so high that the interest rate becomes negative. For example, if the fee is 7% (annualised) and base rates are 4%, the borrower of stock actually deposits cash with the lender and effectively pays 3% on that cash to the lender of the stock! Collateral rates are usually set at around 105% of stock value and are marked-to-market daily.

Figure 1.3: Stock lending money flow diagram

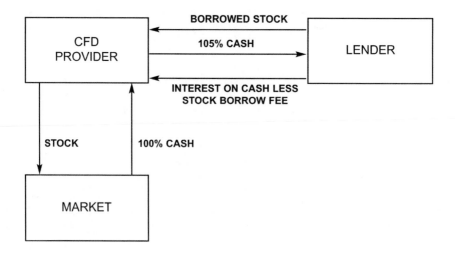

Stock lending is still regarded with suspicion by some institutions in the UK, where it is unfortunately associated with the Maxwell pensions scandal. Institutions are all too keen to suspend lending of stock in difficult market conditions, blaming short selling for market falls, while quietly resuming the practice when conditions improve. In the US there is a much greater general acceptance of it as a legitimate practice.

If hedge funds are suspected of short selling a stock during a rights issue, one way that long-term holders of the stock can help to support the stock is by recalling all lent stock.

Statistics on stock lending

The settlement organisation *CREST* (www.crestco.co.uk) publishes figures pertaining to lent stock but because not all borrowers and lenders participate in the statistics, and the figures are delayed by five working days and only supplied in aggregate, the figures do not represent a complete picture. Stock lent by institutions is only a crude proxy for short selling as one only implies the other, however the figures can give an indication of arbitrage or short selling activity.

> *Note*: Not all lent stock is necessarily used in short selling and it seems unwise to rely on figures that are incomplete. Stock may be borrowed as part of a more complex trade that may in fact have a net market neutral effect.

A better indication is available from Securities Finance Systems (SFS), which pools information from a consortium of lenders with more in-depth detail on price and activity. It also takes daily CREST data to express lent stock as a percentage of market capitalisation, showing how this has varied over time and its relation to corporate events. SFS was rebranded as Data Explorers (www.dataexplorers.co.uk) in April 2004.

Short selling often blamed for market falls

Blaming short selling for sharp market falls is an easy option, but as a recent report by ABN-AMRO found, usually the practice is pro-cyclical and there is no proven relationship.

My counter argument would be that if a stock is sold short heavily below fair value then that in turn offers an opportunity to the investor. The only problem that I think is valid is that if a company's business relationships are jeopardised by a low share price, an issue that is more pertinent than some may think. In other words, other companies stop trading with the company concerned and cancel orders because of worries over: the low share price; its commercial viability; its general financial condition; and ability to pay its bills. Often companies will experience an inflow of orders after a successful refinancing. Invensys secured a £2.7bn refinancing package in February 2004, alleviating customer worries over whether their supplier was still going to be around the following week, and encouraging customers to sign off on contracts which they were reluctant to do beforehand.

Stock lending is not necessarily an indication of naked short selling, as stock has to be borrowed for most arbitrage techniques. Stock lending figures can however offer a clue to a potential trade or arbitrage. The very existence of high demand for borrowing in a stock may alert the trader to a situation that he may not have been aware of. However some apparent arbitrages exist precisely because the cost of borrowing one side of the trade is prohibitively expensive.

Stock borrowing strategies

Typical strategies requiring access to borrowed stock include:

1. **Arbitrage opportunities across exchanges,** such as American Depositary Receipts (ADRs), against the underlying stock.
2. **Stocks which are dual listed but not fungible** (deliverable against each other) such as Anglo-Dutch companies Royal Dutch Shell, Reed Elsevier and Unilever.
3. **Stocks listed in foreign markets** such as SABMiller and Old Mutual which are listed on both the UK and South Africa stock exchanges.
4. Market neutral strategies such as **pairs trading and convertible arbitrage** where hedge funds buy the convertible share and short the underlying stock to capture the implied option value within the trade.
5. When **one company bids for another** in shares there is also an arbitrage opportunity between the two stocks leading to a demand for borrowed stock in the predator.

By and large the system works very well and I think that it is essential for a professional trader to be able to play stock movements in both directions – trading long and short are two sides of the same coin. Like anything, however, it can have shortcomings in extreme situations.

Occasional shortcomings – and the example of Room Service

In November 2003 it became clear that a market maker had built up a short position in excess of the total number of shares in issue of a small shell company called Room Service. There was uproar from investors but the situation was exacerbated by the stock being ramped up on a bulletin board and having a very small market capitalisation.

Market makers are obliged to make continual two-way prices; it isn't always realistic to check that a stock is borrowable every time that you may want to make a short sale. It would be relatively easy for a market maker to build up a big short position in relation to the market capitalisation of a small company if it was within trading limits. Of course, once a stock is suspended, it can be more difficult to deliver a stock as the stock can no longer be traded; normally there is a period of three days between trade and settlement to cover the position or secure a borrow and the market makers net position may have changed several times within that period. If this was deliberate, because they thought there was an impending rights issue where they could cover their commitments cheaply, then that is another issue entirely.

The conspiracy theorists thought there was a plot in the case of Room Service and the FSA did indeed later fine and censure both the market maker and head of market making. In practice, the level of communication between the front office and lending staff can be overestimated. If you checked a stock was borrowable every time you wanted to short sell it naked you would never deal. Normally, even if it isn't borrowable, there is often an opportunity to cover the position while failing on delivery for a few days. It is only when trading is suspended and a market maker is unable to cover his position for delivery that problems can arise.

Because big institutions lend out stock which might be re-registered with the new holder, adding up declared institutional holdings can be misleading, and could, in theory, add up to more than 100% of the number of shares in issue. This is because some institutions may have disclosed an 8% holding in a company and lent out 3% but not be obliged to inform the market of the effective reduction in its holding. The 3% holding may then appear in another shareholder's name.

I'm all for increased visibility, but additional taxation on short selling, or "grit in the system" as proposed by some, is a ludicrous proposal and goes against all my instincts. We are excessively taxed already and the stamp duty regime in the UK does nothing to improve stock liquidity, although the tax is now mainly optional due to financial engineering and CFDs. Stock lending is in the headlines because there is more of it going on, mainly due to the rapid growth in hedge funds and more sophisticated trading strategies. It certainly seems asymmetrical that long positions over 3% in a company must be disclosed under the Companies Act but not short positions of more than 3%.

Cross-border dividend tax arbitrage

Cross-border dividend tax arbitrage is now less extensive than it was, as the tax authorities have now tightened up the regulations, but equity swaps are often structured so that stock can be temporarily switched over the ex-dividend date to a foreign investor with a more beneficial tax status for UK dividend income under withholding tax rules. A UK investor may not want to hold a stock over an ex-dividend date when he can temporarily swap it to a foreign investor who may receive a higher net dividend due to withholding tax rules. Both sides will then split the difference, with the intermediary taking a small fee.

Scrip dividend arbitrage

Some companies, such as Rolls Royce and Standard Chartered, offer shareholders the opportunity to take shares in lieu of a dividend (often sceptically referred to as a mini rights issue). As the election date to decide whether to take up cash or shares is often up to a month after the date on which the exchange ratio is fixed, there is effectively a call option in the situation.

The opportunity is best illustrated by way of an example.

Example: Rolls Royce

Rolls Royce announced interim results on 31st July 2003, and declared a 3.18p net interim dividend and that the shares would trade *ex-dividend* on 15th October. If a holder of 10,000 shares elected to receive cash they would receive a dividend of £318. Alternatively, the holder could elect to receive shares in lieu of the dividend and the company, with reference to the share price, calculates the ratio that determines the number of shares received, over a set number of days.

In this example Rolls Royce used the closing share price of its shares on the five business days following the *ex*-dividend date, from 15th October to 21st October:

- 181.75p, 177.5p, 183.75p, 186.5p, 186.5p.

The average price over these days was calculated at 183.2p and subsequently used to calculate the ratio of shares namely:

```
3.18/183.2 = 0.0173
```

In other words, a holder of 10,000 shares could elect to receive 173 more shares instead of the dividend.

Not particularly exciting, you might think, but there is an option value in the scrip dividend because shareholders do not have to make a decision over whether to take cash or shares until a few weeks later, in December. If the stock weakens it wouldn't make sense to subscribe to the shares, however if the stock strengthens before decision day and trades over 183.2p then it becomes more attractive to subscribe for the scrip.

CFD providers and investment banks that have substantial long positions can often take advantage of this opportunity. A CFD provider may be net long of, say, 1.5m Rolls Royce shares over the ex-dividend date as a hedge against CFD contracts, and will pay its CFD clients the net dividend of 3.18p on the ex-dividend date, but will wait until the last moment before deciding whether to elect for cash or scrip. The risk can be completely removed by short selling the appropriate number of shares (i.e. selling the anticipated receivable scrip shares forward) during the fixing period and electing for stock if the shares are trading above the strike price on election day, or cash if trading below, and buying the shares back cheaper in the market. Often the firm will sell, say, half the appropriate number of shares during the five day fixing period, usually in the closing auction, to create a synthetic put option and buy stock back if it falls and sell more, up to 100% of the appropriate position, if it rises in the same way as an options trader would delta hedge an option.

Another possibility might be to borrow shares over the ex-dividend date in a *guaranteed cash* term deal with a stock lender, whereby the lender only requires the borrower to pass through the cash dividend. Lenders have now wised up to the scrip dividend trade however and the lending rate for stock in this situation is likely to be much higher, to reflect the opportunity in the situation than the normal UK blue-chip borrowing rates of between 10 and 35 basis points.

Foreign holders often cannot participate in rights issues and scrip dividends so UK institutions will borrow the stock over the scrip dividend period, subscribe for the shares and return the stock at a later date to the lender. The lender will receive a fee for his lent stock in the usual way.

Some companies, however, spoil the party by bringing forward the decision date on subscribing to the scrip, thus making the trade a *blind election* and hence much less attractive. This is known as a dividend reinvestment program (DRIP) where the company buys stock in the market in lieu of the dividend in contrast to the scrip option where the company issues new shares.

London Stock Exchange Trading Platforms

SETS

Introduced in 1997, SETS (Stock Exchange Electronic Trading Service) is the automated trading system for the largest companies quoted on the main list of the London Stock Exchange. Trades through SETS match buyers and sellers automatically, cutting out the need for a market maker, which theoretically means a narrower bid-offer spread.

The London Stock Exchange monitors key trading statistics quarterly and reviews whether individual stocks are on the appropriate trading system, although it is more proactive about adding stocks to SETS than taking them off. It also reviews tick sizes (0.25p, 0.5p, etc.) and normal market size for each stock. Changes generally take effect on the same day that FTSE constituent changes take effect. The Exchange also has discretion to add new issues such as IPOs directly onto SETS if appropriate.

Settlement for trades conducted on SETS are for standard settlement (T+3) on CREST, except for nil-paid rights, which are T+1. Trades in SETS securities that are for non-standard settlement must be executed off order book and agreed between counter parties.

Yellow strip

The yellow strip extracts the best bid and best offer to give a 'touch' price, colloquially known as the *touch*.

Level 1

Level 1 only provides basic information such as mid, best bid and best offer as well as opening prices and closing prices.

Level 2

Level 2 provides full market depth, competing quotes for SEAQ stocks and full order book depth for SETS stocks.

The SETS trading screen

A typical SETS Level 2 screen is displayed below.

Figure 1.4: SETS Level 2 screen shot

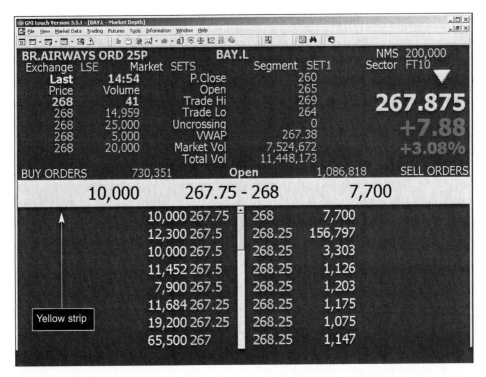

Used with permission from GNI touch®

The yellow strip displays the best bid and offer with the full market depth (or Level 2) below. On SETS, the full market depth consists of limit orders which are executed according to price and then time priority. If an order is amended it will be given a new time stamp and so move to the back of the queue of other orders at the same price. Orders are automatically included in the auction process so it is worth bearing in mind that the earlier you place a limit order the better placed you will be if the auction uncrosses at that exact price.

Note: Some Level 2 providers such as MoneyAM and ADVFN provide sophisticated Level 2 screens, which include colour coding and the ability to set tolerance levels to filter out orders a certain distance away from the current touch price.

Key features of SETS order book:

- **Best bid-offer price and size**: displayed on the yellow strip, and known as the *touch* (267.75-268p and 10,000 x 7,700).

- **Last five trades**: some systems display the associated trade code which can reveal if the trade was done *on-book* or *off-book*.

- **Last traded price including time and volume**: the last trade was 41 shares at 268p.

- **NMS**: normal market size (200K).

- **Company Name**: (British Airways).

- **TIDM**: Company code (BAY).

- **VWAP**: volume weighted average price for the trades conducted on the book (267.38p).

- **Total volume**: volume of all shares traded (11,448,173).

- **Market volume**: the ratio between total volume traded over the day and the percentage of that volume traded on the order book varies from stock to stock. If order book volume is less than 30% of the total volume, the trader should appreciate that a great deal of business is taking place *off-book* in which he cannot participate. Often these will be risk deals of a bigger size negotiated between institutions and principal traders (previously market makers) at investment banks, which are booked out later in the day, often after the close, with various trade codes indicating that the trades have been worked throughout the day. DMA traders generally find it much more attractive to trade stocks where a high proportion of the trades are conducted on the order book as they will be able to participate in, and influence, the order flow (7,524,672).

- **Previous day's close**: 260p.

- **Trade high and low**: 269p, 264p.

- **Total shares on bid and offer**: an unreliable indicator of future market direction (10,000 and 7,700)

- **Opening price**: 265.

- **Uncrossing price**: only applicable during the auction process (0p).

> *Tip: A later order which is input to the auction process at the exact price that the stock uncrosses at may not be filled if there are other residual orders at the same price ahead of it. Consider inputting buy orders with the smallest increment allowed for that stock over a round number, and sell orders with the smallest increment below a round number, typically 0.25p or 0.5p. I have seen many traders miss good fills by lazily inputting trades at round numbers, e.g. 440p instead of 440.25p and seen the auction uncross at 440p and miss an attractive trade. The same practice applies for trades placed on the order book during the day.*

Electronic order book trading offers a number of advantages over trading in SEAQ stocks. The key is to identify these and maximise them to your own advantage. Electronic trading is instantaneous and powerful – it only takes a mouse click. However, care must be taken as I regularly see traders erroneously inputting buys instead of sells, and vice versa. An order entered and executed in error can be reversed by agreement with the counter party but since trading is now anonymous – since the introduction of the Central Counterparty (CCP) (see page 28) – this will not happen often.

The trading day

The SETS trading day consists of three main trading periods:

Table 1.1: SETS daily trading timetable

07.50-08.00	Opening auction
08.00-16.30	Continuous trading
16.30-16.35	Closing auction

The opening and closing auctions are covered below. Continuous trading commences at 08.00, although 30 second random end times to the auction and auction extensions may mean that stocks enter continuous trading at slightly later times.

Trading SETS stocks

An order-driven trading platform

The introduction of SETS and order-driven electronic trading in October 1997 for the most liquid stocks, has made the market place much more attractive for outside participants, and resulted in a major shift in power away from the investment banks, to the individual. Many traders in the UK restrict themselves to trading only SETS stocks for this very reason.

Trading on European exchanges is now dominated by electronic order books, and although I trade predominantly UK stocks, many direct access platforms offer the facility to trade directly in the main European markets as well. Traders will tend to congregate at the point of best liquidity and although some exchanges like the London Stock Exchange have sought to capture liquidity by listing foreign stocks on their own market, the advantage currently resides firmly with the domestic exchange in its own marketplace.

There are around 205 stocks (March 2006) listed on SETS, including:

- all the blue-chip FTSE 100 stocks;
- the most liquid FTSE 250 stocks;
- equities with a LIFFE traded option;
- 29 ETFs; and
- some Euro-denominated Irish stocks.

The advantages of order-driven systems

One of the big advantages of order-driven trading is that by using direct market access (DMA) the participant has the ability to buy on the left side (the bid) and sell on the right side (the offer) without having to cross the bid-offer spread. Also, leaving opportunistic orders on either side of the order book, away from the current trading price, may benefit from badly handled orders, intra-day volatility or a 'fat-finger'. Although there are fewer spurious trades on SETS than there used to be, because dealing is only a mouse click away, errors do occur and if your order is in the order book at that time you stand to benefit. There are, however, risks to being rewarded for providing this liquidity: should any news come out that affects the individual stock or the market in general, you stand to be in the firing line of a sharp stock movement.

> *Note*: The advantages of the electronic order book to me seem neutralised if you do not use direct access. Trading through another company which makes its own prices seems like a move backwards towards the SEAQ system. With DMA you have an opportunity to buy at the low of the day and sell at the high of the day. This can never be done with a firm that makes risk prices to you as there will always be a spread.

Stop losses

Stop losses are also a contentious issue and notoriously hard to apply to an electronic order book, as they are reliant on sufficient liquidity being present at all times to provide a true market price. I am wary of using stop losses with a firm that makes its own prices as it strikes me that there is a potential conflict of interest.

The importance of understanding the trading profile of stocks

Different stocks have different price actions on SETS; some will be very liquid whereas others, such as Man Group and Next, are notoriously gappy. Many traders specialise in trading a list of stocks that they are familiar with and will recognise when the price action is unusual, say a large order being worked in the system that has yet to be printed. Amvescap is one of the most popular stocks to trade among UK traders as it usually offers a good daily trading range, volatility and close correlation with the US indices. It also has a high beta in relation to the US dollar.

SETS definitely provides a higher level of visibility to the participant than SEAQ, and gives them the opportunity to interact with the order book – to see as well as be seen. Traders all over the world can now make the price in Marks and Spencer in London rather than it being restricted to a few market makers with a franchise.

How to use Level 2

Level 2, however, has its limitations and due to the reporting regime – allowing the delay in the disclosure of large orders – I am sceptical of those who say they can 'read' Level 2. Level 2 prices are essential to be on equal terms with the rest of the market, and they are excellent for the timing of trade entries and exits once a possible trade has been identified.

> *Note*: I don't believe, however, that judging the future direction of a stock by the volume on the buy side or sell side is possible. Printed trades are real trades that have happened. Orders on the order book are trades that might happen sometime in the future.

What Level 2 can do is to identify gaps in the order book in which to place limit orders. If there is a large buy order at 290p and you wish to place a limit buy order, it makes sense to place it in front by the smallest increment allowed on the stock, say 290.25p. Similarly for a sell order – not enough traders take advantage of using an odd number such as 289.75p, instead they rather lazily join the round number offer price, at 290p for instance.

Some traders are convinced that tame institutions are represented by odd numbers of shares such as a buy order for 96,214 shares and market makers use round numbers. I'm afraid not. I use odd numbers all the time and a number of the DMA platforms allow you to fill in amounts in consideration to trade, and automatically calculates the number of shares for you, once the price field has been populated, often resulting in an odd number of shares.

Read the timestamp

Timestamps on orders on Level 2 can also give you an idea of how long the order has been present on the order book. Many orders are often reloaded automatically onto the order book day after day until executed.

Computer-driven trading

The fast, computerised order execution systems of today have encouraged the growth of electronic program trading. This type of trading can have quite an influence on the market.

Novice traders can waste lots of time watching or commenting constantly on 'fake' orders – large orders that are placed on the book but disappear miraculously as soon as they are in danger of actually trading, otherwise known as *spoofing*. Often, however, these orders are computer-driven against other contingent orders, such as a key level in another stock, and are working a particular ratio. They may also be arbitrage orders against ADRs or convertibles.

> *Note*: Dealers are far less interested in wasting time submitting and removing 'fake' orders during the day than the conspiracy theorists would believe.

It is possible to identify orders that have been worked over a particular time period, such as VWAP orders or WPA (see page 29) trades, and there can be a corresponding price move when that overhang is cleared.

The impact of electronic trading

Electronic trading will continue to evolve with new, advanced trading software based on algorithms and black box trading models, which can automate complex trading strategies and techniques. Traders in futures contracts are already complaining about the large numbers of *Automated Price Injection Models* (APIMs), which spray out large numbers of orders, clogging up the system during market moving events, like the release of key economic figures. The Exchanges are naturally reluctant to curb this source of liquidity (or *noise* as the traders call it) and rules do exist regarding their use. But the independents are complaining that the system is being slowed down by the large number of updates and is affecting their speed of execution in a fast market.

Even on SETS, it is easy to find automated trading systems that are programmed to jump onto the bid, or to be best offer, or to be second best bid. Touch prices can easily be manipulated by placing your own small orders within the touch price, thereby inducing automated systems to leap-frog your order to become best bid or best offer.

> *Note: Try changing the touch price on a SETSmm stock: you will find that some market makers' quotes will change automatically to be a certain distance from the touch.*

This trend is likely to continue: less manual intervention will be required and algorithmic systems will automatically execute complex trading strategies.

The Flipper

Another scheme is that operated by the likes of the so-called *Flipper*, the nickname given to a big player in the two-year German government bond future, the *Schatz* (traded on Eurex, the German-Swiss derivatives exchange), who places large, fake orders close to the existing touch price. Independent traders who trade short-term small moves like to rely on these orders as a cheap cut, as the price appears to be backed by big volume, but there have been accusations that The Flipper has been gaming the market.

For example, he will post a large buy or sell order close to the existing touch price, inducing other traders to join him in the belief that the price is backed by big volume. That's until The Flipper suddenly disappears off the bid, turns seller and hits all the locals who have been caught on the wrong side of the market.

Moving away from a risk-taking culture

The London market is continuing to evolve from a quote-driven structure that has encouraged a risk-taking culture with trades done in large blocks, to an electronic driven market where more transactions are carried out but deal sizes are smaller. Hedge funds can minimise market impact by feeding multiple orders onto the market, and institutions have recognised that they can reduce commissions by utilising the program trading desks at investment banks and execute several trades simultaneously rather than individually. This is because an institution can benefit from keener pricing if the portfolio to be switched is market neutral, in other words, cash neutral: selling a basket of stocks to buy another basket. If the trades were all done individually the risk price on each stock would be higher as there would be no offsetting trade.

Although there are now no official market makers in SETS securities, large trades can still be negotiated *off-book* between institutions and banks committing risk capital to the marketplace. This has preserved some of the risk-taking culture that has been endemic to London trading for so long, and reporting and publication privileges still exist to encourage this facility.

The electronic order book also makes the price formation process more transparent as prices are based on actual trades rather than on what a market maker's quote thinks they should be. The London Stock Exchange is always keen to point out that average bid-offer spreads have also reduced dramatically to less than 20 bps from over 70bps in 1997, although these figures are only meaningful if combined with the number of shares (liquidity) available at the touch price. But the real advantage of electronic trading is the breaking of the market makers' franchise and the ability to participate in the bid-offer spread.

Despite initial scepticism, particularly from those in whose interest it was to discount SETS (such as market makers in CFDs), there is no doubt that SETS has established itself as the primary source of liquidity and price discovery. Over six million trades are now being transacted on SETS every month, with average daily volume close to 300,000 trades.

Types of order

Market participants can enter five types of order onto SETS:

1. **Limit**: the most common type, specifies price and size and executes immediately if there is a price match, else it remains on the order book. The order may have an expiry date, but the Exchange deletes all orders where there is a corporate action to protect participants from leaving inappropriate orders on the book.
2. **At best**: executed immediately at the best price available.
3. **Fill or kill**: executed immediately in full or rejected. The order may include a limit price.
4. **Execute & eliminate**: similar to *at best* but with a price limit so that it is immediately matched down to the specified price with any unexecuted part rejected.
5. **Market**: unpriced orders which have maximum priority during the auction phase.

Icebergs

Iceberg functionality was introduced onto SETS and SETSmm in November 2003, although it is often confused with computer-driven trading.

Member firms were already using a type of iceberg functionality to disguise bigger orders by only submitting a part of a large order, which was automatically reloaded when the first part was executed. For example, if a firm wanted to sell 1m shares in EMI, but not reveal its intentions by placing the whole order on the order book, it might split the order up into 20 tranches of 50,000, only displaying 50K at a time, and reloading each time the 50K was executed.

The problem was that there was always a risk of missing a further trade execution between the time of execution of the first order and the subsequent reloading of another order, however quick the firm's computer-driven system was.

The London Stock Exchange introduced the iceberg feature to bring this functionality onto the actual order book itself, rather than having to be programmed into the firm's connectivity with the SETS system. Effectively the functionality is now available additionally at the Exchange level rather than just at the firm level. Iceberg orders are colloquially known as *reloaders*.

Placing an iceberg order

When an iceberg order is entered, the participant needs to specify the total order size and the peak size (the maximum to be displayed at any one time); the remainder is hidden from market view. The minimum peak size allowed is 10% of the NMS for that stock, to prevent multiple small orders and to provide some transparency. The iceberg function solves the problem of missing execution due to re-inputting a trade.

For example, previously, if you were bidding 545p for a stock in tranches of 10K and there was a bid behind you of 544p for 25K shares, and someone hit the market with an order to sell 35K at best, you would buy 10K at 545p, but before you had the chance to reload, the 544p bid would be filled as well. With the iceberg function, you always maintain price priority while only showing the peak. So in this example you would buy 35K and your order would leave 5K more showing on the bid at 545p. New iceberg peaks have a new timestamp and so lose time priority to another order at the same price.

If there are two icebergs at the same price, the peaks retain price priority between themselves. If an order comes in that is larger than the sum of the two peaks, then the balance is filled against the iceberg with the higher time priority.

Level 2 and hidden orders

Although Level 2 has brought a greater visibility to the market, it is important to understand the trade reporting and publication regime to realise that underlying price action can be driven by large trades that have yet to be printed. Although there are no formal market makers for SETS stocks, banks will still employ dealers to take on large trades, on risk or otherwise, on behalf of clients which are executed in parts and then booked on completion later.

Before the Central Counterparty (CCP) was introduced, one could check to discover the identity of the counterparty to a hidden or tranched order, by checking the details of a fill. Now the London Clearing House stands in the middle of all trades conducted on SETS.

Access to Level 2 will reveal many of the automated order entry and execution trading programs which allow dealers to leave the desk. There are a myriad of different rules that can be plugged in but some of the most common will react to either volume going through, or a change in the touch price. Orders can be hidden at the Exchange level (icebergs) or tranched in by the member firm. An order may be programmed so as to always best bid, second best bid or a certain increment away from the touch price. Other programs will execute a certain percentage of the volume going through the trade book, for instance as soon as 60,000 shares trade it will immediately sell 20,000 shares, subject to certain parameters, so as to execute 30% of the volume going through.

An understanding of the rules that an automated trade entry system is pursuing can allow the trader to influence its movements. The water can often be tested by moving orders within the order book or temporarily changing the touch price.

Trade reporting and publication

All trades conducted on the order book (*AT trades*) publish immediately, irrespective of size. Other trades conducted off SETS (*off book*) in SETS securities must be reported within three minutes of execution, subject to certain exemptions as detailed below.

Worked Principal Agreements (WPAs)

When a market maker has taken on a large position on risk in a SETS stock, he is afforded some protection from spoiling tactics from other market participants and is allowed a period of time to work the order before the trade is published. A *worked principal agreement* (WPA) is an agreement by a member firm to act as principal to trade a SETS stock at some point in the future. The trade size must be at least *eight times NMS* and once a WPA has been entered into, the dealer must attempt to improve either on the price or size agreed. The trade is colloquially known as a *whopper*.

Only the Exchange is initially notified that a WPA has been entered into and publication of the trade is delayed until 80% of the trade has been covered. If 80% of the trade has not been covered, the trade must nevertheless be reported by:

- market close, if the transaction was entered into **before 15.00**; or
- market close the following day, if entered into **after 15.00** (although the firm can apply to the London Stock Exchange for an extension).

If the WPA entered into is of a size of *75 times NMS* or more, publication can be delayed until market close the following business day.

A portfolio WPA can also be entered into but must contain at least 20 stocks, of which at least one must be a SETS stock. When the trades are eventually booked out they will be marked as *P trades*.

As an example, if Barclays share price was 495-497p with an NMS of 200K, a member firm could enter into a WPA to sell 1.6m shares on behalf of a client and would be able to work the order for a period of time before booking the trade. The trade could be filled in smaller amounts of say 50K and 100K on the order book before the whole 1.6m is later booked out and marked as a *WT trade*.

Volume Weighted Average Price (VWAP)

VWAP has become one of the primary benchmark measures of trade execution, partly because of the greater awareness among institutional investors of the importance of trading costs. Trading costs have a direct impact on fund performance and so the better the trade execution, the higher the fund is likely to feature in the investment league tables.

The calculation of current VWAP for any particular stock is relatively straightforward – the total consideration traded during the day so far divided by the number of shares traded. In other words, for each trade multiply the number of shares (shape) by the price at which it was traded, then add them all together and divide by the total number of shares traded. This gives an average price, weighted according to where the majority of the shares traded.

For example, if Vodafone had only traded five times so far as follows:

Table 1.2: VWAP calculation

No. of shares	Price	Consideration
10,000	140p	£14,000
20,000	140p	£28,000
20,000	130p	£26,000
50,000	125p	£62,500
15,000	145p	£21,750
115,000		**£152,250**

the VWAP would be:

$$152,250/115,000 = 132.39p$$

whereas the mean of the five trades is 136p.

Although VWAP is published by data vendors for every electronically traded stock in real time from the opening bell, usually only those trades that take place on the order book (AT trades) are included in the calculation and those transacted off-book (O trades) are ignored. This is because a broker executing a trade against VWAP cannot participate in orders executed off book or in-house elsewhere, and it is perhaps unfair to judge execution performance against something over which he has no control. Large agency crosses that may also distort VWAP are also usually omitted.

Ten years ago in the UK, VWAP was almost unheard of but the introduction of electronic trading and a growing awareness among institutional investors that a way of measuring trade execution performance was needed has led to it becoming an almost obsessive benchmark.

It also, superficially, neatly transfers the execution risk away from the institutional client; however there are some issues associated with VWAP execution.

Issues with VWAP execution

Placing a VWAP order, which means asking the broker to execute against the VWAP for that stock, seems to offer the client an additional level of comfort, rather than simply comparing an ordinary fill against the day's opening and closing price. A buy order filled below VWAP is generally viewed as a good thing, as is a sell order executed above VWAP. The reverse also applies. If a stock had opened at 140p, closed at 140p and you had given an instruction to buy a large line of stock throughout the day, and been filled at 138p, you may think this was a good fill. But if you later found the stock had actually traded for most of the day at 136p, with a daily VWAP of 136.5p, you might feel somewhat differently.

Clearly VWAP is not dissimilar to the view you get in the rear view mirror, and if a stock is trending down consistently throughout the day, the current VWAP will always be higher than the current stock price. Similarly if the stock is trending up all day, the VWAP will always be lower.

> *Note*: Do not fall into the trap, as I have seen many novice traders do, of thinking that you are entering a good trade simply because you are selling above, or buying below, VWAP.

A typical scenario might be where a designated broker is instructed to buy 10m Unilever and to execute the order against that day's VWAP. This will be a VWAP trade and, in the UK, will have a VW code associated with it when the trade is booked out. The larger VWAP trade will likely be the cumulative total of many smaller trades executed and printed earlier in the day. Many VWAP trades print after the close of normal trading when the booking out is done. However, daily VWAP is only one measure. VWAP can be calculated for any time interval, so another scenario might be to buy 3m Unilever between 09.30 and 11.30, again executing against VWAP, this time for a two-hour interval. As a measure of performance, the client will compare the price that the broker fills him at with the VWAP for the relevant period. The broker will have completed the trade in tranches, or blocks, spread out over the period so as to match the target VWAP as closely as possible. It is very easy to calculate VWAP for a particular time period for a particular stock on some of the more advanced information systems, such as the AQR function on Bloomberg.

Trade activity during the day varies, with higher volumes during the morning and afternoon session (as the US markets open) and lower volumes during lunchtime and pre-US opening. A great deal of activity now also takes place during the closing auction, particularly when index re-weightings are taking place.

Figure 1.5: Intra-day volume for SETS stocks

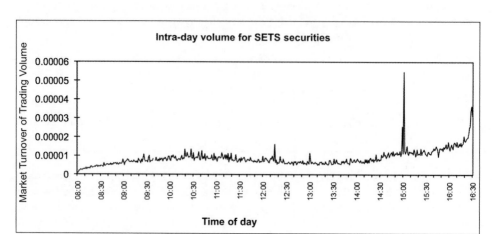

Source: Charlie x. Cai, Robert Hudson and Kevin Keasey of University of Leeds

Note: The peak in volume at 15.00 is due to the release of some key US economic figures.

Execution performance against the VWAP benchmark is usually measured in terms of a few basis points; however there can be problems. If the trader executing a VWAP order represents a large proportion of the day's total volume, the VWAP itself will be influenced by his participation; indeed, large scale VWAP trading throughout the marketplace will affect the VWAP itself. (You can see the dangers of this calculation becoming rather circular!) A broker may consistently deliver excellent trade fills to his client under a VWAP methodology, but as soon as his influence in the marketplace has disappeared, his performance against the next day's share price movement may be poor. In other words, his execution looks good at first glance because he has influenced the VWAP for the day himself, but once free of his influence, the price reverts to its normal trading range.

The industry risks ignoring some of the problems associated with VWAP execution in an effort to embrace the comfort of an order conducted on VWAP principles; VWAP is not necessarily the Holy Grail of broker performance attainment. The situation is not dissimilar to that which exists in index tracking. Passive investment transfers the performance risk from the investment manager, but the mechanism itself is open to abuse. Although less prevalent these days, tracking funds were regularly 'legged over' by proprietary traders who knew that there would be a large buy or sell order in the closing auction on the day that the stock was due to enter or leave an index and took advantage.

Portfolios can also be traded around VWAP, hence the simultaneous booking of large numbers of trades (basket trades) often with some very small shapes. Other large VWAP orders may take place over several days resulting in a stock trading in a narrow range (i.e. the VWAP executor keeps selling when the price rises and buying when it falls).

In effect, VWAP traders seek to execute a large order throughout the day without the risks associated with affecting the trade at one particular time. A good VWAP trader will know the share price action of the stocks that he trades and trade according to prevailing liquidity. He will have to balance the risks of crossing the bid-offer spread to get the order done, against the probability of getting hit on the bid with a buy order, or lifted on the offer with a sell order at a later time. He will only execute large chunks if the price is favourable and he has not left himself exposed to trading ahead of himself. If he has executed 5m shares of a 10m VWAP order before half the day's trading volume has occurred he leaves himself open to a price move against him that may not be recoverable.

Note that when VW trades are printed, they represent the booking out of several trades conducted earlier in the relevant time period and are aggregated. As such they are not good indicators of future price movement, rather confirmation of earlier volume.

VWAP also anaesthetises the good trader's skill as his performance is now based against only one benchmark – VWAP. For the reasons discussed above, it doesn't necessarily show a good fill, particularly if there is discretion over the cancelling of trades or postponement to another day in the event of a sharp price move.

SEAQ

The majority of small to mid-cap UK companies, currently numbering 1,946 quoted securities (March 2006), including AIM stocks, still trade under the market making system of competing quotes called the Stock Exchange Automated Quotation (SEAQ).

Order-driven systems not suitable for small stocks

Until the introduction of electronic order-driven trading in 1997, all UK stocks traded under this system, and although it is generally accepted that SETS is a better system for blue-chip, liquid shares, the poor liquidity of smaller company shares makes them unsuitable for trading on an order book. Electronic order books work very well for high volume, high liquidity blue-chip stocks, but are dependent on participants submitting orders to build a good market depth. It is counter productive if a company's shares have no orders displayed for hours at a time and hence no real reference price. With a quote driven-system, although the bid-offer spread may be wide, there will always be a reference price, so that at the very least RSPs will be able to execute orders.

Many modern, active traders are wary of trading SEAQ stocks and restrict themselves to specialising in order book stocks, whereas other UK traders are SEAQ specialists relishing the challenge of dealing against a market maker.

Note: There is no doubt that trading a stock on SEAQ is very different from trading a SETS stock, and the price action between stocks can vary significantly depending on the platform they are traded on.

The liquidity in a SEAQ stock is dependent on the number of market makers and the risk capital available. The smaller the company, the fewer market makers there are likely to be and the more likely that a small order will affect the share price.

Some features of SEAQ trades:

- **Usually executed by telephone**, with a broker approaching the market maker by phone on the Stock Exchange internal telephone exchange (STX).
- **RSPs are utilised for 90% of trades**, but these are the smaller trades, normally below NMS.
- **Each stock must have at least two market makers** but there is no maximum number.

SEAQ Level 2 Screen

A typical SEAQ Level 2 screen is shown below.

Figure 1.6: SEAQ Level 2 screen shot

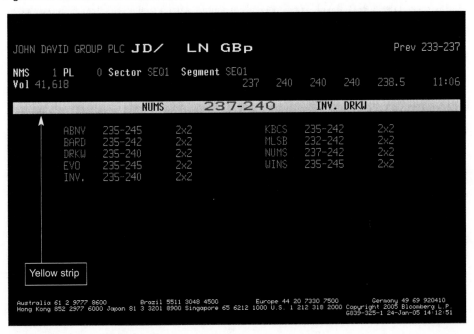

Used with permission from Bloomberg L.P.

The screen can be split into two halves; above and below the distinctive yellow strip.

Lower part of screen

The lower part of the screen incorporates the full market depth, or *Level 2*, displaying each market maker on a separate line in alphabetical order. Each market maker will have a:

1. **mnemonic** (e.g. WINS is Winterflood);
2. **two-way price** (to buy and sell);
3. **minimum size** his quote is good for (2,000 shares in this case); and
4. the **time that the quote was last revised** (not shown in this shot but provided by some vendors).

(A list of market maker mnemonics is included in the Appendices.)

In this case, Numis (NUMS) is making the most competitive bid for stock at 237p and Investec and Dresdner are offering the cheapest stock at 240p.

Upper part of screen

The top half of the screen contains additional information such as the previous day's closing quote, shown here as 233-237p in the top right – so we can see that the stock is trading up on the day slightly. On the left, NMS (1000) is displayed, next to the publication limit (PL) and also which sector classification the stock belongs to (Smaller Companies) and the means of trading (SEAQ).

Below that is the:

1. **total traded volume** (41,618) reported so far (remember, publication of some trades may be delayed);
2. **recent trades** with trade code, the most recent being at 238.5p, on the far right with a time stamp (11.06); and
3. **stock code**, or Tradeable Instrument Display Mnemonic (TIDM) – previously known as an EPIC code – is at the top, and in this example is JD (John David Group Plc).

Other key features include the day's high and low traded price, and opening price for the stock. The *publication limit* is normally a multiple of the NMS but is zero in this case, suggesting that the stock may be in an offer period, as defined by the Takeover Panel, requiring all trades to be published immediately.

A *backwardation* occurs when a bid is higher than an offer, and the yellow strip turns red. This only happens in SEAQ stocks when changes in market maker prices happen so quickly, usually on a profits warning or similar event, that one or more market makers get left behind. A backwardation never happens for SETS or SETSmm stocks as there would be automatic instantaneous execution.

Figure 1.7: Sanctuary Group (SGP) – stock in backwardation on breaking news

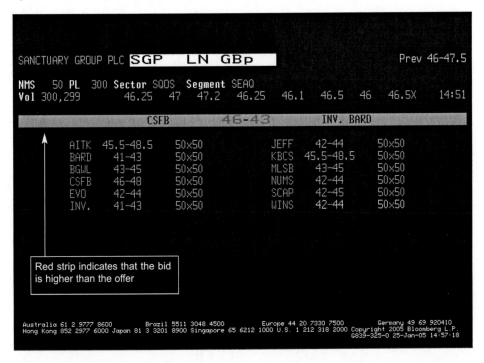

Used with permission from Bloomberg L.P.

When the best bid and offer are the same, the touch price is referred to as *choice*. The screen shot below shows the same stock (Sanctuary Group) with a *choice price* – often only a temporary phenomenon. This situation will not last long as the London Stock Exchange Rulebook requires the two market makers making the touch price to trade with each other at the earliest opportunity and adjust their prices accordingly.

Figure 1.8: Sanctuary Group (SGP) – Level 2 choice price

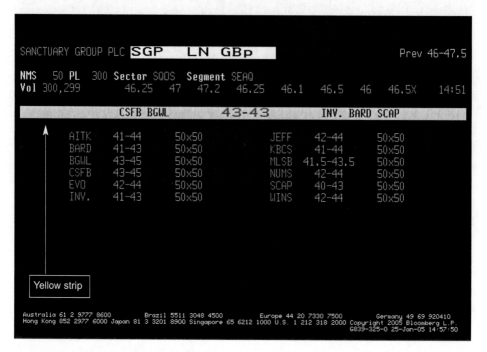

Used with permission from Bloomberg L.P.

Can Level 2 forecast stock movements?

Level 2 offers key price information to an active investor and help in the timing of trade entry and exit points. However, I am sceptical of its value in signalling the possible future direction of a stock.

Like the chart of a share price, I believe Level 2 is an essential tool; I simply don't instigate trades based on the information available on Level 2. Once I have a trade idea, though, I will usually check Level 2 before trading. Level 2 gives me an indication of:

1. how many market makers there are in the stock;
2. whether the current spread is representative (i.e. 295-296p might look attractive until all the quotes change to a more normal 290-300p); and
3. the time when each market maker's quote last changed.

The information on the screen cannot tell you what else is going on behind the scenes, such as whether:

- large orders are being worked that have not yet been published;
- the market is net long or short of a stock;
- a stock is being moved around on no trading volume; or
- two market makers are co-operating or trying to make things difficult for each other.

There may be a residual long or short position in the market from the previous trading day or a large order being worked over several days. It also can't tell you whether a market making firm is net long or short from the previous day's or week's trading.

> *Note*: Features on websites that try to categorise individual trades as buys or sells are suspect not just because trade publication can be delayed, but because portfolio trades, for example, are often printed at middle prices to avoid disclosing whether the stock is coming into or out of the market. Adding together printed buy and sell orders to judge a stock's future move is pointless.

Level 2 information should be taken in context.

If, for instance, there is only one market maker on the bid and five on the offer *this is not necessarily any indication of the future direction of the stock.*

Time stamps can be of some assistance, enabling you to judge which was the last market maker to change his price, but in any given stock some market makers shuffle down automatically whereas others actually do have significant flow and are adjusting their prices accordingly. The market maker on the bid in the SEAQ Level 2 screen shot may or may not be a big buyer, in fact he is just as likely to be a seller; maybe he is holding the stock up. Sure, he is obliged to buy 2,000 if he is challenged by a broker or another market maker, but if he is trying to place say 100K shares on behalf of a client, that may be a cheap option while making the market price look firmer.

Normal Market Size (NMS)

Each stock has an NMS associated with it, which is assigned by the London Stock Exchange based on the value of shares traded in the last twelve months. The NMS classifications are reviewed quarterly and the most common bands are:

200K, 150K, 100K, 75K, 50K, 25K, 15K, 10K, 5K, 3K, 2K, 1K, 500 and 100 shares.

The NMS is the minimum quote size which market makers are obliged to trade in if challenged by another market maker, and are also used as the basis for determining the threshold for delayed publication of larger trades. All SETS stocks also have an associated NMS which is used to determine publication limits.

Some market makers can register as *reduced size market makers*, which means that they can display prices in a size below NMS.

Despite being reviewed quarterly, NMS classifications can be inappropriate for a stock which may have much better liquidity than the NMS suggests. Many of the bigger firms are quite comfortable making a two-way market in excess of NMS. If you are trading a stock regularly, it will soon become clear if there is more liquidity in a stock than suggested by the headline NMS.

Market maker obligations

Market makers are obliged to offer continuous buy and sell prices between 08.00 and 16.30 (the *mandatory quote period*).

A market maker may quote a larger size than NMS so, for example, although the NMS is 5,000, his price to a broker dealer, should he wish, might be firm for 50,000 shares. This means that:

- if a broker calls the market maker on behalf of a client *acting as agent*, the market maker is **obliged to deal** in a minimum of his quote size;
- if the market maker is approached by another member firm that is acting in a *proprietary capacity*, in other words trading for himself, then the market maker is **not obliged to deal**.

This is an important point for those traders utilising a CFD provider which hedges all its transactions in the cash market, as, in the eyes of the marketplace, the CFD provider is acting as principal because the stock never transfers to the client. It stays on the CFD broker's book as a hedge against the CFD he has written the client. The market maker can decline to deal if the broker is buying stock as a hedge against a CFD, whereas if the broker is acting for his client as agent in a normal transaction, the obligation stands. Be aware that when trading CFDs, this may mean that you could miss a price that you would be entitled to when dealing 'agency' i.e. trading normal shares.

Market makers can challenge each other as long as their respective screen prices are different, but are only obliged to deal in the NMS. Trades executed between market makers are marked with an 'M' code.

Rules of engagement

There are certain rules of conduct between broker dealers and market makers that many traders may not at first be aware of.

- Just because a SEAQ screen may display six different market makers all offering 20K shares at 120p, does not mean that your broker can go round and buy 120K simultaneously – 20K from each market maker. The broker is required to inform the market maker of the whole size of the order if he approaches him to transact a part of it. The market maker will always want to see the full transaction as a split order or multiple orders can ruin his opportunity to cover the position.
- Even if the broker dealer has got through to the market maker on the telephone he may be unable to deal if the market maker declares *dealer in front*. In other words, he is currently quoting that stock to another member firm, or has executed a trade and has not had a reasonable opportunity to change his price. The situation can be further complicated if the broker dealer receives two orders in the same stock in the same direction from two different clients, typically momentum traders.

- The market maker is only obliged to quote in one stock per single phone call, although the broker dealer can get another stock quoted if the market maker calls *dealer in front*.

- If a broker executes a trade with a market maker in a size larger than the displayed quote, then the broker is obliged to offer any subsequent business in that security of greater size than NMS to the same market maker.

- A market maker that has business disclosed to it by an enquiring member firm, but does not complete the transaction, should not prejudice that transaction for at least three minutes. He may offer 'protection' (see later) and send him on.

- A broker dealer (member firm that is not a market maker) proposing to execute an agency cross, or riskless principal trade at, or outside, the best price displayed by a market maker, must give the market maker displaying the best price in the nearest size the opportunity of participating in the trade to level his book or fill any later orders that he is working. Regardless, the market maker is entitled to participate at the indicated dealing price up to the NMS.

- When a market maker is going round the market, he may engage the help of several dealers so that he can make several calls at once, but his displayed price must be different. If this has happened it will be in evidence on the screen as several M codes will be appended to trades, normally in the NMS and printed in quick succession.

- Orders left with a market maker: if the market maker moves his bid price to the same level as a sell order left with him, or his offer to a buy order, he is obliged to deal at that price.

The ongoing relationship between broker and market maker is key and should be borne in mind by the client who may be trying to execute an opportunistic trade or 'pick-off' a market maker.

Price and size

Market maker etiquette demands that the broker only shows an order at one place rather than going round the market executing a 50,000 order in 5 clips of 10,000. Not enough traders take full advantage of their brokers when handling bigger orders, as price improvement can be a matter of skilful negotiation.

Generally speaking, a market maker will make a wider price for a bigger order that he will be taking on risk. For instance, if a stock was showing 290-295p on the screen with an NMS of 25,000 the market maker might be prepared to make that price in the NMS or in the size that he is displaying. The broker might ask for a price in a bigger size, with or without disclosing whether he was a buyer or seller. The market maker might say:

- "290-295p in 25K";
- "288-296p in 50K"; or
- "286-296p in 100K",

depending on his existing position (the prices in this example strongly suggest that he is a seller by choice), any business he may have on, and the liquidity of the stock.

'Going round the market and M trades'

A number of momentum traders specialise in tracking M (market maker) trades throughout the trading day, but they are inevitably unpopular with market makers. There will always be an inherent conflict of interest between market makers and short-term traders:

- *Market makers* want large tame institutional orders to 'work'.
- *Short-term traders* want to buy something that is on the move but refuse to accept (or choose to ignore) that, unlike an order-driven system, there will always be a lag between actual trading and screen prices.

A stock can rise all day for no apparent reason – then, when the trade that has been worked all day by the market maker gets trade-reported very late, all becomes clear. Scanning the market for M trades can easily be done on websites such as ADVFN (www.advfn.co.uk) and MoneyAM (www.moneyam.co.uk). The theory is that if one market maker is prepared to deal with another either directly, or anonymously, the current screen price will change to reflect the new level that the stock is trading at.

In the coming example, just prior to this screen shot being taken, CES Software was quoted at 192-193p. A market maker, who was on the offer, then went round the market and sold two lots of 5,000 at 192p by challenging the market makers who were on the bid, and the price quickly sagged to 190-193p as other market makers shuffled their prices down. The two M trades can be seen on the trade ticker at the top.

Momentum traders wait for these trades to go through then send their brokers into the market to try and get the screen price before it changes. Needless to say, the strategy isn't popular with the market makers and can ruin relations between brokers and market makers, to the detriment of other clients. However, it is not unknown for market makers to print M trades deliberately for that reason between themselves to create a smoke screen.

Figure 1.9: M trades in a SEAQ stock

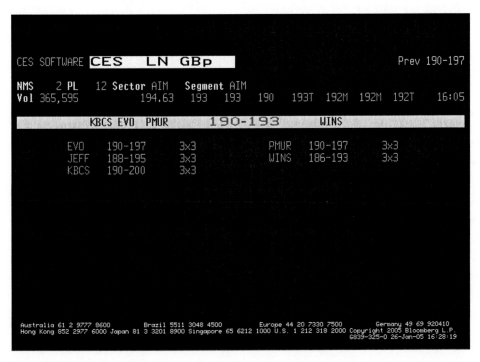

Used with permission from Bloomberg L.P.

Trade reporting and publication

Trades can be reported from 07.15 until 17.15 and although the mandatory quote period is from 08.00 until 16.30, market makers will sometimes open their screen quotes early, from 07.15 onwards, although they are indicative prices only. Therefore it is possible to request a broker to deal by phone with a market maker before 08.00, although the market maker is not obliged to trade.

Similarly, quotes are indicative from 16.30 until 17.15 when SEAQ closes.

Normal trades must be reported within three minutes of execution or a fining system operates. Publication of larger trades will be delayed to protect the risk taker, as detailed later.

For SEAQ stocks, market makers enjoy delayed publication of larger trades to protect their position and the risk capital that they deploy.

Protected or 'worked' trades

Working a trade

Orders of any size can be left with a market maker to *work* and the trade will not be reported until the transaction is complete or towards market close, whichever is earlier, when there is no further delay in publication. The client may be protected in a certain minimum size at a certain price on the understanding that the market maker will try to improve on the price originally quoted.

For example, you might want to sell 50K shares in a stock, which is quoted in 15K (i.e. the market maker is making a price for 15,000 shares). He agrees to do 25K on risk on the basis you leave the balance with him to work. You are therefore guaranteed to do a minimum of 25K. But remember to leave a time limit to avoid later misunderstandings over when the commitment expires. Worked orders are printed as 'T' trades, which often print towards the end of the day when the transaction has either been completed or booked out because it was only partially filled.

Swap limits

The market maker may also agree to *swap limits* on the understanding that if the stock moves against the client he will have a guarantee of a fill with the chance of an improvement. For instance, you might offer the stock to a market maker at 4 and he bids you 3. These will also be marked as T trades.

Trades in SEAQ stocks that are part of a portfolio trade (twenty securities or more) can be worked until market close when they will be reported and published as P trades.

Spotting worked trades

It is clearly not in the market maker's interest to disclose if he is working a protected order for a client, but there can be some clues. If one of the bigger players suddenly joins the bid in a stock after a period of inactivity and remains there in spite of being hit by several sell orders, he may be filling a much larger order for an institution. Often this large trade will not print until later in the day, or after the market closes at 16.30 or even until a few days later. Unusual price action can often be reconciled against trades that are not published until much later. Once a protected buy order has been completed the stock may well move down as normal selling pressure resumes, or vice versa in the case of the completion of a large sell order. All stocks will have market makers who are major players and others who try to avoid being caught on the bid or offer.

Ordinary O trades

Although reported immediately, O trades of greater than six times NMS are delayed from publication to the general marketplace.

- If the *NMS of the stock is 2,000 or more*, publication is **delayed for 60 minutes**.
- If the *NMS is less than 2,000*, then it is **delayed for 120 minutes**.

The same rules apply for publication trades in SEAQ stocks that are part of a non-protected portfolio (twenty stocks or more).

Publication of reported trades below six times NMS are immediate.

Block K trades

Block trades are much larger.

For stocks with an NMS of 2,000 or more, a trade can be classified as a block trade if it is at least 75 times NMS. For stocks with an NMS of less than 2,000, the level for definition of a block trade is set at 50 times NMS.

In both cases publication is delayed for five days or until 90% of the position has been unwound.

Other trade publication rules

- **Agency cross deals** are subject to immediate publication, essentially because no risk has been taken by a member firm.
- Trades in **smaller companies with an NMS of 500** or less are published the next business day with a price but no volume.
- Transactions in stocks that are in an **offer period** (i.e. listed in the Takeover Panel's daily Disclosure Table), are subject to immediate publication and also via the regulatory news services by noon the next day if the holder controls 1% or more of the shares.
- Trades **conducted and reported after 17.15** are published between 07.15 and 07.45 the next trading day (trade identifier is overnight, also an O).

There is a comprehensive list of trade type indicators in the Appendices.

Inter-dealer brokers (IDBs)

Market makers are able to deal between themselves anonymously using *inter-dealer brokers* (IDBs). For years market makers had four different IDB screens on their desks, but the introduction of SETS and SETSmm has reduced demand and now only Cantor Fitzgerald handles the majority of screen-based inter-market deals.

If a stock shows, say, 234-236p on the screen, the market maker can show an anonymous 234.5p bid on the IDB screen and, if he gets hit, the trade will be reported as an M trade. The reason that some of the dealing prices are a bit odd is that the seller reports the trade and pays the commission, so if he hits the 234.5p bid it may print at something like 234.42p.

Occasionally a market maker quote will be closed; this may be a system or communications problem preventing the firm from updating their price, or because the firm is suddenly connected with a corporate action involving the company.

Trading SEAQ stocks

The arrival of the internet and electronic trading has not had the same impact on SEAQ trading as it has on the top blue-chip stocks. In fact many UK stock traders refuse to trade SEAQ stocks as it is still based around a market maker, quote-driven, system.

> *Note: The methodology involved with trading SEAQ stocks is certainly different from trading stocks on SETS and a different approach can be appropriate.*

Personally, I want the ability to trade all stocks in the UK, not restrict myself to those just traded on SETS, but SEAQ trading certainly requires a good understanding of the market structure. I think it is important to keep a balanced view of the needs and obligations of different market participants.

Why banks become market makers

By electing to make a market in certain stocks, banks are committing risk capital as well as trader resource, and, not unreasonably, they expect a return on that investment. There may be all kinds of reasons why a bank elects to be a market maker in a stock, including a corporate relationship with the company, (whereby making a secondary market in the shares maintains that relationship), or because that particular sector is one in which the bank wants to be represented. Stock liquidity can increase dramatically when a new firm takes up market making in a stock. Before stamp duty exemption was widened in 1997 with the introduction of SETS, it would be common when a company was subject to a takeover bid, or when trading the shares offered a new arbitrage opportunity, for investment banks to start market making in a stock to take advantage of the stamp duty exemption and to see the order flow.

Some market makers, like Winterflood, have traditionally been small cap specialists and will make markets in most small companies, whereas the bigger investment banks, like Merrill Lynch and Deutsche, may be more selective about the smaller companies they will make markets in.

How market making has changed

Staffing levels are way down on what they were ten years ago when I was at Smith New Court, when there were almost a hundred market makers covering UK stocks on different *pitches*. A pitch will specialise in one particular sector such as Banks, Insurance, Retailers or Oils. These days market makers have restructured and one pitch will cover the FTSE 100 stocks for instance, and another all the FTSE 250 constituents. There might be only two or three dealers covering more than a hundred stocks. Market making now exists only in SEAQ and SETSmm stocks as there are no longer market makers in the electronically traded stocks on SETS, although many ex market makers have now become principal traders in these stocks.

The importance of relationships between market makers and brokers

In recent years there has also been the growth of Retail Service Providers (RSPs), which allows electronic execution of smaller orders. However, the majority of larger orders are still executed over the phone and this is the crux of the matter. When you instruct your broker to execute your order he has to deal over the phone with a market maker who will be taking the other side of the trade, sometimes on risk, and the price that is struck is greatly dependent on the relationship between broker and market maker.

> Trading on SEAQ is heavily based around relationships and what a number of newer traders fail to realise, or choose to ignore, is that there is an intrinsic conflict of interest, particularly where very short-term trading is concerned.

In return for making continuous, firm two-way prices, market makers benefit from a number of concessions, including:

- stamp duty exemption;
- the ability to borrow and short sell stock; and
- delayed publication of trades to protect any order that they may be executing (or 'working').

Some market making firms will be more risk-averse than others, depending on current market conditions, stock volatility, liquidity and the attitude of the bank to risk. Ideally, market makers like to enjoy a quiet life buying at 2 and selling at 3 with good deal flow from tame institutions. Other firms have wider trading limits and more risk capital available and are comfortable running directional positions.

Quite often a good relationship between broker and market maker will result in a good price, usually because there is a bigger picture, maybe because the market maker knows that he will get the first call when the broker gets a big order in the same stock or sector at a future date. So, it is crucial to understand that trading in SEAQ stocks is heavily reliant on the relationship between broker and market maker. Because of the way that a firm may structure its market making, a badly handled order may damage the relationship between broker and market maker and affect future execution in what may appear to be completely unrelated stocks.

The majority of trades are struck within the market spread on the screen; screen prices should only be regarded as indicative. I call them tourist rates. SETS traders complain about wide bid-offer spreads on SEAQ stocks, but that does not make them untradeable. Sometimes quite astonishing prices can be obtained for a number of reasons that are not visible to the screen watcher. On occasion I have *sold* stock above the displayed *offer* price and *bought* stock below the *bid* price.

Be wary of Level 2

In the same way that Level 2 on SETS stocks should be viewed with a great deal of caution, so the same should be said of SEAQ stocks. Market making is a franchise and screen prices only tell part of the story. There can be a variety of reasons why the screen price may not represent the true current market price. A market maker will use all means at his disposal to generate a flow of trades, and will jealously shield his exposure from the marketplace, possibly moving prices around even when there are no apparent trades going through.

A constant stream of client buying should imply that a price may move up, but that may not be in the best interests of the market maker and he may seek to hold the price down. Unlike order-driven trading it is important to realise that with SEAQ stocks the market maker has taken the other side of the trade. So, if the client has bought, the market maker has sold. He can utilise the bid-offer spread to protect his position, widening it to make it less attractive for short-term traders, or narrowing it to induce more flow. He benefits from delayed publication of trades and he has the ability to change screen prices to cover his tracks. This can create a conflict of interest if the client is a short-term trader.

Generally, market makers are there to provide a two-way market, but their primary objective is to make money. They are rarely concerned with a company's fundamentals and are simply wholesalers of shares, trying to establish equilibrium between buying and selling. Usually position taking is short-term, with the book in each stock fluctuating between net long and net short.

Market makers and risk

Some market makers' appetite for risk is bigger than others. While some firms impose strict trading limits, meaning that a market maker can only hold prices down so long in the face of persistent buying, other bigger houses have more of a free rein and can run much bigger positions. His overall market exposure, or his net bull/bear, may also influence his position in one stock. In other words, if the market is trending upwards and he is very short across a number of stocks he may take appropriate action. If the market maker has a large position in a stock, either by choice or because he has taken it on risk, or as part of a program trade, he will seek to maximise his price for it as he feeds it out to the market. It can be more difficult to influence prices in liquid stocks where, with many more market makers, the market will have much more capacity to absorb or release stock, somewhat like a shock absorber.

Market makers may also be under pressure to give a better price to an in-house order, where there may be a commission for the firm's sales trader, than from another member firm, particularly one acting in a principal capacity.

The difficulty of analysing trade flow

Some traders try to evaluate if the market is net long or short a particular stock. The delayed publication regime and the ability to price report at middle prices, particularly for a program trade, where the risk profit is embedded in the commission, makes this a suspect pastime. In the same way that Level 2 only provides a two dimensional image of supply and demand, so time and sales information will never offer a complete picture of trade flow.

Each stock has market makers who are the main players in the stock and others who only occasionally have significant flow. If you specialise in only a few SEAQ stocks, it is possible to follow which market makers simply follow the pack with their quote and which ones are continually on the bid or offer in a particular stock. A market maker that suddenly has form in a stock, in which it is never normally a player, may be working a large order. Flow can often be all one way, particularly in smaller cap stocks, perhaps one which has been tipped somewhere, and a single market maker like Winterflood may be experiencing most of the flow through their RSP facility. Protected orders will not print until later, so a market maker who is sitting on the bid – absorbing stock or constantly selling it – may be filling a much larger order which is yet to print through the system. Quite often significant price moves are accounted for later in the day when a delayed trade finally gets printed.

> It is pointless counting buys and sells, as I have seen a number of traders try to do, as the market often has a residual net position from the previous day's trading and delayed trade publication results in a complete lack of transparency.

If a stock has moved up recently, an order going through at what appears to be the bid may actually have been a buyer earlier in the day when the price was lower. In addition, RSPs are utilised by market makers to advertise prices that they may not necessarily want to show on the screen.

Below is a good example of the true market price of 6.50-6.51p for Eurodis Electron, whereas the SEAQ price for the stock at the time was 6.50-6.75p. I have even seen instances when the RSP quote is in backwardation – in other words, the offer price is below the bid price on the SEAQ screen. This happens rarely but is perfectly feasible, as the quote will reflect the extracted best bid and offer from a number of different market makers anonymously, and if one wants to offer stock cheaply without disturbing the screen quote, he may do so via the RSP. Without the knowledge of the true market price, a trade at 6.51p may be interpreted as a sell. In addition, the net buy/sell counters on some websites will also incorrectly interpret the trade.

Figure 1.10: RSP screen shot for Eurodis Electron (ELH)

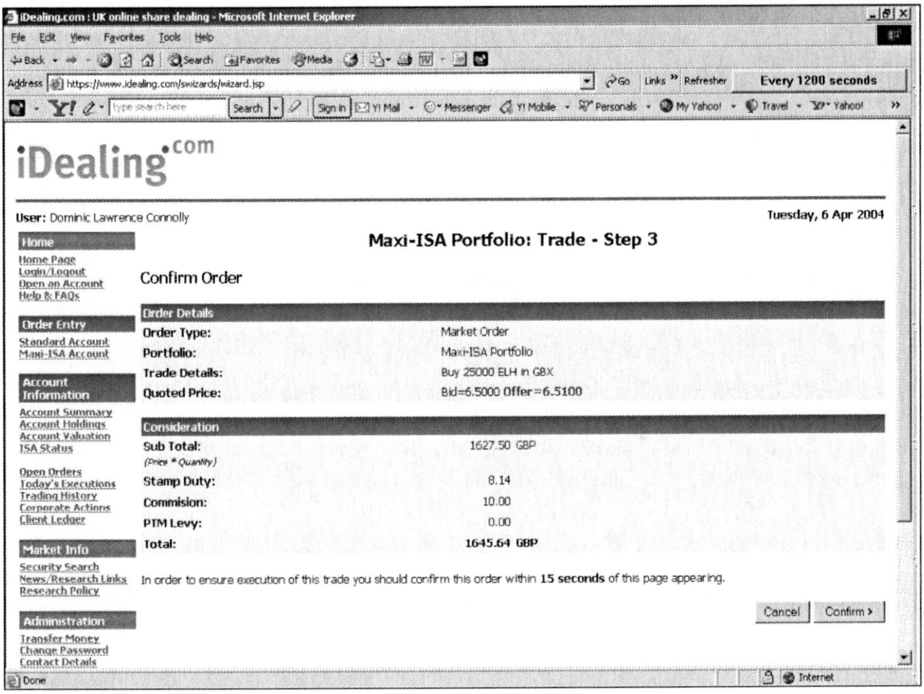

Source: iDealing.com

Screen quotes are a one-way communication street and market makers may move quotes around even when there is no trade going through simply to try to generate flow. Most traders are unaware that market makers occasionally selectively trade report on virt-x, a rival electronic exchange, thereby avoiding reporting unsuitable trades on the main market.

Institutional selling and buying

Following RNS announcements relating to the buying or selling of a particular share by big institutions can be helpful, but is only of limited use. The standard disclosure level under the Companies Act is 3%, so, once an institution falls just below that, you have no idea whether they are still selling or whether they have stopped. In addition some institutional investors and fund managers have exemption on disclosures up to 10%.

It can sometimes be possible to match up which market maker an institution is using by the screen activity – seeing who is consistently on the bid or offer, watching for the publication of protected and block trades, and RNS disclosures. It may take days or even weeks for an institution to sell or buy a large holding in a less liquid SEAQ stock, and this will be the predominant influence on that stock during that time. If the order is transacted aggressively without too much regard to price, the move in the stock price can be severe and relentless. I have been caught on several occasions on the wrong side of a very large institutional order where the buying or selling pressure will be remorseless until it is either complete, or the stock has moved to such a price that they are unwilling to continue chasing it. Certain institutions can have very deep pockets; be very wary about taking a position in the opposite direction of a persistent buyer or seller, such as the fund manager Fidelity. Once a large institution has decided to buy or sell a stock, it will often deal in the 'Unit Size' for that fund. In other words, it might buy chunks of, say, £2m worth at a time. So the number of shares will vary slightly each time with the price transacted.

The bid-offer spread

The gap between bid and offer can also be an effective deterrent in trading SEAQ stocks: wide spreads discourage dealing, narrow spreads encourage traders.

Bid-offer spreads are generally a reflection of liquidity, certainly for electronically traded stocks. It is very easy for a market maker to chase a bid right up behind an offer, so long as the trading is occurring with other market makers, and then to retreat if they haven't encouraged the other screen-quoted market makers to join them. Some market makers will change their quotes regularly simply to move a stock and induce retail buying and selling but will rapidly retrace on only a few small trades.

Figure 1.11: Healthcare Enterprise Group (HCEG) – deceptive narrow bid-offer spread

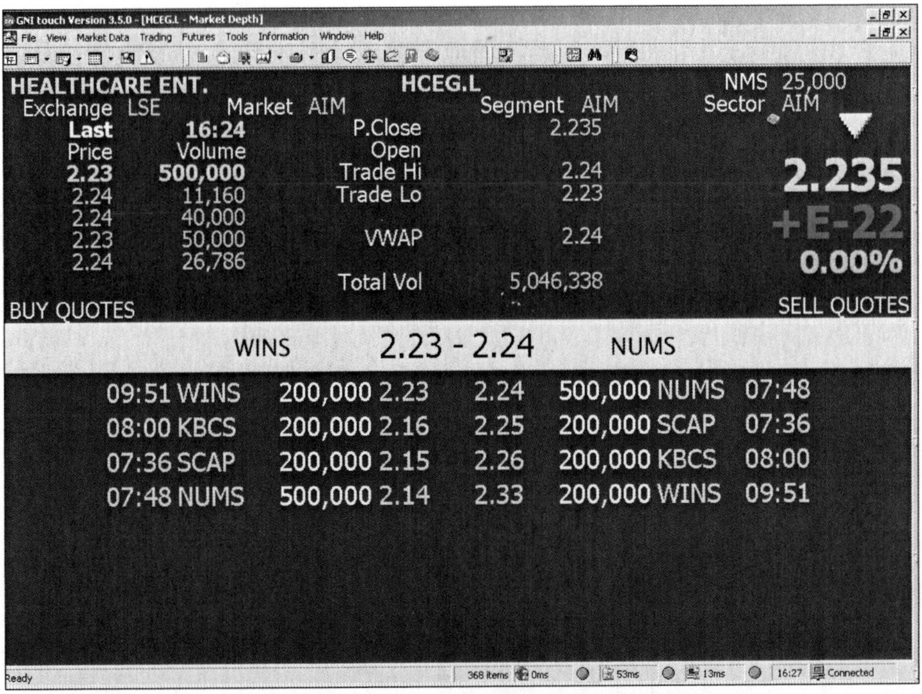

Used with permission from GNI touch®

In the example above, the market maker on the bid has chased the stock right up to the offer price so that the bid-offer spread is very narrow. Anyone without Level 2 who was unfamiliar with the stock and was checking it for the first time might think that the current touch price (2.23-2.24) was reflective of normal liquidity in the stock. This is where Level 2 and knowledge of a stock can be useful.

There can be a number of reasons to narrow the spread like this – after all, to be the best bid in this example requires the market maker to bid only 2.17 rather than 2.23. One reason is that the market maker concerned may actually be long of stock and trying to give an impression that the stock is a better market than it really is. He is only committing to buy 200,000 shares, worth around £4,000; not a huge position. Also, that price is only firm by telephone and there is no guarantee that by the time your broker has got through the price will still be there. It might, however, encourage buyers through the RSP system, and the price on the RSP may bear no relation to the screen price whatsoever. The same market maker may be bidding 2.23p for 50,000 but offering 200,000 shares at 2.24p. If a competing market maker is on the offer and trying to hold the price down, and also making prices via the RSP, he may find himself selling stock too as a direct result of the bid being pushed up so far, although prices made via the RSP can be subject to size constraints that can be changed at short notice.

Neither is it a good indication of future stock direction. Just because a market maker appears to be aggressively bidding a price up does not mean he is short of stock. As the screen shot below shows (taken early the next morning) the stock has in fact moved down and the bid-offer spread has widened out to a more normal 3 points. Notice here that Numis is prepared to make a firm price in 500K shares, whereas the other market makers are making a price in 200K and the NMS is just 25K. A good example of the NMS being unrepresentative of typical liquidity.

Figure 1.12: Healthcare Enterprise Group (HCEG) – normal bid-offer spread

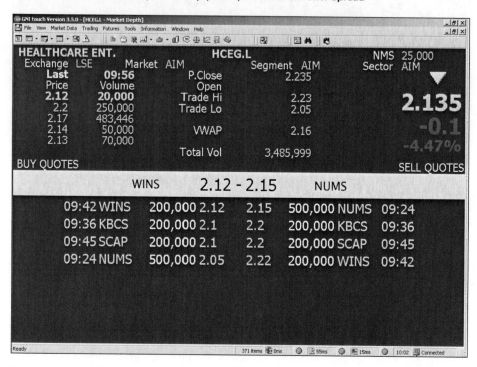

Used with permission from GNI touch®

The following screen shots are a good example of how screen prices can be unrepresentative. Here the SEAQ market price is 5.75-6p in Eurodis Electron, but a quick check on the RSP shows that the real market is 5.75p choice. For a number of days there was heavy selling in this stock and it was disclosed shortly after this screen shot that Kleinwort (KLWT) had been handling a large sell order for an institution, despite being consistently on the bid (of course)!

Figure 1.13: SEAQ price for Eurodis Electron (ELH)

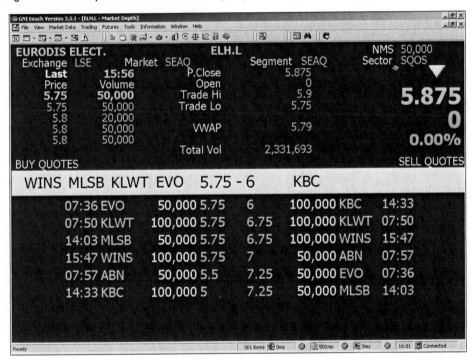

Used with permission from GNI touch®

Figure 1.14: Choice RSP price for Eurodis Electron (ELH)

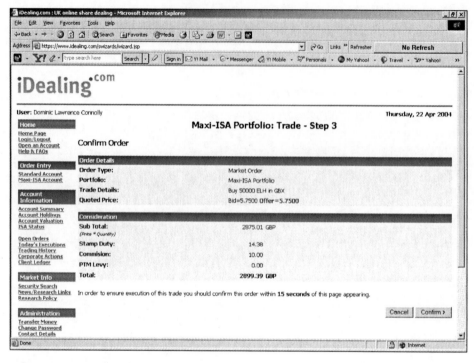

Source: iDealing.com

Momentum traders place great significance on M trades between market makers but market makers are not immune from executing an M trade between themselves in the NMS to encourage retail players in. If the trade is of insignificant size in relation to the larger order it can be worth giving an impression that the stock is a 'better market' than it really is.

If a market maker is placing a large line of stock at a discount to the prevailing price, say at 340p compared to a quote of 352-355p, he will almost certainly sit on the bid. He can afford to take a few hits while he gets the bigger line placed.

> *Note*: Only when you have understood that a stock can be 352p bid for 5,000, but offered in 5m at 340p by the same firm, have you grasped the significance of the screen franchise.

Laws of supply and demand govern market markers

Market makers are primarily concerned with flow and can often end up having large positions in a stock, not always through choice. Market makers may be reluctantly sitting on lines of stock, holding the price up, six months after having to buy some illiquid stock in 100 times the NMS, because a line of stock was sneaked into a large program trade by an institution.

Each market maker will have a different appetite for risk; some will take on big directional trades and will try to influence the market, others won't and will seek to find the other side of an order without taking any risk on their own book. Supply and demand will eventually determine the price for a stock. Those who believe in the efficient market hypothesis, whereby a security's price is determined by all known information at that time, simply don't understand the laws of supply and demand. Some market makers co-operate, whereas others are barely on speaking terms and will do anything possible to spoil the other's market.

SEAQ compared with SETS and SETSmm

There is no doubt that the price action in SEAQ stocks is different from SETS stocks, which is different again for SETSmm stocks. A number of UK traders, specialising in SEAQ stocks, found it extremely difficult to adapt when some FTSE 250 stocks moved from SEAQ to SETSmm in November 2003 and the market became more difficult to read. This may be because some traders find it hard to adapt to an electronic order book where there can be hundreds of iceberg and hidden orders, as well as multiple orders driven by complex algorithmic software, which may in turn be dependent on prices in other assets.

Software can be programmed to execute an order:

- against VWAP;
- to be the best bid or second best bid; or
- to execute *one-third volume*.
  (This automated order type reacts every time an order is conducted on the order book and seeks to trade one third of the market volume between two time intervals. Traders may have subconsciously seen this program in action, when, after hitting a bid in say 30,000 shares, an order immediately enters the book and buys 10,000 shares at the offer price, or any number of permutations.)

Stock volatility

Stocks traded on quote driven systems tend to have lower stock volatility on a comparable basis. It isn't correct to compare SETS volatility with SEAQ volatility because SETS is orientated around large stocks, whereas SEAQ is orientated around small cap stocks. When SETS was introduced in 1997, a number of investments banks took big bets that there would be a large increase in volatility and were proved correct. They did this mainly through the buying of option premia (long volatility). Being *long volatility* means being long options or premium that will bring a profit if actual stock volatility is higher than the implied volatility in anticipated option prices. Quote-driven systems react more slowly and have an ability to absorb stock both coming into and going out of the market. Electronic trading is instantaneous and is a direct reflection of current trading, not what someone thinks the price should be.

My advice with SEAQ stocks is that:

- If you are **executing a tame order** and the stock is not on the move, get on the phone – there is usually a deal to be done inside the spread.
- If you are **chasing stocks on the move** all the time, you will put the relationship between your broker and the market place under strain, which will be to the detriment of other clients. At some point your broker will have to trade with the same market maker again and all he will remember is the last hot order he gave him. He won't be interested in hearing that it is for a different client. Because of the way that pitches are organised it might be the same market maker for a completely unrelated stock in a different sector.

Market makers want order flow

At any one time, institutions will have preferred relationships with particular market makers. An institution looking to buy stock may not always go to the market maker on the offer but to whom he thinks will perform best to fill the order. This may be dependent on a variety of factors, including the handling of recent larger orders, or because a market maker is known to be strong in that particular stock or prepared to take on more risk and make a risk price in bigger size. Larger firms such as Merrill Lynch and Kleinwort usually strive to facilitate, as they want to see the order. Many firms have a policy of matching the current touch price in at least some size, even if they are not currently offering the best bid or offer price.

This can create a virtuous circle as the more flow that the firm sees, the greater its placing power, and its ability to both source and place stock to match business. Other firms without access to substantial flow will be more reluctant to take on larger positions on risk, as it will be more difficult to find the other side.

Sometimes there may be a bigger picture. A firm may take on a position that it would normally be reluctant to, in order to maintain a good relationship with the client. It may be anxious to see the next big order and in the process accept what is likely to be a loss-making position.

Dealing in smaller stocks

It should be remembered that with smaller stocks, it can be very easy for a market maker to become quite short of a stock through multiple small orders; particularly if the stock is subject to bulletin board speculation and the flow of business is only one way. It can be difficult to cover a position and often market makers will simply keep selling stock at higher and higher prices to average their position. In such situations:

1. Opening up and tightening the spread as well as changing the price are legitimate techniques to induce retail buying and selling.
2. He may utilise the reporting and publication privileges for the stock concerned: as smaller trades print immediately and larger trades may be delayed, he may be keen to print small trades at a price which may give the impression of selling while he is actually trying to cover a short position.

3. It is not unknown to challenge another market maker to create an M trade to give the impression that he is a seller rather than a buyer, as the size of the stock transacted may be small in relation to the bigger picture.

4. If a position is really hurting and a market maker has found himself on the wrong side of the market in the stock, for instance caught very short, it may be in his interests to hold the stock down right until the bell so that he can distribute a bad loss over more than one trading day. This can sometimes have the effect of artificially limiting the movement of a SEAQ stock in one trading day. Distributing a bad P+L over two or more days looks better from a risk management point of view than a single bad hit in one day.

Tree shaking and dead cat bounce

Two expressions that are commonly used in trading stocks are:

- *tree shaking*: where market makers shuffle a share price back on little or no volume after a sharp rise to induce profit takers to sell stock, allowing them to close short positions at more favourable prices;
- *dead cat bounce*: where a stock is rallied upwards on similarly low volumes after a sharp fall to encourage buyers and give the impression of a rally before the price resumes its slide southwards.

Both effects can be seen if a stock is traded on an electronic platform too, but the dynamics will be different and it is often easier to catch the turn with an order book stock than with a market making stock, when instantaneous dealing in size may be difficult and the stock is being manoeuvred on quotes rather than actual trades.

SEAQ Crosses

Although SEAQ Crosses still take place daily at:

- 09.30, 11.00, 15.00, 16.45

with a blind cross along the same lines as the POSIT system, the facility has fallen into disuse and is of little use to active traders. Any trades taking place under the SEAQ Crosses mechanism are marked with an ST code (SEAQ trade).

SETSmm

The SETSmm platform was introduced by the London Stock Exchange on 3 November 2003, building on the success of the introduction of the SETS electronic order book in 1997. Recognising that electronic order-driven trading had been proven successful for the top blue-chip stocks with improved liquidity, lower transaction costs and tighter bid-offer spreads, SETSmm was introduced as a hybrid market.

SETSmm is based around the FTSE 250 stocks not already traded on SETS, FTSE 250 reserves and some Irish and other securities. As such, the UK market has now effectively become a three-tiered market:

1. **SETS**: Top 205 blue-chip stocks, including all FTSE 100 and reserves.
2. **SETSmm**: FTSE 250, FTSE 250 reserves, some Irish and others, around 652 stocks.
3. **SEAQ**: Most other securities, currently around 1,946.

SETSmm is an electronic order book supported by continuous liquidity provision from committed market makers. Some features of SETSmm are:

- Each stock has a minimum of one **registered market maker** providing two-way prices in a size of at least 25% of the NMS for that stock.
- **Market maker prices are embedded in the order book**, with market makers' names displayed alongside, although they are also allowed to enter anonymous orders like other market participants.
- Trades executed on SETSmm are for **standard settlement like SETS**.
- SETSmm securities are **reviewed quarterly** like those on SETS.

SETSmm combines the advantages of:

1. order book trading, which for the active trader with direct access means being able to show the marketplace his price; while
2. benefiting from continuous two-way prices provided from committed market makers.

Electronic order books work especially well with large liquid stocks as their success depends on good liquidity and depth on both sides of the order book. Electronic order-driven trading works less well when few participants enter orders and the stock becomes illiquid and trades infrequently. SETSmm has been structured so that there is always a minimum level of liquidity. Stocks have been added to the SETSmm platform in a staged process. In July 2005 the top 200 smaller companies were transferred followed in December 2005 by the remaining 100 small caps and AIM 50.

SETSmm is very good news for the active trader as it allows participation directly with the marketplace. Many SETS traders who had been reluctant to trade SEAQ stocks now find a wider universe of over 850 stocks available to them.

A Level 2 screen shot of a SETSmm stock is shown below:

Figure 1.15: SETSmm Level 2 screen shot

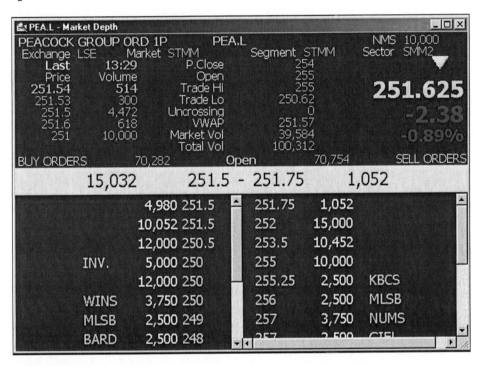

Used with permission from GNI touch®

As can be seen above, the SETSmm screen incorporates the characteristics of an order book screen such as SETS with market maker quotes embedded. Note again that different market makers are prepared to quote different sizes.

Daily timetable

The SETSmm trading day is structured in a similar way to SETS, with trade reporting from 07.15 and order entry allowed from 07.50 onwards until the opening auction uncrosses at 08.00. Continuous trading is then in operation until 16.30 when the closing auction period begins, which completes at 16.35.

Market maker obligations

Although there is a minimum of one registered market maker for each stock, the average number is around eight, with each stock currently having at least five. In total, 31 market makers support the 652 SETSmm stocks.

Market makers are no longer obliged to make a price over the telephone in SETSmm stocks, as their obligations have now moved to the order book. The prices market makers display on the screen are for electronic execution only.

Market makers must make a maximum spread and a minimum size in each stock. SETSmm stocks are allocated to Band 1 or Band 2, depending on liquidity; the maximum spread for Band 1 is the greater of either 10% of the previous day's closing price or 3p. For Band 2 stocks it is 5% of the previous day's closing price.

The minimum size for SETSmm stocks is a quarter of the NMS. In the example MLSB, BARD and KBCS are making a price in the minimum size allowable.

Under current rules, market makers are able, but not required, to participate in the opening auction, but must make prices in the closing auction.

Price monitoring

On both SETS and SETSmm the Exchange operates a price monitoring algorithm where each incoming order, which potentially would activate an execution on the order book respectively, is compared with a reference price. For the opening and closing auction the tolerances are 5% and 15% for Band 1 stocks and 10% for Band 2 stocks. Unlike SETS, there is no closing auction volume check, so there is no minimum required volume in the uncrossing, even after the necessary extensions.

Trade reporting and publication

Delayed trade reporting and publication, similar to the other platforms, is in place to protect the providers of risk capital. The rules are similar to those for block trades for SEAQ and WPAs for SETS.

All trades executed on the order book are published immediately and trades conducted off book must be reported within three minutes. Portfolio transactions of at least twenty stocks benefit from delayed reporting requirements, so long as at least one stock is quoted on SETSmm.

Worked Principal Agreements (WPAs)

WPAs are transactions of at least eight times NMS, which can be worked throughout the trading day and are reported when 80% offset or at the end of the day, whichever comes first. Once reported they are published immediately.

Block trades

Block trades for SETSmm stocks are set at 75 times NMS. Publication is delayed for three days or when 90% offset, whichever is earlier. Unlike SEAQ stocks, the delay period is the same whatever the NMS for the stock.

Statutory exemptions

The Companies Act requires the disclosure of holdings of 3% or more; however, market makers have some exemptions to protect their trading positions. The Exchange acts as policeman by requiring market makers to disclose holdings of 3% or more to the Exchange itself within two business days of the interest first being held. The following business day the Exchange will publish the holdings via RNS, but only if they breach the following thresholds:

- **FTSE 350 securities**: 5% or more.
- **Non FTSE 350 securities**: 10% or more.

Movements through a whole percentage point are also published while the holding remains above the publication limits.

SETS and SETSmm auctions

In May 2000 the London Stock Exchange introduced the auction process as a refinement to electronic trading on SETS and this was extended to stocks traded on SETSmm in November 2003. Although some people find the auction process confusing, it is actually quite simple once the concept of the *uncrossing price* is grasped.

Each trading day there is:

- a **pre-market auction for each stock** between 07.50 and 08.00;
- a **post-market auction** between 16.30 and 16.35; and
- **intra-day auctions** that can be triggered if an attempt is made to match a trade on the order book outside a certain price tolerance level for that stock. (Note that the trade does not actually have to take place, just an order submitted that would result in it.)

No trading takes place during the auction process while market participants enter limit buy and sell orders. During the auction period, the Exchange automatically calculates and displays the uncrossing price in real time, which is that price at which maximum volume can be executed, providing that a stock is crossed (i.e. a buy order is equal to or higher than a sell order).

At the end of the auction period, orders can be deleted but not entered, and the uncrossing will take place within a random 30-second period. Unlike the normal trading day, *at-market* orders can also be placed which will be executed at the best available price. The uncrossing price is calculated in real time throughout the auction process by the Exchange, and it is important to remember that all trades which take place at the end of the auction process take place at the uncrossing price or not at all.

Opening auction

Before continuous trading commences at 08.00 there is a pre-market auction between 07.50 and 08.00, known as the *auction call process,* where limit and market orders can be entered and deleted. No execution takes place during this time, but an indicative uncrossing price is calculated by the exchange and displayed in real time. At 08.00 those stocks that are crossed will start to uncross at a price allowing maximum executable volume within the next 30 seconds, introducing a random element to the timing to prevent manipulation. Additional orders can be entered and deleted in this time but run the risk of inadvertent execution.

Occasionally the auction process can be extended under two circumstances:

1. **Market order extension:** where there is an incomplete market order because there is insufficient liquidity on the other side of the order book to complete it. The auction process is extended by two minutes followed by a random 30-second end period.
2. **Price monitoring extension:** where the uncrossing price would be more than 5% away from the base price, which is usually the previous day's closing price. In this circumstance the auction is extended for five minutes with a random 30-second end period. This often happens when there is overnight news or price-moving results are released pre-market. The London Stock Exchange does not allow market orders in the opening auction if a new stock has listed, as there is no prior base price. The base price may also be adjusted if there is a corporate action.

Extensions can only occur once, but can happen in either order with market order extensions receiving priority.

Closing auction

After continuous trading finishes at 16.30 there is a 5-minute closing auction period between 16.30 and 16.35 followed by a random 30-second end period. Between 16.35 and the uncrossing, orders can be deleted but not entered to avoid manipulation.

Like the opening auction, there can be market order and price monitoring extensions.

1. **Market order extension**: where there is an incomplete market order because there is insufficient liquidity on the other side of the order book to complete it. The auction process is extended by two minutes followed by a random 30-second end period.
2. **Price monitoring extension**: where the uncrossing price is more than 3% away from the base price for FTSE 100 stocks, or more than 5% away for other SETS stocks, there will be a 5-minute extension and random 30-second end period. The base price is the volume weighted average price for the last ten minutes of normal trading (16:20-16:30). If there is no VWAP, then the last order book trade (AT) is used as reference. If the uncrossing price is still outside these parameters, a second price monitoring extension period is initiated for a further 5 minutes and random 30 seconds.

The closing auction usually generates the official closing price except when there was no uncrossing in the auction or when the volume that crossed was so low as to not be representative. Usually this is half NMS or less than 2,500 shares for securities with an NMS below 5,000.

Again, extensions can only occur once but can happen in either order with the market order extension receiving priority.

Iceberg orders can participate in the auctions and although only the peak shows, their presence can be revealed, as the full size will show in the uncrossing volume.

Intra-day auctions

Intra-day auctions can occur during the trading day where an order is entered which would cause a stock to trade more than 5% away from the last trade on the order book (although some less liquid stocks have a higher tolerance of 25%). Note that the auction is not triggered after the trade has taken place but if an order is entered that would execute more than a certain percentage away from the last AT trade. Very liquid stocks don't generally have intra-day auctions because, even if there is breaking news and the stock gaps up or down rapidly, the increments between trades are often below 5%. However, where there are big gaps in the order book between prices, intra-day auctions can be triggered by inadvertent dealing or stock moving on breaking news.

Intra-day auctions last for five minutes with a random 30-second end period. There can be a two-minute market order extension but price monitoring extensions do not occur.

Traders who are not participating in the opening and closing auction are not giving themselves access to the day's whole trading range, as auction imbalances can often present the best prices of the day for those looking to close a trade and also those opening a trade who are prepared to take some overnight risk. It would be helpful if the London Stock Exchange introduced a minimum uncrossing volume for the opening auction as well, as there regularly seems to be small numbers of shares uncrossing at spurious prices, which give an unrepresentative opening price reference for the rest of the day.

If a stock were to uncross at 1100, then all buy orders at 1100 and above would be executed and all sell orders at 1100 or below would be executed at the same price of 1100. If you left a limit order to sell at 1095 you would trade at 1100, and if you left an order to sell at 1150 you would not trade. If you left an order to sell at 1100 you may trade depending how far up the queue you are. Orders at the same price take time priority, not size priority, so if you leave a limit order on the book early in the day, which is automatically placed into the closing auction, you have a better chance of execution than an order left in later at the same price. If your limit price was exactly at the uncrossing price then you could of course end up with a partial fill.

For all SETS stocks, the auction-uncrossing price is marked with the UT trade code and usually becomes the official closing price. For SEAQ auctions (crosses) it is ST.

A *market order* is an order without a specific price attached, which will be executed at the best prevailing price, maximising the chance of execution. Market orders take price and time priority in the auction.

A screen shot of a stock in auction is shown below.

Figure 1.16: Tate & Lyle (TATE) – auction screen shot

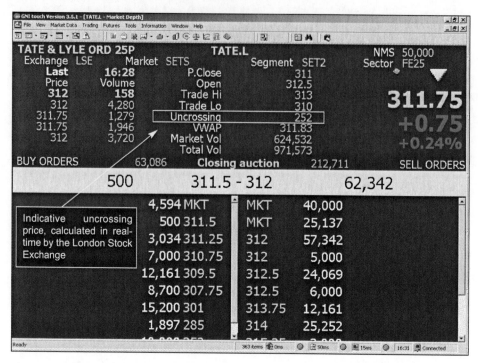

Used with permission from GNI touch®

Here, the *at-market* orders on both sides of the strip can clearly be seen at the top of the book, although the larger market order on the right (sell side) is forcing the indicated uncrossing price down to 252p, in contrast to 312p where the stock was trading shortly before the auction commenced. This shot was taken early in the closing auction; by the end of the 5-minute period it can be expected that the uncrossing price will be closer to 312p as balancing liquidity comes to the market from other participants.

Auctions take place for all SETS and SETSmm stocks, but a stock will not uncross if there are no orders in the system to execute.

A screen shot of the order book for Amvescap taken at 16.34, near the end of the closing auction, is illustrated below:

Figure 1.17: Amvescap (AVZ) – auction screen shot

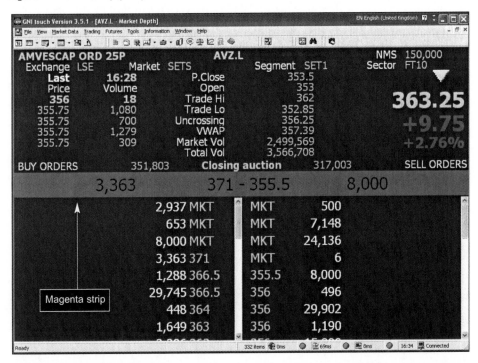

Used with permission from GNI touch®

Here the indicated uncrossing price is shown as 356.25p and, in addition to at-market orders on both the buy and sell side of the book, there are limit buy orders at a higher price than some corresponding limit sell orders. During normal trading these orders would, of course, instantaneously match and create an execution (an AT trade) but in the auction, the order book remains 'crossed' with the 'touch' displayed in a magenta background, rather than the more normal yellow.

At 16.35, the 'closing auction' message in the middle of the screen will change to 'delete only' and the order book will 'uncross' during the next 30 seconds (the random uncrossing period) at the uncrossing price, with all limit bids at or above the uncrossing price and all limit offers at or below the uncrossing price matching and executing at the uncrossing price.

There are a number of reasons why participants want to deal in the auction:

- The completion of an order that has been worked throughout the day.

- To guarantee the buying of a stock at the closing price, as the closing price in the auction is usually also the official close for the stock. The closing price for a stock can be important because derivative instruments may be priced at that time, it may be used as a reference for stock options or a corporate transaction may be based on it.
- Some participants may also want to guarantee dealing at the closing price, particularly if a stock is being added or re-weighted in an index, and the auction process prevents manipulation of a closing price based on the last traded price. This can, however, offer opportunities to a trader prepared to accept overnight risk if an imbalance in the closing auction pushes a stock price away from its previous trading range.

SEATS Plus

SEATS Plus (Stock Exchange Alternative Trading Service) is a hybrid trading service that combines an order-driven service with competing quotes. The service is used for some AIM stocks and also stocks on the Official List with only one market maker (stocks with more than one market maker are moved to SEAQ). Hence trades can be conducted over the telephone with the market maker or electronically by placing a buy or sell order on the trading screen. Although the hybrid quotes and electronic system is similar to SETSmm, the screen is kept separate in two parts but not amalgamated like SETSmm.

Figure 1.18: SEATS Plus screen shot

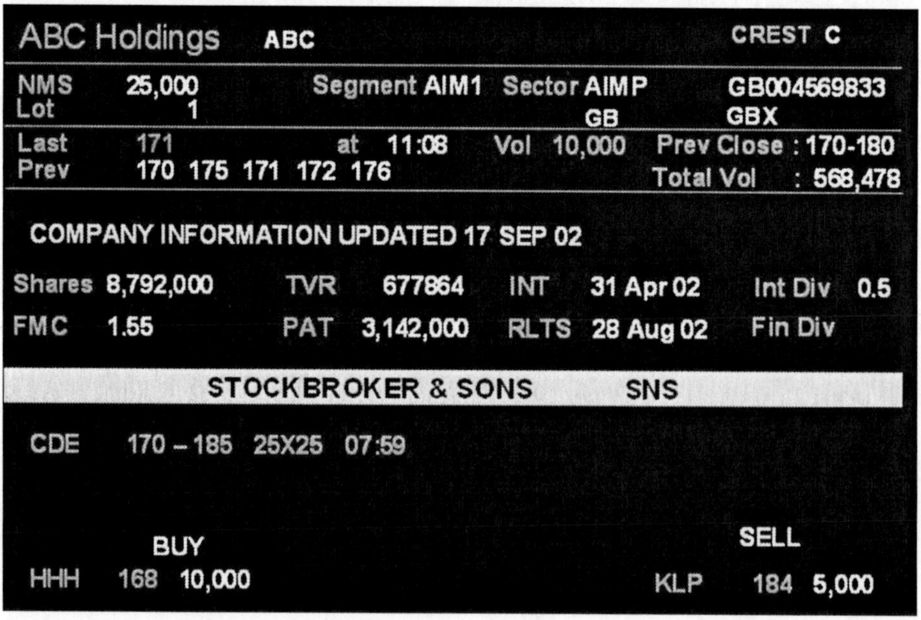

Source: London Stock Exchange

The NMS for SEATS Plus securities is set at 1,000 shares, although AIM stocks have the same NMS regime as SEAQ stocks. A generic screen shot for SEATS Plus stocks is shown in Figure 1.18 (provided by the London Stock Exchange; there are currently 146 securities quoted on SEATS Plus).

Share Certificates and CREST

Stockbrokers have increasingly encouraged clients to use *nominee accounts*, where shares are held centrally in the electronic settlement service called *CREST*, as they are cheaper and faster to use. There are around five million retail shareholders in the UK who hold their shares in dematerialised form in nominee accounts.

Electronic holdings guarantee stock delivery, meaning that settlement is typically T+3, compared to typically T+7 for share certificates. However, investors utilising nominee accounts do not enjoy shareholder rights, such as copies of reports and accounts, voting rights, notices to meetings and shareholder perks and have to request a proxy card to vote.

CREST sponsored membership

Those unwilling to lose these benefits, but wanting to benefit from the quicker settlement and other advantages of CREST, can elect to have a *CREST sponsored membership*. Under this system, stock is held electronically in CREST, and the broker still acts as sponsor, but the accounts are held in the shareholder's own name, meaning that all communication goes directly to the address that the shareholder has registered. Expect to pay around £50 per annum for this service.

Shareholders do not lose their rights if they have a CREST personal membership, therefore it seems unfair that there is a distinction between the rights of legal and beneficial (nominee) owners. Brewin Dolphin has now rolled out the *CREST proxy voting system* from institutions to private clients. Brewin clients can now send their voting instructions online, with Brewin subsequently submitting them through CREST.

The providers of risk capital should have voting control of the firm using that capital, not the people who manage it, and a web-based world might just provide it. This is a move in the right direction despite hysterics from some saying, "This is crazy. You could get the noisy minority actually voting for the silent majority".

It seems inevitable that electronic voting will come in sooner rather than later, and although the facility already exists via CREST, the UK settlement agency, there has been a slow uptake.

It is a shame that the internet, which has transformed so many other different aspects of life, has failed to have an immediate impact on bringing the suppliers of capital closer to the users of it. Electronic voting, which should improve corporate governance, is an inevitability, despite feet-dragging by custodians and proxy voting agencies.

Contracts For Difference

The last few years have seen a dramatic change in the visibility and accessibility of the UK stock market as the process of *disintermediation,* to use a popular media term, accelerated by the growth of the internet, has changed the nature of trading. A growing number of individuals, disillusioned by the financial services industry, have recognised that it is now possible to actively trade the UK markets for a living. The arrival of electronic trading in 1997, the availability and evolution of new retail derivative products, such as CFDs, and the popularity of spread betting, together with widespread use of Level 2, has resulted in a significant shifting of financial power from the investment banks and financial institutions to the individual.

Origins of CFDs

Contrary to popular belief, equity *contracts for difference* (CFDs) are not a recent innovation but have been utilised in the UK since the early 1990s. Originally available only in the institutional marketplace, the widening of stamp duty exemption and introduction of electronic trading in 1997 allowed other stock exchange intermediaries, as well as market makers, to offer the product to their clients.

Before 1997, the UK stock market was based around a quote-driven market making system (Stock Exchange Automated Quotations), and smaller capitalised UK stocks still trade on this SEAQ system today. Trading was predominantly by telephone and market makers had to provide firm, continuous two-way prices during the mandatory quote period (i.e. opening hours). In exchange for this obligation, market makers were extended a number of privileges including exemption from stamp duty and the ability to borrow stock from institutions through intermediaries for short sale. Stock lending and borrowing is a legitimate activity that assists market liquidity and allows hedging of derivative products and other activities. Many long-term holders of shares, such as tracking funds, lend their stock out for a small fee (normally expressed as an annual percentage), as the fees earned improve the fund performance.

Many market-making firms (or *stock jobbers* as they were known) were bought by large investment banks in the 1990s for their franchise, and integrated into banks' equity divisions. Non-member firms that wanted to short stock (perhaps to hedge a convertibles book, or to execute market neutral trades) approached the market makers to structure a product whereby they could benefit from this exemption, and the CFD product was born.

So, if the client wished to short sell 100,000 shares in Vodafone, he would call the market maker's CFD desk with whom he had a CFD arrangement, the desk would state the firm's current price in Vodafone, say 130.5-131p, and the client could elect to sell at that price. The CFD desk would sell 100,000 Vodafone shares to its in-house market maker at 130.5p, and so have a short stock position hedge against the long CFD with the client. The client would be short the same number of CFDs as was his original intention.

> The introduction of electronic trading has allowed hedge funds to trade synthetically on the order book, via direct access, avoiding the costs associated with traditional share dealing.

What is a CFD?

A CFD is an agreement between two parties to exchange, at the close of the contract, the difference between the opening price and the closing price of the contract, with reference to the underlying share, multiplied by the number of shares specified within the contract. In the institutional market, CFDs are often structured as equity swaps because single stock futures were, until recently, prohibited in the American market.

The principal advantages of CFDs are that under current legislation:

- **no stamp duty is payable** on CFD transactions;
- **short selling** is as easy as establishing long positions; and
- CFDs are **traded on a margined basis** like a futures contract. In other words, CFDs offer gearing as the user need only put up a percentage of the underlying contract value. The remainder is borrowed from the CFD provider at a pre-agreed interest rate, normally expressed as a percentage over base rates.

Although CFDs do not generally confer the right to vote as the user does not actually own a stake in the company, most other aspects make trading CFDs almost identical to trading shares. Voting at AGMs is low down the list of trader priorities.

In the case of a corporate action in the underlying stock, providers will generally facilitate the client's wishes, although there is no written agreement. Sometimes the client will assume that because he has a position the firm will be able to execute his wishes in the underlying stock; however, it is often forgotten that the firm's net position may be different to that of an individual client's, due to simultaneous long and short positions with different clients which creates a different net market position.

CFDs, the instrument of choice for proprietary and active traders

CFDs are now firmly established as the preferred primary equity-trading instrument in the UK for market participants such as hedge funds and proprietary traders operating outside a stamp duty exempt trading institution. Most of the professional traders that I know in the UK who are trading for a living make active use of them. Trading actively in traditional stocks and paying 0.5% stamp duty for the privilege on every purchase is not economically viable.

CFDs are generally available on all but the smallest stocks (the original £50m market cap limit has been reduced further by most firms to around £10m), including stocks quoted on AIM, although margin rates may be higher on less liquid, smaller capitalised companies.

Although there are currently around a dozen retail providers of CFDs, not all CFDs are the same as some providers structure them in a different way to others. The choice is effectively between:

- **direct market access**; and
- **quote-driven** trading.

Retail CFD providers are usually London Stock Exchange member firms with stamp duty exemption, and the majority take little or no risk and simply hedge all transactions in the underlying stock (or cash market).

Example: CFD transaction

If a client places an order to buy 5,000 Barclays CFDs, the provider buys 5,000 shares in the marketplace, the trade prints, and the client simultaneously establishes their long contract of 5,000 Barclays CFDs. The CFD provider holds the 5,000 Barclays stock on his book as a hedge, and is short 5,000 Barclays CFDs to the client. The stock stays on the provider's book and does not move to the client otherwise stamp duty would be payable.

The transaction is reversed when the client comes to close the trade: the stock is sold in the cash market and the CFD contract closed out at the same price as the hedge is traded at. Hence, the client will usually see the shadow transaction print in the cash market.

CFD charges

The CFD provider takes no risk in the above example but charges a commission on each transaction. Standard retail commission charges are around 0.25% (25 basis points) but are generally negotiable and are inversely proportional to trading activity and trade size. Institutional rates can be as low as a couple of basis points. As the client only has to put up around 10% of the underlying contract value, the provider lends the client the remaining 90%, which is charged at a financing spread over base rate. This can be as high as 3% over base rate for less frequent retail clients.

Note that if positions are only run intra-day and not overnight there are no financing charges.

Most CFDs can be traded over the phone or online, and different CFD providers have different strengths. Some will provide value added services such as research and an account handler, whereas others concentrate on lower costs but a more basic service. A resilient and powerful online trading platform will be more important to some traders than others. One big factor is that of direct market access (DMA), or *synthetic DMA* in the case of CFDs.

Short-term trading is inevitably orientated around taking positions, sometimes sizeable, for short periods of time, and without margining that would be extremely capital intensive. Margin rates of 10% allow the user to be comfortable with several simultaneous positions without being capital constrained. Having said that, just because he has 10:1 gearing available doesn't mean he has to use it all the time, but it does allow him a great deal of flexibility. Most experienced traders always have something in reserve for the unexpected. Running a margin account permanently fully leveraged allows no room for manoeuvre or the ability to benefit from a sudden opportunity without liquidating something.

Personally, I prefer to close a position at a time of my choosing rather than the market's. Capital is the most valuable commodity that a trader can have. Without it he cannot participate.

Direct market access (DMA) and quote-driven trading

Trading costs

One of the big advantages for the private investor in having electronic order-driven trading in the UK is not only the increased visibility but also the ability to participate indirectly within the market spread of the cash market, hence reducing execution costs.

The bid-offer spread is the most important of all costs that the trader encounters – and the most pernicious.

Other costs such as commission, stamp duty (where applicable) and subscription fees are tangible and usually appear on contract notes where they are easy to quantify. However, after buying a stock at 7 and then ten minutes later selling at 5, the trader is often left feeling that he has done a bad trade or got it wrong in some way. All too often that is simply the cost of dealing in the market, which he has failed to fully take into account. Every position established has, at some point, to be exited. It is very easy for costs to be buried in the bid-offer spread and ignored, as they are not easily identifiable on paper.

Minimum increments are another often forgotten factor. There was a profound effect on the US market when decimals were introduced to replace sixteenths, resulting in a squeeze in market-making profits and narrower spreads. Minimum spreads effectively offer the market maker protection. There are still some stocks that appear to trade on increment sizes that seem inappropriate and should be narrower. Examples include:

- **Vodafone**, which is incredibly liquid and, despite trading around 130p has a 0.25p increment, equivalent to 0.2% (0.1p would be more appropriate); and
- **Invensys** which also bizarrely trades on 0.25p increments (equivalent to 1%) despite a share price of 23p at the time of writing.

Synthetic direct access

Up until recently it has been difficult for the trader to gain direct access to the market but three of the highest profile CFD providers, GNI, IG Markets and E*Trade, now offer what is effectively *synthetic direct access*. In other words, when placing your CFD order in a stock which is traded on SETS or SETSmm, the corresponding hedge transaction is automatically generated electronically allowing the participant to trade within the market spread. This level of participation is crucial for many traders although individual trading style will dictate which system works best.

Quote-driven prices

CFD providers that wish to trade the client flow that they receive, and take on proprietary risk, structure their CFD offering differently. Here, the provider will make its own quote-driven prices based around the underlying cash market, not dissimilar to a spread betting firm, or that of a bookmaker, offering his own two-way prices.

There are pros and cons to both methods. Although commission-free trading may at first sight appear cheaper and more attractive, this must be tempered with the fact that the relationship between provider and client is completely different. With a broker, where you pay commission, there is little, if any, conflict of interest and every incentive for the broker to get the best price for his client. Some traders may also be uncomfortable with their provider knowing their position because at some point they will have to exit the trade. The instantaneous dealing that direct access providers offer can be a major factor as you are not going to suffer from:

- re-quotes;
- "your stop is under review";
- "your deal ticket is being reviewed by a dealer"; or
- "stock temporarily suspended"

before being accepted.

Speed of execution is very important to me: if something is available on the screen I should be able to trade against it.

The UK market has successfully embraced electronic trading and moved away from the old quote-driven model. It seems to me that if you continue to use a firm that only offers a quote-driven service, that is a step backwards and the full benefits that the modern market have to offer are not being fully utilised.

Although some ridiculed SETS when it was brought in as not being reflective of the true market, it is inarguably now the primary source of price discovery in the UK, with over 60% of all trades being executed electronically through SETS. With direct access, the individual now has all the advantages that were previously the reserve of the investment banks and can trade alongside them on equal terms.

Trading in the underlying cash market allows access to the best prices for the day, often achieved in the pre- and post-market auctions. It is also possible, by being able to submit limit orders within the spread, to literally buy at the low of the day and sell at the high, something that is not possible if trading with a firm that makes its own prices; it is the firm that gets the best prices in that case, not the client.

The argument that it is always better to go direct to a market maker in CFDs rather than a broker is specious and misrepresents the structure of the market. It is not like buying insurance. Market makers in stocks display competing prices on a screen but there is a single central point of liquidity and dealing as well as settlement. Having bought from one market maker today I can sell to another tomorrow. However, market makers in CFDs display their own prices in their own environment. If you choose to deal with them on their risk price, the position needs to be closed with them at some point. A conventional broker hedges everything in the underlying market, and the dealing price in the CFD is always the same as the price of the underlying stock execution.

It is very hard to accurately demonstrate a direct comparison of costs between trading commission-free but at someone else's prices, and paying a fixed cost per trade but being able to trade at the underlying market price, or even better through DMA. It will depend on which stocks are traded, the prevailing liquidity and the style of trading.

Firms that offer their own prices, or make markets in CFDs, can be very competitive in the blue-chip stocks but spreads will inevitably widen in smaller stocks.

My own trading style, which is opportunity-driven, is to have access to the whole universe of stocks in the underlying cash market and use my strong position of reasonably high frequency trading and decent size to negotiate very competitive commission rates. I am uncomfortable relying on one firm's prices when it comes to exiting a trade; I much prefer to trade in the deepest pool of liquidity, where I can have access to other participants' orders and they can see mine. I expect to deal within the market spread most of the time in SEAQ stocks, unless I am in a hurry to do something. When you are committed to opening and closing a trade with the same person, you're running the risk of not getting the best price.

Choice of CFD provider – quote-driven or order-driven

An individual's choice of CFD provider will depend on the instruments that he wishes to trade and on his style of trading.

My priorities are direct access, comprehensive coverage of all UK stocks and direct access to the FTSE 100 futures contract for hedging and speculation. A broker with a strong SEAQ dealing capability and access to crossing networks such as POSIT is also useful. Trading out of hours is not for everyone and is a low priority for myself, as I like to shut down at 16.35. I also specialise in UK stocks, so have no requirement to trade currencies, commodities and options, although I will occasionally trade European stocks.

It can also be wise to have more than one provider with good telephone back-up in case of internet failure.

Headline commission rates are usually negotiable based on trade activity and size traded. In my experience many UK traders seem afraid to negotiate. It must be something to do with English reserve!

Whichever firm you choose to trade CFDs with, it will be via one of the following three structures:

1. Trading with a firm that **offers synthetic direct access**, in other words takes no risk itself and hedges everything in the underlying market. Utilising this method you will usually see the *ghost* print of your CFD trade report in the cash market. Trading in SEAQ stocks may involve a dealer handling your order (e.g. GNI), or utilising an embedded RSP where the firm converts the trade into a CFD for you (e.g. IG Index).
2. **Trading on risk prices** – better suited to the blue-chip, more liquid stocks. The provider will claim that as the client is not paying for the clearing and settlement costs associated with hedging in the underlying market, and it adopts a portfolio approach to hedging with a business model based on principal risk, the benefits are passed onto the client. I find this argument somewhat specious. I would much prefer to be a price maker than a price taker, and not be subject to re-quotes or "your stop is under review".
3. A **best execution model** along the lines offered by City Index where not everything is hedged, but market prices are restricted in size.

Despite claims from one CFD firm that they defined CFD trading as "share trading only better" (they didn't), commission-free trading makes a good headline but misses the main issue – that of the bid-offer spread.

Are you trading on the wrong side of the spread?

DMA and low commission costs are essential to the professional daytrader playing for very short-term, low margin trades, often in response to breaking news. Quote driven systems are more suited to position-taking over a longer time scale where the conflict of interest between client and provider is less operative.

The prices provided by quote-driven systems are often referred to as *prices on risk* or *risk prices,* and it should always be remembered that risk prices come at a premium. In addition, dealing may not be instantaneous like DMA, and bid-offer spreads are usually a reflection of stock liquidity. Average bid-offer spreads throughout the trading day on an electronic platform like SETS start with the widest spreads occurring during the first hour of trading as orders are submitted to the market, but as liquidity builds up, the market starts to establish a 'fair' value for each stock.

Figure 1.19: Intra-day bid-offer spread for SETS stocks

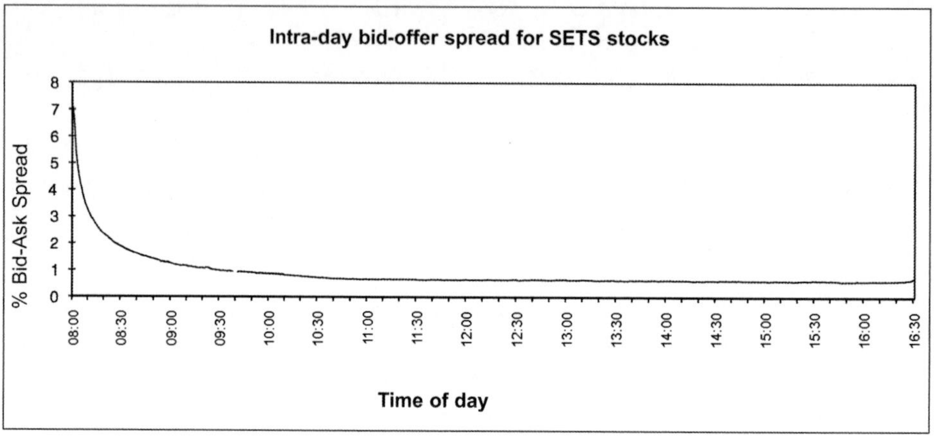

Source: Charlie x. Cai, Robert Hudson and Kevin Keasey of University of Leeds

DMA also allows the user the flexibility of submitting limit orders and improving on price by not crossing the bid-offer spread and trading patiently, against the certainty of dealing by actively crossing the spread in the same way as a market order. Different circumstances will dictate the appropriate strategy.

Funding costs – CFDs and traditional share trading

CFDs are short-term trading instruments and due to their characteristics they are neither a substitute for, nor an alternative to, long-term investment. For short-term trading, however, they remain one of the most cost-effective means of dealing.

CFDs are a margined product and hence involve borrowing from the provider. If the provider charges, say, 3% over a base rate of say 4.5%, then it costs around £5 per day to finance a £25,000 position, assuming the financing is charged on the whole position. Strictly speaking it is 90% of the position that is being borrowed, but if the trader looks carefully he will see that some CFD providers charge on the whole position but credit the client positive interest on the 10% margin that he puts up (at a slightly lower rate of course).

For the purposes of simplicity I will assume that the financing costs apply to the whole position. Putting aside for one moment the issues of dealing methodology, bid-offer spreads and commission, it is relatively straightforward to calculate at what point the extra cost of funding the CFD position overtakes the saving in stamp duty.

CFD funding cost vs stamp duty

When comparing funding costs between CFDs and buying shares in full, it is important to remember that the position needs to be funded when buying shares, whether from a building society account or existing funds. So, assuming that funds are available at around base rate, the opportunity cost in using CFDs is the additional funding cost associated with the spread that the providers add on above base rates. This can be compared to the up-front cost of paying stamp duty at 0.5% to calculate after how many days the cost of running the position in CFD form overtakes the saving in stamp duty. Rationalising, and assuming a standard additional financing cost gives us:

```
0.5% = (y/365)*3%
```

where y is the number of days,

Solving for y gives:

```
y = (0.5*365)/3 = 61 days
```

In other words, positions held for longer than two months, with a financing spread of 3%, will have attracted a funding cost in excess of the original stamp duty saving. Similar calculations can be carried out for financing spreads of 2% (91 days) and 1% (183 days).

The crossover points are illustrated below:

Figure 1.20: Cost comparison of CFDs and normal stock

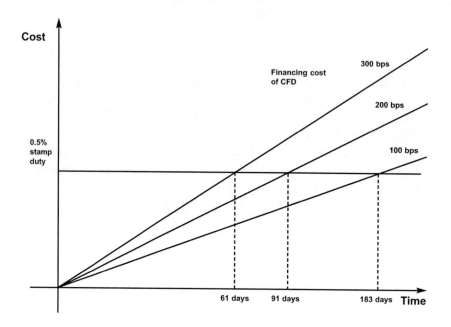

Trading via CFDs also has some additional hidden option value in that the trade may be closed much earlier than expected, or indeed be opened and closed several times. That allows much more flexibility than incurring a prohibitively high up-front cost every time one trades when paying stamp duty. It should also be borne in mind that most providers will allow you to later materialise a CFD position into a real stock position, for those trades that become 'investments', although stamp duty will then be payable and the additional funding cost ceases.

Positive funding with short sales

Short CFD positions generate positive funding, another concept that some find hard to grasp. When a short sale is effected, that sale generates a cash payment on settlement and the CFD provider will pass on some of that interest receivable on the cash, typically 3% below base rates (which with rates currently being so low, is almost negligible). It is slightly gratifying to know, however, that if a stock that you are short of is moving sideways, you are generating a small positive financing flow.

Some stocks that are less liquid and more difficult to borrow may incur special borrow fees. Your CFD provider usually provides a list of these. If the borrow fee is particularly high it can actually mean that a short position becomes negative funding.

For example, with base rates at 5% and short rebates set at 3% below base rates, the client will expect to receive 2% interest on his short position. However with a special borrow fee of 4.5% in addition, he will actually pay a net 2.5% for the privilege of running the short position.

The timing of funding costs

Often funding costs are charged daily and interest payable credited monthly. GNI charges funding on the whole consideration of a position, so if a £100,000 position is established, with a margin rate of 20%, an initial equity of £50,000 (the free equity in this example being £30,000), the funding costs are charged on the whole £100,000 on a daily basis but interest is credited on the net equity – not free equity – monthly; so the client effectively loses the financing spread on the margin component. As the margin rate is set at 20%, the client puts up that amount and the CFD provider puts up the remaining 80% to finance the position.

Similarly, short positions are credited daily but could be negative if interest rates are low. For example, with base rates at 2% and the provider crediting the client interest payable on short position of LIBOR less 300 bps, there will be a funding charge of 1%.

Funding costs are usually calculated on the value of the position marked-to-market, not the opening value.

Collateral to fund CFD accounts

Many providers allow clients to use physical stock as collateral as an effective way of funding short-term trading with longer-term positions. There are restrictions placed on the stock that might be used as collateral, which typically must be:

1. a member of a major European or US Index or FTSE 350 stock;
2. held in Crest; and
3. not the same stock that the CFD is established in.

A *haircut* may also be applied, so £10,000 worth of Barclays Bank may be given a haircut of 20% allowing £8,000 worth to be used as trading capital.

Voting rights and dividends

Generally speaking, CFD holders have no voting rights over the underlying stock, although most corporate actions are reflected in the CFD.

Recently, however, the boundaries have been pushed further and voting rights have been granted to holders of large CFD positions in stocks such as Moss Bros. and Regus by one CFD provider. In these cases it is likely that the underlying hedge position, which resides on the CFD provider's book, is ring fenced, and not borrowed against, to preserve the voting rights and clear ownership of the stock.

Dividends are reflected in the CFD as *cash adjustments* and, in fact, there is a cash flow advantage in holding a CFD. In the UK a stock trades *ex-dividend* on a certain date, now usually a Wednesday since T+3 settlement was introduced, and most CFD providers credit clients with long CFD positions the corresponding cash adjustment on the next trading day. In contrast, traditional shareholders often have to wait up to three months after the ex-dividend date for companies to send dividend cheques.

For companies in the FTSE All-Share, the average time delay between declaring dividends and paying them is around 67 days.

There is a 10% tax differential between net and gross dividends in the UK, so if the company declares a net dividend of 8.7p per share, expect to receive that if you are long. If you are short, however, over the *ex-dividend* date you will usually pay the provider 9.67p or 100% of the declared gross dividend.

Stock/CFD conversion

Many CFD providers will allow you to convert stock into a CFD to release funds, or convert a CFD position into real stock (although CFD contracts do not confer this absolute right). Converting stock into a CFD with a 10% margin requirement will release 90% of the value of the stock as free equity with which to trade.

When you convert a CFD into stock, perhaps because you wish to run the position longer than originally intended, expect to pay stamp duty as the stock will be beneficially registered in your name, even if held in a nominee account.

Short selling

One of the main advantages of CFDs is the ease with which short selling can be executed. *Short selling* is the selling of a stock one doesn't currently own in the anticipation of a fall in the share price. Subsequently the position can be bought back, hopefully at a lower price, and the difference can be pocketed.

It can be a difficult concept for many people new to the stock market to grasp, and it goes against human logic to sell something one doesn't own, but it is an absolutely essential concept for any professional trader to understand. Short selling is second nature to experienced traders and is as natural as going long: they are effectively two sides of the same coin. Short selling is necessary to provide liquid markets and allow hedging techniques. For example, imagine that you wanted to buy a put option from an option trader and he had no means of hedging himself by selling short. He would not be able to make you a price for the option.

Short selling is a simple process, that has been championed by professional traders such as Simon Cawkwell (Evil Knievil), but it is important to understand the mechanics behind how the short sale is effected.

Settlement periods

Today in the UK, settlement takes place three days after trade date (T+3) when purchases are paid for and stock delivered. In the past, the UK market operated on a fortnightly account basis, with all trades settled at the end of this period. This meant it was possible to buy shares at the beginning of the account and sell them towards the end, without having to pay for them. Similarly, it was also possible to sell at the beginning of the account in the anticipation of a share price fall and to buyback later in the account, without ever having to deliver the shares. Another popular way to trade both long and short was to trade T+10 or T+20 (with the agreement of your broker), which means that settlement is effected ten or twenty days later. Some brokers still offer this facility, although it is not very cost-effective.

Risks of short selling – tight stocks

When trading CFDs, the trader need not concern himself with the mechanics of borrowing and settlement of stock as this is taken care of by the CFD provider. However it is important to be aware of the mechanics, and that not all stocks are borrowable. Therefore there may be restrictions on shorting a share. Most CFD brokers provide a list of stocks that are either unborrowable, or *tight*, and the situation can change daily. A stock may become tight if there is:

- a **corporate action** associated with it and the lender requires the return of the stock;
- a **rights issue**; or
- a **takeover**. When one company bids for another with shares rather than cash there is an arbitrage opportunity between the two shares (see *Risk Arbitrage*), creating borrowing demand for the shares of the bidder.

Example – Short selling, Regus

A good example of the risks involved in short selling occurred in Regus, the world's largest provider of serviced offices, in late 2003. I had followed Regus for quite a period of time since it came to market in October 2000, although CEO Mark Dixon still retained a 63% stake. I never really bought into the concept of serviced offices and the expansion in the US seemed ill-advised. Nevertheless, I quite clearly remember giving up on the market's seemingly unlimited enthusiasm for the stock and cutting a substantial short position I had been holding at 365p, almost at the very top. Of course, ever since it has been downhill for the share price, and the company has been a popular short selling target for several traders. I had been somewhat more wary of getting involved again for two main reasons.

Beware of limited free floats

Firstly, the stock free float is relatively small at less than 40%, and that presents extra risk as stocks with small free floats can be extremely volatile and illiquid, as any trader in Burberry will tell you (GUS retained a majority stake). However, under the terms of stock lending agreements, lent stock can always be recalled and, although the stock can often be borrowed from elsewhere, there is

---

Example – Short selling, Regus (contd.)

always a higher risk when there is a limited free float, as the holder of the large stake may not want to lend the stock out to others to short sell – for obvious reasons. They may also recall the stock at short notice. That is why taking a short position in a stock with a limited free float is always riskier.

CFD providers with large positions

The second reason why I had become wary is that for a number of months two CFD providers had been accumulating substantial stakes, accounting for more than 20% of the shares in issue, almost certainly as a hedge against long client CFD positions. Large positions taken by CFD providers in a stock are always of interest to me as stake building is often a prelude to a corporate action of some sort. Holding positions for a long time via CFDs is not normally cost-effective so it is not unreasonable to expect something to happen sooner rather than later.

Disclosure

The level of disclosure had been very good in Regus as the stock entered an offer period on 7 January 2003, which required higher levels of disclosure of dealings under the Takeover Code. Up until that point stakes had been disclosed under the Companies Act that requires declarations if a holding above 3% is amassed. However, once a stock is in an offer period, under Rule 8 of the Code, any dealings in the stock by an offeror, related party, or any person who controls 1% or more of the stock, must be publicly disclosed by noon on the next business day. (Incidentally under Rule 4.2, an offeror is not allowed to sell shares in the target company during the offer period.) In June 1996, as a result of dealings in CFDs during the Trafalgar House bid for Northern Electric, dealings in derivatives by related parties, including CFDs, now fall within the disclosure requirements.

There had also been some confusion during December and January with both Indigo and Cantor Fitzgerald declaring increasing stakes under the Companies Act disclosure requirements, although it later became clear that the Cantor Fizgerald stake was in fact comprised mainly of the stock hedge for Indigo's CFD position.

The disclosures that are made are generally net positions so if, for instance, the CFD provider has clients who have long CFDs of say 500,000 and short CFDs of 300,000 the overall net hedge position in the eyes of the market would be 200,000. The net position fluctuates as trades are executed and if the firm happens to have equal and opposite orders at the same time it can cross the CFDs in-house and not trade in the cash market, so there will be no transaction print and the firm's net position can remain unchanged. It is the overall net position that gets disclosed via the regulatory announcements. Note that if the firm is net short, it will not show up. Things start to get interesting if a firm has a big long position as it may allow other clients to effect short sales; because the firm does not have to go to the lending market to borrow the stock, it simply borrows from its own long position. This is fine as the long holders don't sell, but if they do the firm's net

Example – Short selling, Regus (contd.)

position may turn short (negative) and if the stock is not borrowable the firm will ask its clients who are short to close.

Quite often a stock becomes difficult or impossible to borrow if there is a corporate action such as a rights issue, as the lending institution often likes to have the stock back under its own roof and they may wish to sell at short notice, particularly if the stock is rising quickly. This appears to be what happened in Regus. Lenders of the stock wanted to take advantage of the rising share price and recalled their stock. Remember, lenders retain all rights associated with the stock. It is the policy of many lenders to recall stock during a corporate action such as a rights issue.

Regus announces a rights issue and the stock surges

On 13 November 2003, Regus announced that its US interests were coming out of Chapter 11 and that it was launching a fully underwritten 1 for 3 rights issue at 28p. There was an abrupt change of sentiment in the stock with more than twenty new institutions coming on board and the news was interpreted positively, with the stock rising from 32p to over 60p in a matter of days on huge volume, even with the price adjusted for the nil-paids that were now trading separately. A number of traders who had sold the stock short got caught out, not only because of the rising share price, but worse because they were asked by the CFD providers to close their positions as the shares had become unborrowable.

There was more than one reason for this:

- Regus was conducting a rights issue and there is always a demand for borrowed stock during a rights issue, because there is an arbitrage between the ordinary shares and the nil-paids when they trade separately.
- The clients holding long CFD positions were taking advantage of the price rise to sell their profitable positions. That had the effect of reducing the CFD firms' net positions to such an extent that it was no longer possible to borrow from themselves.

Volume picked up dramatically as the stock started to accelerate and the cash market easily absorbed the profit-taking CFD sellers which rather suggested that there was very good institutional demand for the stock and indeed it continued to perform strongly – so this could be a useful indication to look for in the future. As soon as the rights issue was announced, those with an understanding of the market would have realised the significance and the possible dangers ahead of remaining short. Those who closed immediately got off lightly compared with those who reluctantly had to close somewhat later.

Short selling risk – positions grow larger when they go wrong

There is a further, almost insidious, risk to short selling that is often overlooked. Traders are used to having their books marked-to-market daily, and this can help good discipline in that the opening level of a trade can be distanced from the book position and helps the trader avoid falling into the trap of trying to extract a certain set profit from a trade. However, it is one thing losing a certain amount on a trade and coming in the next day having taken the loss, but with a short position, the overall risk will have increased because the outstanding exposure is now bigger than originally intended. The situation is the exact reverse with long positions, where a stock halving may be painful but at least the outstanding risk has halved. Portfolios are full of stocks that have become penny shares and where it is economically unviable to sell a position because it is so small, unless it later becomes necessary to crystallise a loss for tax purposes.

Short selling risk – open offers

A further risk to short sellers are 'open offers' that give shareholders an opportunity to subscribe pro-rata to their existing holdings on the record date, but which trade *ex* the corporate action immediately. This can be a big risk for traders who are short CFDs, as they will find their accounts will become short of the rights too with little warning.

Example – Open offers pose risk to short sellers

Three recent instances of open offers being suddenly announced to the market have been extremely expensive for short sellers.

On 3 October 2001, **Colt Telecom** launched a rescue open offer to shareholders of 23 new shares for every 25 held at a price of 62p per share, the same as the previous day's closing price. Fidelity, which held 47.7% of Colt, had agreed to take up not only its own pro-rata share, but also to subscribe to any unsubscribed shares and, if necessary, additional shares to take its holding to 54%. This vote of confidence put a rocket under the share price and the shares closed at 83p that day, and within a fortnight were trading at 130p. Great news for shareholders who had an option to apply for new shares at 62p but the shorts, meanwhile, got hit by a double whammy:

1. The share price was heading northwards rapidly, but worse still
2. they were short an additional 920 shares for every thousand that they were short (at 62p), effectively almost doubling the size of their short position.

The shorts that got hurt least were the ones who appreciated the severity of the situation and covered immediately.

Figure 1.21: Colt Telecom (CTM) – share price

Used with permission from Bloomberg L.P.

A similar situation happened in **Corus,** which announced a placing and 5 for 12 open offer at 23.5p on 12 November 2003 to raise £307m, prompting a sharp squeeze in the share price, which closed at 26p on the first day.

In the case of Corus, as the nominal price of a share cannot legally exceed the issue price, the share structure was altered by subdividing and converting each existing 50p ordinary share into one new ordinary of 10p and one deferred of 40p nominal.

Finally, **Invensys,** which announced an open offer and placing on 5 for 8 terms at 21.5p on 5 February 2004, compared to a closing price the previous day of 22p. The stock closed on 5 February up 20% at 26.5p.

The moral for short sellers in stocks with open offers is to manage the risk quickly.

Note: Unlike a rights issue, in an open offer, any shares not applied for are not sold in the market, but placed with Placees at the offer price. The invitation to apply is not transferable or tradeable.

Momentum trading

Momentum trading works best in trending markets, buying shares that are consistently performing well and selling those that are performing badly. The attraction is that no fundamental research is needed, purely access to recent historical price action. A market that is whipsawing is much harder to momentum trade.

SEAQ stocks popular with momentum traders

Very short-term momentum plays in the UK are particularly popular in SEAQ stocks, with traders watching for M codes. This can create problems in the relationship between market makers and brokers. Many market makers regard short-term momentum players as simply traders trying to take advantage of moving prices by catching them on the hop or 'picking them off'.

Momentum traders don't really care why a stock is going up or down, they simply follow what it is doing on the basis that the people who are moving the share do know. It was interesting that many momentum traders found that some shares that they had previously traded successfully became impossible to read when they moved from SEAQ to SETSmm. There is no doubt that the different platforms suit different trading styles as the price action of electronically traded and quote-driven shares is quite different.

Criticism of momentum trading

The issue cited by some commentators is that momentum investors bring no efficiency to the market and can even disrupt it. Paul Woolley of GMO Woolley in his somewhat accurately named paper *Momentum: Private Gain, Public Cost* argues that:

"their actions do nothing to promote the efficient pricing of stocks"

and that:

"momentum is the enemy of fair value".

All perfectly valid perhaps, but of little interest to a momentum trader who is participating in the markets for short-term gain, with little interest in efficient market pricing. Momentum trading is unlikely to die as a popular trading strategy as it requires minimal research but instant gratification for the lazy trader. However, like all strategies it is completely dependent on favourable market conditions and that intangible quality 'market sentiment'.

Spread Betting

Spread betting is an excellent entry-level product. It has the attraction that, unlike CFDs, profits are not taxable; although that also means that any losses incurred are gone for good and cannot be set against further gains.

Trade size

Spread betting allows speculation in smaller sizes, where CFD trading may not be appropriate due to minimum ticket charges and the overheads of a trading platform. For full-time active trading, however, in larger sizes, where a minimum ticket cost is less relevant, the bid-offer spread will become a much more central factor.

Time frame

The shorter the time frame, the more effective CFDs are, especially when combined with direct access.

Leverage

Spread betting also allows the individual to use leverage by trading on margin, to go long or short and trade shares without paying stamp duty.

Short selling

As short selling is inherently difficult in the UK, spread betting provides a useful mechanism to do so, leaving the technicalities involved with the hedging to the spread betting firm.

No certificates

The transaction is also clean without the requirements of share ownership or certificates, as well as the ability to trade out of normal market hours.

Tax

The tax situation also makes it attractive to run positions for slightly longer, although most spread bets will have an expiry date associated with them and will need to be rolled over. CFD holders, meanwhile, will always be aware that the financing is ticking day by day and will eventually overtake the stamp duty savings.

However, it should never be forgotten that spread betting is not really tax-free; the additional bid-offer spread is a tax in itself. In effect it is a transfer of tax revenue to the spread betting firm. With spread betting, the user will never have the satisfaction of buying at the low print of the day, or selling at the high print: accessing the full day's trading range including pre- and post-market auctions where the day's best prices are often available. A significant percentage of the highs and lows of a stock's daily trading range occur in the daily auctions.

Spread betting often involves the counter parties taking equal and opposite positions, however temporarily, especially if the spread betting firm is operating a discretionary hedging policy and so there will be an inevitable conflict of interest, particularly if the trading tactics involve trading breaking news, or trades over a very short time frame. Much better in my opinion to trade anonymously with the cash market where the relationship is not in jeopardy or subject to dealer referral and trades can be conducted instantly.

Benefits of spread betting over CFDs:

- Spread bets can often be made when the markets are closed, providing out-of-hours dealing for those that want it, and many spread betting firms provide free live prices on the underlying instrument.
- There will often be a market available on a new issue (the grey market), before official trading begins on the exchange, although most CFD providers also offer dealings in stocks that are trading on a when-issued basis. This can give an advantage to the CFD trader who can deal immediately, whereas retail investors may have to wait until unconditional dealings commence (usually about a week later).

Spread betting prices, unlike CFD prices, are usually based on the future price of the instrument and are priced as a futures contract. In other words, dividends and financing are factored in, although spread betting firms retain the right to adjust prices if there is a special unexpected event, such as a share split or a dividend falls in a different period than that originally anticipated.

Most spread bets are based around quarterly expiries (March, June, September and December) and spread betting is best suited to the more liquid blue-chip stocks. CFDs, meanwhile, incur a daily financing charge and are adjusted for corporate actions as they happen on the ex-date. A bet is also for a fixed term and has to have an outcome, whereas CFDs are open-ended.

The main difference between trading CFDs and spread bets will always be the relationship between firm and client. I am far more comfortable with direct access to an anonymous market than taking an equal and opposite position to the firm. In the end there will always be a conflict of interest, particularly in the short term.

Messages such as "dealer referred order", "your stop is under review" or re-quotes don't work really for me. Instantaneous dealing counts for a lot, particularly in fast markets or in the context of breaking news.

Stamp duty revenues

Proof that more and more share transactions are being transacted synthetically is reflected in the continuing fall in stamp duty revenues. Despite the value of shares transacted only falling by a few percentage points since the boom of 2000, stamp duty revenues have more than halved from £4.5bn to less than £2.2bn.

Other Trading Instruments

Universal Stock Futures (USFs)

Universal Stock Futures (USFs) were launched by Euronext.liffe in early 2001, and are equivalent to single stock futures in the US. As their name implies, they are futures contracts linked to individual stocks, rather than broad indices.

With contracts available on over 100 European blue-chip stocks, they offer the comfort of dealing on an Exchange, as well as the ability to go short. They also offer substantial gearing with margin rates set around 10%.

They would probably be more successful if they had been launched before CFDs had come into existence, but with the CFD product now so strong in the UK, linked to synthetic direct access, and the ability to trade across the whole spectrum of UK stocks, without the need to roll positions, I find their attraction limited.

They may be more appropriate to institutional users who are restricted to dealing on Exchanges, without the administrative issues of trading over-the-counter instruments like CFDs. The main difference between CFDs and USFs is that CFDs are non-expiring and financed on an on-going basis, whereas USFs are futures contracts with an expiry date and therefore have an associated premium included in the price.

Exchange Traded Funds (ETFs)

ETFs were pioneered in the US in 1993 and launched in Europe in 2000, and are effectively shares in a fund designed to track an index. The attractions of ETFs in the UK include:

- They are tradeable on SETS, and through an RSP via a stockbroker.
- ETFs are eligible to be placed in an ISA.
- They do not attract stamp duty (as they are domiciled in the Republic of Ireland).
- They do not trade on significant discounts as investment trusts can.
- Their dealing costs are lower than unit trusts.
- Exposure to a whole index or sector can be easily gained through the purchase of one share.

However, despite their attractions, ETFs have not been as well received in Europe as they have been in the US. A reason for this may be that instruments based on sectors are not popular with retail investors. Also, the ETF based on the FTSE 100, although cheap to trade, as well as allowing the investor to go short, is over-shadowed by the extremely liquid and developed FTSE 100 Index futures contract traded on LIFFE.

Most UK traders already have an active futures account with which to hedge general market risk. The stamp duty exemption is also of limited value, as one can trade a CFD on an ETF through several CFD providers, and UK ETFs are not exempt from capital gains tax. In the US however, they enjoy a tax advantage over mutual funds, as they are not liable to capital gains tax when investors sell out, which may explain why they have not taken off in Europe to the same degree as they have in the US.

Institutional investors in Europe who want to gain rapid equity exposure to an index can participate in the electronic, highly liquid futures market, whereas in the US ETFs offer an alternative to trading in the US's open outcry futures markets.

In the UK, ETFs are not particularly attractive from a short-term trader's point of view, although retail investors may find the low fees associated with them beguiling. The total expense ratio (TER), which includes all costs such as custody, auditing and administration, is between 0.2% and 0.55%, depending on the ETF, which compares well with unit trust trackers.

Unlike unit trusts which are priced daily at noon, ETFs trade electronically throughout the day and are kept in line with the underlying indices by arbitrage, so rarely trade at a premium or discount unlike investment trusts.

In September 2003, Barclays Global Investors (BGI) closed nine of its sector-tracking ETFs, including the Technology and Pharmaceuticals ETFs, due to a lack of demand. Part of the reason that sector ETFs did not take off was that they were based around relatively unknown Bloomberg benchmark indices.

There are now 29 ETFs (known as iShares) quoted on SETS – 25 equity ETFs (listed below) and four bond ETFs.

Table 1.3: UK ETFs trading on SETS

ETF Name	Code	ETF Name	Code
AEX	IAEX	FTSE UK Dividend Plus	IUKD
DJ Euro STOXX Mid Cap	DJMC	FTSE/XINHUA China 25	FXC
DJ Euro STOXX Small Cap	DJSC	MSCI AC Far East ex-Japan	IFFF
DJ Euro STOXX Growth	IDJG	MSCI Brazil	IBZL
DJ Euro STOXX Value	IDJV	MSCI Eastern Europe	IEER
DJ Euro STOXX Select Dividend	IDVY	MSCI Emerging Markets	IEEM
DJ Euro STOXX 50	EUE	MSCI Japan Fund	IJPN
DJ STOXX 50	EUN	MSCI Korea	IKOR
FTSEurofirst 100	IEUT	MSCI Taiwan	ITWN
FTSEurofirst 80	IEUR	MSCI World	IWRD
FTSE 100	ISF	Nasdaq-100 European Tracker	EQQQ
FTSE 250	MIDD	S&P 500	IUSA
FTSE/EPRA European Property	IPRP		

The most liquid ETFs in the US are:

- NASDAQ 100 Trust (code: QQQ), which tracks the NASDAQ 100 Index; and the
- S&P 500 SPDR 'spider' (code: SPY), which tracks the S&P 500 Composite.

They are popular among both investors and short-term traders and are now some of the most heavily traded instruments on the US market with daily volumes approaching 100 million units.

Reference
BGI: www.ishares.net

Covered warrants

Covered warrants were launched by the London Stock Exchange in October 2002, and offer an alternative form of geared investment to CFDs.

Covered warrants are securitised derivatives which can be traded in their own right before expiry and are issued by investment banks such as: Goldman Sachs, JP Morgan, SG and TradingLab. Like other kinds of warrant they are linked to a particular underlying asset, but do not offer the option of converting into ordinary shares at maturity, being usually cash-settled. In the UK, they are available on a number of blue-chip stocks, but it has been the warrants on the FTSE 100 Index that have proved most popular.

Like traded options, if the price of the option is known as well as all the parameters (such as exercise price, expiry date, interest rates and future dividends), the implied volatility of the warrant can be calculated. This is the single most important value for any warrant, and should be compared to historic volatility.

Although put warrants are also available to benefit from a fall in the markets, as a delta one trader, warrants are not a particularly attractive instrument to trade as they can't be shorted and, like traded options, there is always a premium involved which is vulnerable to changes in implied volatility.

In the UK they have got off to a slow start, and have a limited appeal to an active stock trader, or traders comfortable trading delta one instruments.

Benchmark Certificates

Benchmark Certificates are listed on the London Stock Exchange, and have no management fees. The company backing the certificates (TradingLab) makes its profit on the bid-offer spread.

Indices covered include FTSE 100, Eurostoxx 50, Dow Jones Industrial Average and Nikkei 225.

Note: Although exempt from stamp duty, it is not possible to place them in an ISA.

LyxOR Gold Bullion Securities (GBS)

A special purpose listed company, established by the World Gold Council, offering a way to invest in the gold bullion market without having to take physical delivery. The security, listed on the London Stock Exchange's SETSmm platform in December 2003, is backed by one-tenth of an ounce of gold.

There is also an Australian affiliate, Gold Bullion Limited, listed on the Australian Stock Exchange.

Low transaction costs compare favourably with that of the underlying, which average around 0.7%, and the management fee of 0.3% per year covers custody costs and other incidental expenses.

The stock does not qualify for inclusion in any stock indices as it is backed by a physical commodity. As of January 2005, the total gold held in trust was 57 tonnes, of value US$790m.

Figure 1.22: LyxOR Gold Bullion Securities (GBS) screen shot

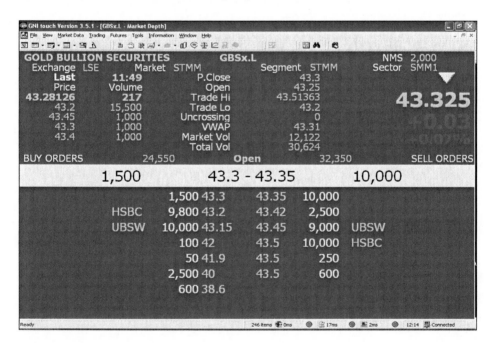

Used with permission from GNI touch®

Reference

LyxOR Gold Bullion Securities: www.lyxorgbs.com

American Depositary Receipts (ADRs)

ADRs exist on a number of UK shares to encourage US institutions to invest in UK companies. The first ADR was pioneered in 1927 by JP Morgan on Selfridges, to allow American investors access to the British retailer. Features of ADRs include:

- They are **denominated in US dollars**, and represent a receipt for shares lodged with an American bank.
- **Stamp duty** is not payable on ADRs, although there is a one-off creation fee of 1.5%.
- **Dividends** are paid to the issuing bank, which pays them to ADR holders after converting them to dollars.
- Although ADRs confer **voting rights**, they cannot participate in rights or bonus issues; nil-paid rights are sold for cash with the proceeds distributed to ADR shareholders.

UK investors perceive that the US market trades on a higher rating than the UK, and a new pool of potential investors can only be a good thing.

> Expect a company's shares to rise on the announcement that they are seeking an ADR listing.

For example, GeneMedix sought an ADR listing to increase its marketability to US investors, as some US investors are restricted from investing in foreign companies not listed in the US.

There are two levels of ADR:

- A sponsored **Level 1** ADR means that the ADRs are traded on the American OTC market and the company does not have to comply with US Generally Accepted Accounting Principles (GAAP) or SEC disclosure.
- A **Level 2** ADR program allows a company a full US listing, but requires full US GAAP and SEC compliance.

A number of companies, including Autonomy and United Business Media, have recently abandoned their ADR listings, citing the cost of complying with SEC regulations and rules under the Sarbanes-Oxley Act.

Unfortunately, ADR arbitrage is efficient

Arbitrage between the underlying shares and the ADRs is extremely efficient (meaning there are few profitable opportunities), and the two quotes rarely move out of line. Investment banks with trade flow in both the domestic and ADR are best placed to carry out the arbitrage, and it isn't really attractive for individual traders to get involved.

Example: Ryanair

Anomalies do occur, however, and Ryanair's ADR trades at a premium of around 17% to its theoretical level as there is a restriction on the percentage of the company that can be owned by non-EU shareholders.

Figure 1.23: Premium of Ryanair (RYA) ADRs to ordinary shares

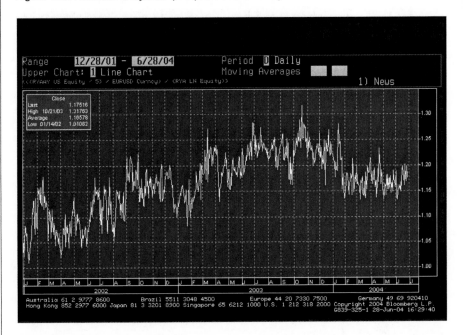

Used with permission from Bloomberg L.P.

Reference

A list detailing which UK stocks have ADRs is included in the Appendices

J.P. Morgan: www.adr.com

The Bank of New York: www.adrbny.com

SEC: www.sec.gov/answers/adrs.htm

Portfolio/Basket Trading

In recent years an increasing amount of trade volume has been transacted in the form of *portfolio* or *program trading*. The introduction of electronic order-driven trading and improved market transparency has lent itself to the simultaneous execution of baskets of stock far more cost-effectively than was possible previously. Most investment banks and major market makers have dedicated program trading desks that will handle the execution and risk of such transactions.

Program trading generally falls into two main types:

1. **principal transaction**: where the bank will quote a price and take on the risk of the execution; and
2. **agency transaction**: where the bank acts as agent and executes on behalf of the client on a best endeavours basis.

The major players in London who are prepared to devote substantial amounts of risk capital to program trading are:

- Deutsche Bank
- Goldman Sachs
- Lehman Brothers
- Merrill Lynch
- Morgan Stanley
- UBS

Programs can be carried out for a number of reasons and are often cheaper for the institution to execute than trading the stocks individually. A transitional trade where one fund manager has lost an investment mandate to another will often be structured as a program, as the new fund manager will take the opportunity to re-weight the portfolio as he sees best. Many programs are conducted on a pan-European level with the program desk utilising the index future in individual markets to hedge net market exposure.

Principal portfolio trading

A client, typically an institution with a basket of stocks to buy or sell, will approach several investment banks for a quote.

Only general portfolio characteristics are given at first

For instance, the institution may have a list of twenty-five stocks that it wishes to buy and twenty-five stocks that it wishes to sell, perhaps to re-weight a portfolio. Rather than execute every stock separately, the fund manager may ask the investment bank to quote on risk. Only basic characteristics of the trade are revealed at this stage, for instance the size of the long positions to sell and securities to buy (for example £120m long to sell and £100m new positions to buy), percentages of average daily volume, NMS multiples, correlation with an index, etc. The portfolio desk will then respond shortly with a two-way quote expressed in basis points around middle prices and the institution then usually awards the business to the most competitive desk.

The winning firm is then provided with the details of the portfolio, securities and number of shares to be transacted a few minutes before the agreed transaction time. Pre-hedging, where the firm starts to cover its risk on the transaction early, as soon as it is aware of the details of the trade, is legal so long as the client is informed that it intends to do so. The client has to balance the risk of giving specific constituent information to a firm that may not eventually win the mandate, against receiving a less competitive quote for more general portfolio characteristics.

The prices, usually middle prices, are then frozen at an agreed time, avoiding times when key figures such as non-farm payrolls and interest rate announcements are released. To protect the firm from spoiling tactics, the trades are usually reported at the prevailing middle prices and the firm's risk premium is taken in the commission agreed.

Often portfolio trades will be executed on the market open, or at-market close, or on the hour during the trading day at the request of the client. These simultaneous multiple trades can account for some of the odd looking at-market orders in the opening or closing auctions, or for strange short-term moves in individual stocks during the trading day.

Aggressive portfolio desks

Periodically, to win business, a bank may take a very aggressive stance in bidding for portfolio trades, even to the point where it is not commercially viable, in an effort to buy market share. Trades will often be priced based on the firm's relationship with the client, although there may sometimes be a bigger picture and the deal may be aggressively priced to buy order flow. Bigger firms with large amounts of capital available to deploy and big flows with an opportunity to match business, may be better placed than smaller ones. A strong presence in program trading can create a virtuous circle with increased flows to the cash equities desks, improving execution and pricing. The firm may hope that the successful execution of a portfolio trade for a content client may win business for other parts of the firm, perhaps in cash equities, block deals or corporate finance. A presence in portfolio trading also makes a clear statement of commitment in the business. However, direct access to the cash market and crossing networks may, in the future, pull some liquidity away from the portfolio trading desks.

Portfolio trades are easy to spot and the trade codes usually used for principal transactions are 'N' and 'P'. There have to be at least twenty stocks for the trade to be classified as a portfolio trade by the London Stock Exchange.

Basket trade is now a generic term but strictly speaking a basket relates to a group of stocks delivered in proportion to their weighting in a particular index or benchmark.

N non-protected portfolio

N trades will quite often appear across several stocks simultaneously as the basket is reported within three minutes of trading. The prices will have been struck at an agreed time and the trades automatically have a publication delay of:

- 120 minutes for **SETS stocks**; and
- 60 minutes for **SEAQ stocks** with an NMS of greater than 2,000.

The prices will sometimes seem odd and may run to two decimal points or more as, for instance, the middle prices will be frozen and an offset applied. Sometimes the price is struck at middle prices and the bank's profit (risk premium) will be incorporated in the commission charged (e.g. 6-8bps).

P protected portfolio

Unlike a non-protected portfolio, the market maker benefits from a delayed reporting of the trades, normally until the end of the day or when the risk is 100% offset. Similar to the protection in an individual stock, the institution is guaranteed a certain minimum price for the portfolio, but, if the execution goes well during the day, may receive an improvement in prices.

Protected means that there is an intention to improve on the transaction within a specified period. Of course this is at the discretion of the market maker and his relationship with the institution. A flurry of P trades will often go through the market in the last fifteen minutes or so of trading, as the orders that have been worked are trade reported and published immediately. Reporting the trade as a protected trade allows the firm to benefit from not having to report the transaction until the end of the day when publication will be instantaneous.

Again, the improvement in price may be reflected in a reduction in commission charged rather than an adjustment to the actual reported prices.

Anything between 0-5 basis point's slippage is regarded as reasonable execution. It is not in dispute that the introduction of electronic trading has reduced bid-offer spreads, as the London Stock Exchange is always keen to publicise, although it is not a full picture without knowing what size is on the bid and offer! It may only be ten shares. However, average spreads for FTSE 100 stocks are now less than 15bps, with FTSE 250 typically less than 65bps.

Agency portfolio trading

Here the firm executes the portfolio on a best endeavours basis and the client takes the execution risk. The client may give the firm some criteria to execute against such as:

- VWAP;
- the previous night's closing price;
- dealing on the close; or
- tranching throughout the day with some residual execution left for the closing auction.

For example, if the trade consisted of selling £40m of stock to buy £30m, the client may ask the firm to raise £10m immediately by selling 25% of the portfolio then transact on a money for money basis.

Transaction-based management systems allow the client to monitor progress of the order electronically as it is being executed and he can adjust his instructions accordingly. If some stocks have been difficult to execute against a VWAP target for instance and suffered from slippage, the firm may smooth the prices by adjusting the better-executed transactions to allow a better fill for the worse ones. In other words, if some prices were more than 10bps away from VWAP, both better and worse, the prices of the worst trades would be adjusted to make the spread tighter with an overall range of say +/- 3 basis points.

If a firm guarantees execution against VWAP then any improvement in execution goes in the firm's pocket, but the firm also takes the risk of slippage. Agency portfolio trades generally attract commission levels of less than 10bps, but there seems only one way that commission levels are headed.

One contentious area is *chopping,* where an unexpected improvement in execution is retained by the firm instead of being passed onto the client; however, modern online order management by the client in real time makes the process more transparent and the client can always request full time and sales details if suspicious.

Risk of execution against VWAP

Guaranteed execution against VWAP carries some risks. Suppose, for example, a desk is asked to sell 10m Shell shares during a day's trading and to match VWAP, and the average daily volume in Shell is 100m shares. By lunchtime the firm has executed half the trade and, as expected, 50m Shell has traded so far, with the price staying stable at 375p. Some unexpected news comes out and the stock rallies dramatically to 390p, where heavy trading takes place, and at the end of the day 150m shares actually trade, with the day's VWAP somewhere near 385p. The broker now has no chance of matching VWAP as most of the volume has taken place at the higher price. Also, because the day's volume was bigger than expected, he sold too much too soon.

The booking of portfolio trades at the end of the day represents the aggregated total of many transactions that have taken place during the day and can often explain sharp stock moves earlier in the day. Many novice traders do not realise that simply watching buys and sells going through the market is not an indication of the whole picture, due to the delays in trade reporting and publication enjoyed by the providers of risk capital.

It is a feature of the European, and in particular the UK markets that a substantial amount of price-sensitive information is released throughout the day, unlike the US, where most announcements are made pre- or post-market. This policy of not suspending stocks gives a big advantage to direct access traders in the UK, but can be tricky for dealers working an order against VWAP, or as part of a program trade, and can be a big shock for US program trade experts who are brought over to Europe, having previously only traded the US domestic market.

Futures and index arbitrage

The FTSE 100 Index futures contract is the most important contract as far as a UK trader is concerned, although it will be influenced by movements in other European indices and, of course, the major US indices. The FTSE 100 future offers a cheap means of speculating on the future direction of the UK market, hedging a position, or arbitraging between the future and the underlying cash indices. A detailed explanation of futures contracts is beyond the scope of this book; however, I do believe it is important to understand how the futures contract can be utilised, what its relationship with the underlying cash market is and how that can affect moves in the underlying cash market.

FTSE 100 Index

Trading the FTSE 100 contract allows market participants to gain exposure to the main UK blue-chip benchmark index through a single contract. The FTSE 100 is a capitalisation-weighted index of the top 100 (actually 102, as two companies, Schroders and Royal Dutch Shell have two classes of share) blue-chip UK companies, representing 80% of the UK market by value. *Capitalisation-weighted* means that a 5% move in a large company such as BP will have a bigger effect than a 5% move in a smaller company such as Sage Group. There is also a futures contract on the FTSE 250 but that is relatively illiquid.

FTSE 100 futures contract

The FTSE 100 futures and options contracts are cash settled at the Exchange Delivery Settlement Price (EDSP). This means that if you buy a futures contract and hold it until expiry, you do not take delivery of the underlying basket of stocks, but receive or pay a cash figure depending on the difference between the opening price and EDSP.

Until November 2004, the EDSP was based on the average value of the FTSE 100 Cash Index every fifteen seconds between 10.10 and 10.30 on expiry day, which is always the third Friday of the delivery month. Of the eighty-one measured values, the highest twelve and lowest twelve were discarded and the remaining fifty-seven averaged to calculate the EDSP.

In November 2004, the London Stock Exchange introduced a new procedure whereby the final EDSP was calculated using an intra-day auction in the underlying stocks, using the same concept as used in the closing auction except that there is no volume check. Expiry now starts at 10.10 with the uncrossing taking place at 10.15, plus a random start time. This new procedure was introduced to concentrate expiry liquidity into a shorter period of time to avoid the wild swings that have occurred in the index during previous expiries.

Note: SETS random periods are a maximum of thirty seconds, whilst SETSmm are a maximum of sixty seconds.

Futures contracts trade on a quarterly cycle of March, June, September and December so there is an expiry every three months. The most liquid contract is usually the closest to expiry – the *front month* – until very close to expiry when the next contract out will become the more actively traded. Trading hours are 08.00 to 17.30.

Fair value

The key feature of futures contracts is the concept of *fair value*. Normally the futures contract trades at a premium to the underlying index, even though the two are guaranteed to converge at EDSP at contract expiry. This is because if you were to buy a basket of stocks now, you would need to finance the position until expiry date, so it is more cost-effective to buy the futures contract. This is reflected in the premium that the contract trades at. However, stock indices contain companies that pay dividends, and if the stock goes *ex*-dividend between now and the expiry date you receive that dividend by holding the basket of stocks but not if you hold the futures contract. Therefore the fair value of a futures contract can be calculated based on current interest rates and expected dividends.

Say the FTSE 100 is trading at 5000 and there are 80 days until expiry, with interest rates at 5%. The cost of financing a long basket of FTSE 100 stocks will be:

```
5000 x 80/365 x 5/100 = 54.8 index points
```

If you have also calculated that there will be expected dividends worth 22 index points, then the fair value for the futures contract will be:

```
5000 + 54.8 - 22 = 5032.8
```

So if the futures were trading at fair value, with the cash Index at 5000, you would expect the future to trade at 5033.

Arbitrage keeps the futures close to fair value

Of course, the futures contract will fluctuate with supply and demand; however, if it rises too far arbitrageurs will step in and sell the futures contract to buy the underlying stocks, hence pushing the cash market up. Similarly, if the futures contract falls, they will buy the contract and short the underlying stocks. Due to the cost of executing transactions in the underlying market, such as the bid-offer spread, there will be an arbitrage channel, within which it is not worth executing the trade.

Take an underlying cash Index value of 5100, with a bid-offer spread of say 0.2% (equivalent to approximately ten index points); the bid price of the index constituents all added together might be around 5095 and the offer price 5105. If the fair value of the futures contract were, say, 55 index points, and an arbitrageur wanted to lock in a profit of at least 20 index points, he might not start selling the futures contract until it reached:

```
5105 + 55 + 20 = 5180
```

Possible risks with arbitrage

Contrary to popular belief, index arbitrage is not risk-free. A couple of interesting situations can occur:

1. If you are running a long stock basket/short futures arbitrage position and a **stock is suspended** and removed from the index at a certain price and replaced with another, because the stock is removed at the suspended price you take the hit if it subsequently turns out to be worthless. This is because the index has not fallen, as it would have done if the stock had been removed at zero.
2. **Cash flow** can be an issue. If you are short a large futures position in a rising market, you will be required to post additional variation margin with the futures exchange; similarly with a long futures position in a falling market. This can lead to serious cash outflows and although you are fully hedged you will receive no credit for the hedge position in the cash market.

There is also the execution risk involved in unwinding the transaction on expiry day, covered in a later chapter.

Fair value is not the same for everyone

Fair value is a subjective calculation and may vary between firms, depending on their internal financing costs and assumptions on forward dividends. In addition, different firms may value the dividends differently based on their own tax position. Firms with large amounts of capital and flow in the blue-chip stocks will be particularly well placed and there will be a close interaction between the cash desks, the program trading desks, and the index arbitrage desks.

The multiplier on the UK FTSE 100 futures contract is £10 per point so buying one futures contract at 4550 gives effective exposure to £45,500 of FTSE 100 stocks. The Exchange has the right to raise margin rates at times of high volatility but usually the margin rate is around £1,500 per contract, which, with an index level of 4500, corresponds to around 3% or 30:1 gearing.

Index arbitrage no longer a monopoly of major market makers

Until the introduction of electronic trading in 1997, index arbitrage was the franchise of the main market makers as they had a monopoly on making prices, the ability to borrow stock to short sell and to trade without paying stamp duty. Now automated index arbitrage trading strategies allow computers to automatically execute optimised baskets against the FTSE futures contract.

As an aside, it is interesting to note for technical traders that the charts of the underlying FTSE 100 cash Index have changed demonstrably since 1997. This is because the Index was calculated by taking the middle price of the competing market makers quotes in all stocks pre-1997 and often there would be a gap up or down in the opening Index price when market makers reacted to significant overnight news. In other words the Index was being calculated based on simultaneous quotations rather than actual trades. Now the Index is calculated on the last traded price for each stock and, as it may take some time until all stocks are traded after the open, the cash Index tends to creep up rather than gap up because with electronic trading the stocks come up in turn.

Exchange for physical (EFP)

An institution may approach an investment bank to transact an *exchange for physical* transaction or vice versa. A simple example might be where a fund manager has bought 500 FTSE 100 futures contracts as a quick and cost-effective way of gaining market exposure and now wants to convert into the underlying stocks. If the fund manager wanted the exact constituent stocks of the underlying index, this would be a very simple transaction and might even suit the existing book of the investment bank. The arbitrage desk may have a short futures long stock position established for a differential of, say, 68 points with fair value currently 52 points. Running this to expiry will guarantee a profit of 16 index points, after execution slippage. Here, however, the bank may offer the exchange to the fund manager at, say, fair value or slightly below. The 500 contracts are crossed in the futures market at the prevailing market rate, so the fund manager closes his long futures position and the investment bank closes its short, and the investment bank delivers the basket of stocks to the fund at prices representing an effective index value of 52 index points below the level at which the futures were crossed.

This is a simple example. What is more likely to happen is that the fund manager wants a specific basket of stocks that may be similar to the underlying basket of the futures contract but not identical. The bank will then price the trade according to the residual risk involved in handling the skewed weightings.

The futures and cash markets

It is overly simplistic to define any one trading day as futures-driven or cash-driven, but because of the strong interaction between the two markets, linked by arbitrage activity, it is important if trading one to keep a close watch on the other. If an investment bank takes on a large program trade in the cash market that is heavily weighted to a net large long or short position, it will almost certainly seek to hedge some of that exposure in the futures market. Institutions seeking quick exposure to UK equities can buy futures quickly and inexpensively, and then later switch these into a basket of stocks.

Quite often, therefore, the balance of the day's action will be in one or other of the markets and one will lead the other. It is essential for the UK trader to have a live FTSE 100 futures feed as well as to keep a close eye on the other main European index futures markets and the early show for the US futures markets. The Dow Jones, S&P 500 and NASDAQ futures all trade pre-market during UK morning hours, giving an early indication to the open of US trading.

Equity block trades and bought deals

The UK market has always embraced a principal, risk-taking culture, although the process is now far more refined than it was. The two big risk-taking houses, Smith New Court and Warburg, dominated the late eighties and early nineties at the time, particularly the former, whose placing power was second to none.

Risk prices

If an institution or shareholder with a chunky stake in a company wanted to sell that stake in one transaction, rather than drip feed it onto the market and depress the share price, they would approach one of the investment houses for a risk price. The broking firm would then bid the shareholder a price at a discount to the prevailing market price of, say, 5-10% on risk, depending on the liquidity of the stock, market sentiment at the time, and the bank's perception of the risk. If the price was accepted, it was then up to the bank to go to work and place that stock as cleanly, quickly, discreetly and efficiently as possible, before the market place got wind of the placing and the share price faded. This was much easier to do before electronic trading arrived, as all stocks were quoted on SEAQ, and a market maker could sit on the bid and make the stock look better than it actually was.

For simplicity's sake take, for example, a stock which is quoted at 545-550p. The investment house may have agreed to buy the stock at 521p and place it at 525p, simultaneously making a turn of 4p per share. It doesn't sound much, but when you are placing 50m shares, that adds up to £2m on a £260m order. The house conducting the business would invariably sit on the bid and hold the stock up for as long as possible, to make the deal look as attractive to institutions as possible. It is one of those rare situations where a stock can be offered in big size at 525p but be bid for 545p in the normal market size. The booking of the trade would obviously take place later or at the end of the day, giving the house some protection from spoiling tactics.

Nowadays the business of bought deals is far more sophisticated, and the monopoly that was enjoyed by the big two market makers has been relinquished to the main global investment houses like Goldman Sachs, Morgan Stanley and Deutsche Bank.

Book building exercises

A bank will often use a *book building* exercise to gauge market sentiment, rather than attempting to estimate the right risk price itself by offering the shares at a fixed price. Although the risk, of course, is that like any big deal, everyone wants to buy the last 500,000 shares when it is clear the placing will be a success. The investment bank will also try to avoid overnight risk; you can only get a certain amount of protection from index futures hedging, and correlated indices and sectors offer little protection.

Backstops are commonly used, where the bank guarantees a minimum price to the seller and takes the risk of the deal on its own book, absorbing any loss. If a price improvement is achieved the difference is shared between client and bank or a fee paid.

Corporate relationships are critical and bought deals will often be part of a bigger picture bringing pressure to bear on winning the mandate. In other words, the bank may be prepared to accept a thinner margin than the risk of the deal implies for the sake of maintaining a good relationship with the client.

Pressure on banks to take on large trades

Contrary to popular belief, taking on bought deals and large program trades for clients is no less risky than proprietary trading. A proprietary trader always has the choice of whether to take on an opening position, whereas the firm may be under client pressure to put its own capital at risk and take on a large trade initiated by the client. A reputation for taking on large trades increases the probability that the firm will have an opportunity of seeing the next trade. With pressure on banks to maintain their global ranking in equity market league tables, the business has become much more about balance sheet strength than placing power. Prevailing market sentiment on the actual day will always play a big part in the success, or otherwise, of a placing.

The market is so competitive and keenly priced, that sometimes the investment bank will misjudge the risk and appetite for the stock and be forced to take a lower price to get the stock off its books. Both Goldman Sachs and Morgan Stanley took hits in bought deals that they bid for in late 2003; the former while placing Texas Pacific's 21.8% stake in Punch Taverns; the latter in placing the Italian government's stake in energy group Enel.

The effect of a bought deal or placing on the market rather depends on how it is handled and whether it leaks out. It is much easier with an electronic market (Central Counterparty preserves anonymity) to spoil someone else's deal, by short-selling stock aggressively, whereas previously the telephone had to be used, and the market maker had much more control over the quote on the screen.

Clients will be mindful of share price performance leading up to the execution of the trade to gauge the real discount to the market price that they are accepting. If a tight lid is not kept on the transaction, share prices can magically weaken ahead of the placing.

Booking of large trades

The booking out of the trade will actually take place later in the day, and the single large transaction that goes through the trade ticket will represent the aggregated opposite side to the many smaller transactions going through earlier.

Large trades that are booked out and appear on the ticker at prices significantly different from the prevailing market price are likely to have a significant instant effect on the share price.

Example: Geest

Geest shares shot up immediately on 28 May 2004, when 3.4m shares went through the ticker at 580p printed at 15.26 in the afternoon. It was later revealed to be a stake taken by the Icelandic group Bakkavör.

Figure 1.24: Geest reacts to large trade at a premium to prevailing price

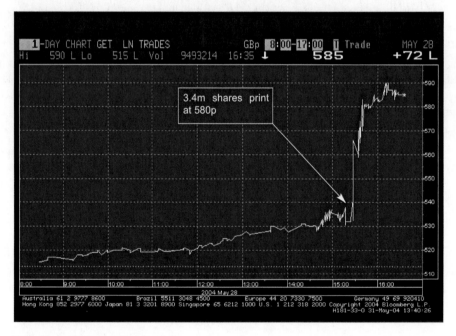

Used with permission from Bloomberg L.P.

Reverse bought deals

Reverse bought deals happen rarely but are utilised when a company makes a dawn raid on another company, bidding for a chunk of stock at a premium to the prevailing market price.

A frisson of excitement goes through any dealing room whenever any large program trade, or bought deal, is taken on by a member firm on risk; followed by the elation of success accompanying the Head of Sales Trading shouting the magic words "offer closed" when the deal is successfully completed.

Hanson's raid on ICI

One of the most famous cases was Hanson's raid on ICI in 1991, when Smith New Court raided the market on Hanson's behalf. The deal was taken on risk, in other words Smith undertook to deliver the stock to Hanson at a fixed price, rather than as a less demanding agency trade, in keeping with its risk-taking culture. Smith bought stock quickly and efficiently in the market.

In those days, Smith was a quoted company trading on a sliver of capital, often taking on large bought deals and program trades, brokered by veteran jobber Michael Marks, many times the size of its market capitalisation.

Its cause in this instance though was helped by not revealing the name of its client, and some institutions were furious when the declaration was made later that evening, just before the news services closed, that it was Hanson that had bought the stake.

I was fortunate enough to observe the whole process first-hand, and some days later I looked across the dealing room and caught sight of Hanson gazing silently across the feverish dealing room. After taking a phone call I glanced back again, but he had disappeared as silently as he had appeared. In some ways almost reflective of his silent and unoticed movements through the world's capital markets.

Section 2

Trading Notes & Strategies

Daily Diary

Basic structure of the UK trading day

Table 2.1: Timetable of UK trading day

07.00	Regulatory News Services open
07.50-08.00	Pre-market auction
08.00	UK market and FTSE 100 Index futures open
08.00-16.30	Continuous trading
14.30	US markets open
16.30-16.35	Post-market auction
17.30	FTSE 100 Index futures close
18.30	Regulatory News Services close

07.00-08.00: Pre-market preparation

The period before the market opens at 08.00 is the most important hour of the day, and by the time the opening auction begins at 07.50 traders will have a clear idea at what price any particular major stock should be opening.

Forward diary of announcements

Scheduled announcements are normally regulatory, and having a good idea of the companies that are reporting for the forthcoming week is essential. Some of the forward diaries produced by the investment banks are extremely comprehensive, and some brokers, such as GNI, also provide excellent reference material such as *The Week Ahead*. Digital Look also has a good forward diary detailing forthcoming company results, economic figures and EGMs/AGMs.

Reference
Digital Look: www.digitallook.com/cgi-bin/digital/event_diary.cgi

Early morning checks

At this hour, traders should be checking:

- the movement of the **major stock indices** overnight;
- the early show for the **futures contracts** on the main indices;
- any **US company results** that were released after hours – unlike the UK, in the US it is common for companies to release results after the markets close; and
- the **ADR** closing prices for any dual listed shares, or shares with good liquidity overseas, like Brambles or Rio Tinto, so that you can anticipate what the opening price is likely to be, adjusted for any overnight currency moves.

Trading before the official open

Although order entry commences at 07.50, Good Til Canceled (GTC) orders that have been input from previous days are left on the order book. Trade reporting commences at 07.15 (closing at 17.15). It is also possible to get a price in a stock from a market maker before the official open, although he is not obliged to make one (remember there are no market makers in SETS stocks; any price will be from a firm prepared to make a risk price), so it is often possible to gauge the opening level of a stock from trades going through before the open at 08.00 (distinguishing from those that are late bookings from the previous day).

Watch out for unaccounted price moves. This is usually down to a broker upgrade or downgrade, some overnight news that you have missed, or a newspaper report. Alternatively, it could be something that the market has got hold of but is not yet general knowledge.

Weekend news

Monday mornings are particularly tricky as the Sunday newspapers will have written up many business stories, as well as tipping shares. In addition, a number of takeover reports (sometimes later confirmed) will get their first mention in the Sunday press, which seems to pride itself in getting the odd scoop. The *Weekend City Press Review* does an excellent comprehensive round-up of the weekend's press, and is available by subscription.

Reference
Weekend City Press Review: www.news-review.co.uk

UK market news can be leaky

The UK market is notoriously leaky and rather than battling against the current, sometimes it can pay to swim with it. A couple of examples:

On 8 October 2003, Amersham opened up strongly at 558p and continued heading northwards to 580p, despite there being no regulatory news release. Sure enough, shortly after 09.30 that morning, a "Statement re share price movement" was released by the company confirming a bid approach and the stock took off, closing the day at 640p.

Figure 2.1: Amersham (AHM) – company news occasionally leaks

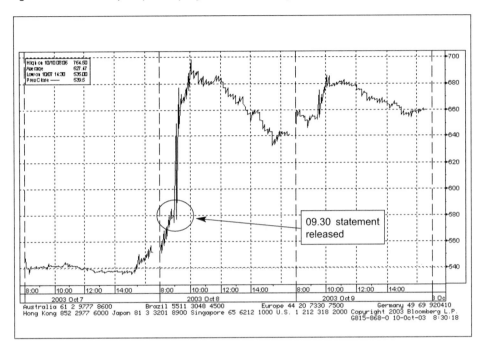

Used with permission from Bloomberg L.P.

Similarly, on 29 October 2003, BOC shares opened lower right from the opening trade and continued heading south on no regulatory news. At 09.00 the company finally confirmed that it had lost a welding fumes lawsuit relating to an allegation over a connection to Parkinson's disease in Madison County, Illinois (nicknamed Plaintiff's Paradise). This was poor form from the company, as it should have got the announcement out before the market opened, rather than allowing a privileged few to benefit.

Newspaper round-up

I think it is essential to get hold of a general newspaper round-up, as well as reading a comprehensive financial paper like the *Financial Times*. Rather than buying all the newspapers, make use of one of the excellent round-ups provided free online by websites such as Digital Look. You can subscribe for this to be delivered by email before the market opens by signing up free at the website. The *Newspaper Watcher Alert* contains a comprehensive round-up of business stories from the day's newspapers in alphabetical order, with links to the online version. Not only are the main English broadsheets and tabloids covered but there are also sometimes stories from Scottish newspapers and some of the US papers, which may not be as well-read in the Square Mile. In the past there have been less widely reported stories on Scottish based companies, such as Indigo Vision, or Scottish based entrepreneurs such as Tom Hunter, that do not become general knowledge until later in the trading day, providing a short-term trading opportunity.

Figure 2.2: Newspaper round up (Digital Look)

Digital Look — Newspaper Round-Up

This alert contains a comprehensive round-up of business stories from today's newspapers.

See the latest newspaper articles online now.

Aberdeen Asset Management (ADN): Aberdeen Asset to launch £50m trust
2005-02-01 (The Herald)

Alliance and Leicester (AL.): A&L hits cashback clients
2005-01-31 (Daily Mail)

BT Group (BT.A): BT leads businesses in fight for £20bn tax rebate
2005-02-01 (Times)

Cable and Wireless (CW.): Lapthorne extends contract at C&W
2005-02-01 (The Independent)

Capital Radio (CAP): Jono Coleman loses Heart
2005-02-01 (Guardian)

Chrysalis Group (CHS): Theakston drafted in to give Heart a lift
2005-02-01 (The Independent)

Chrysalis Group (CHS): Jono Coleman loses Heart
2005-02-01 (Guardian)

EMAP (EMA): Jono Coleman loses Heart
2005-02-01 (Guardian)

Filtronic (FTC): Filtronic jobs go in China move
2005-02-01 (Telegraph)

Friends Provident (FP.): Shares bounce fails Friends Provident
2005-01-31 (Daily Mail)

Friends Provident (FP.): In brief
2005-02-01 (Guardian)

Friends Provident (FP.): A little help with Friends
2005-02-01 (Sun)

Digital Look Featured Services

Your Money - A range of educational trading and personal finance guides to help you make informed and sensible decisions about your finances.

Free Annual Reports - Receive free annual reports delivered to your home.

Broker research - Access premium broker research that you cannot afford to miss.

Funds - Digital Look now provide comprehensive research on investment trusts and unit trusts.

Heat Maps - A powerful visual representation of the stock markets covering share price or RiskGrade risers and fallers, director buying and selling, broker recommendations, and lots more.

Manage Your Account

Your account code is: ▮▮▮▮▮, and this alert was sent to you at
▮▮▮▮▮▮

Unsubscribe from alerts
Forgotten your password?
Change your profile
Contact Digital Look

Digital Look - Free Company Research and News Alerts

Web: http://www.DigitalLook.com
Wap: http://wap.DigitalLook.com/
Email: info@DigitalLook.com

Click here to find out more about **advertising** and **sponsorship** opportunities with Digital Look.

© Digital Look Ltd 1998-2005 – Terms and Conditions

Source: Digital Look

Reference

Digital Look: www.digitallook.com

Influential publications

On Thursdays and Fridays expect moves, particularly in smaller caps, from stocks tipped in *Investors Chronicle* and *Shares* magazine.

On Mondays stocks can react to stories not just in the weekend press but also periodicals like *Barron's*, the well-read and influential US journal, which will occasionally cover a European stock in depth. Barron's roundtable selected Countrywide as a pick on 21 June 2004, and although the stock was due a leg up (there had been some recent significant directors' buying), the subsequent sharp rise may have been due, in part, to the write-up.

Figure 2.3: Influence of Barron's write-up on Countrywide (CWD)

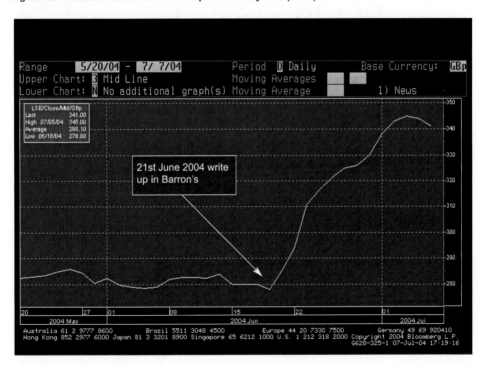

Used with permission from Bloomberg L.P.

Breakingviews issues about six stories in the morning at around 10.00, and a further three or so mid-afternoon. The editorial team, led by ex-Lex writer Hugo Dixon, is highly rated and as the readership is heavily based around the City, I have noticed that on occasion the stories will have an influence over the share price, particularly in special situations.

Websites like mergermarket.com summarise the latest takeover news and gossip.

Of the newspapers, the *Financial Times* (particularly the Lex column) is widely read, and although *The Times* and *The Telegraph* are the most widely read broadsheets, both *The Independent* and *The Guardian* often have takeover stories early.

Reference

Investors Chronicle: www.investorschronicle.co.uk

Shares: www.sharesmagazine.com

Barrons: www.barrons.com

Breakingviews: www.breakingviews.com

Mergermarket.com: www.mergermarket.com

07.50-08.00: Opening auction

There are fewer opportunities in the opening auction than the closing auction, partly because there are lower volumes in the opening auction. In addition it is safer to trade against an at-market order, than against several orders from several other participants that appear to be at the wrong price. They have almost certainly seen something that you haven't.

When a stock opens sharply up or down on significant news in the UK, both scheduled and unscheduled, it is a very common feature that the uncrossing price in the opening auction does not fully reflect the full day's move. It is difficult to be sure of the reason for this, but it is a characteristic that I have seen repeated many times. It may be because not all market participants trade in the opening auction, and so the price may not be fully representative of the market's consensus on the new 'fair' price for a stock. I guess there will always be someone who was the right way round and will therefore be an early profit-taker. It is a feature worth looking out for, however, as it provides trading opportunities; often the opening move is an underestimate of the full day's move. An example is shown opposite where Nestor Healthcare issued a profits warning before the market opened on 13 May 2004 and the stock uncrossed in the opening auction at 163p, down from the previous night's close of 210p. However, the fall continued throughout the day until the stock finally closed on its lows of 127p. Every situation is different of course, but a salutary lesson for those trying to catch a falling knife.

Figure 2.4: Strong moves in the opening auction – Nestor Healthcare (NSR)

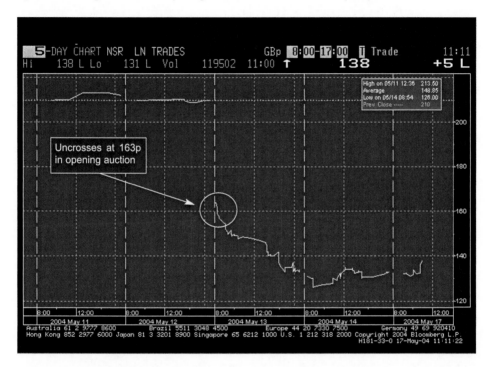

Used with permission from Bloomberg L.P.

Despite representing only a small proportion of the total day's volume, the opening uncrossing trade will often be (or be very close to) the high or low trade of the day for that stock. Traders who are not participating in the opening and closing auctions are simply missing out on some of the day's best prices.

08.00: Market open

By 08.00, as the UK market opens, a trader should be fully prepared for the day's trading.

The main European markets open at the times given below.

Table 2.2: Opening times of European exchanges

Country	Exchange	Open (CET*)	Close (CET)
Belgium	EURONEXT (BE)	09.00	17.30
Denmark	Copenhagen	09.00	17.00
Finland	Helsinki	09.00	17.00
France	EURONEXT (FR)	09.00	17.30
Germany	XETRA (DE)	09.00	17.30
Greece	Athens	10.00	15.30
Ireland	XETRA (IE)	09.00	17.30
Italy	Milan	09.05	17.40
Netherlands	EURONEXT (NL)	09.00	17.30
Norway	Oslo	10.00	16.10
Spain	SIBE	09.00	17.35
Sweden	Stockholm	09.30	17.30
Switzerland	Virt-X, SWX	09.00	17.30
*CET: Central European Time			

08.00-16.30: Continuous trading

Trading is continuous until 16.30, during which time there are key economic figures to look out for, as well as both ad-hoc and scheduled announcements.

Some companies' scheduled trading figures come out at midday, particularly companies that are dual-quoted, such as Reckitt Benckiser and Carnival.

Monthly traffic figures from the airlines are released on certain days of the month; British Airways normally releases its traffic figures at around 14.15. The UK is unusual in this feature, which gives a huge advantage to those with direct market access.

US index futures should be monitored throughout the day, as well as other influential continental indices such as Germany's DAX Index.

Reference

Futures prices can be monitored at:

Chicago Board of Trade: www.cbot.com

CNN Money: money.cnn.com/markets/data/premarket

Traders will often concentrate on watching the higher volatility shares, as these provide the most trading opportunities, although many will add 'guest' stocks to their watch list, and go to where the day's action is and join event traders. Such stocks are often high beta, liquid stocks and will include companies such as:

- Reuters;
- Amvescap (which correlates closely with the US indices and is one of the most popular UK trading stocks);
- Vodafone; and
- Cable and Wireless.

Stocks to watch during the day include the biggest movers on the day (both risers and fallers), those experiencing high volume, and constant gainers (popular with momentum players).

Those concentrating on trading breaking news as it occurs throughout the day will almost certainly use direct access, as there is an almost unavoidable conflict of interest between very short-term trading and a CFD or spread betting provider who is taking the other side of the trade and not necessarily hedging it immediately.

> Volatility is a trader's oxygen; low volatility can slowly grind away at a trader's patience.

Philadelphia Stock Exchange Semiconductor Index (SOX)

A price-weighted index composed of eighteen US semiconductor companies, including Intel and Novellus Systems, primarily involved in the design, distribution, manufacture and sale of semiconductors.

SOX is one of the most closely watched of all sector indices, and although it is orientated around computer chip companies it has often been regarded as the bellwether for the wider technology market.

Reference

Philadelphia Stock Exchange: www.phlx.com

Intra-day opportunities

Stocks react differently to news throughout the day. For example, house builders can be very susceptible to changes in interest rates, and so they will be in focus on days when interest rate announcements are made and during Budget Day, when an expected hike in stamp duty could affect share prices. This type of news will come out intra-day and professional traders will be fully prepared with deal tickets at the ready beforehand.

Different stocks will exhibit different price action depending on which platform they are traded. Some momentum traders specialise in SEAQ stocks, as they have different trading characteristics to order book stocks. Indeed, when some stocks migrated from the SEAQ trading platform to SETSmm in November 2003, some momentum traders had to abandon trading the stocks completely.

Several investment banks took a big bet when SETS and electronic order trading was introduced in the UK in 1997 that there would be a rise in implied volatility, and this proved to be the case. This is because the market-making element in quote-driven stocks often absorbs stock flows without changing the quoted price. Electronic trading, however, is instantaneous and transparent. SEAQ stocks will often have risk capital associated with them supplied by investment banks, which acts as a shock absorber, and will tend to trend one way or the other more markedly.

Direct access allows traders to benefit from leaving opportunistic orders on the order book to benefit from 'fat finger' syndrome. This is where a trader inadvertently keys in a large order with the wrong limit price, sending a stock sharply up or down. If there is sufficient liquidity on the order book the stock may not go into an intra-day auction, but if there are big gaps in the order book, the attempted trade will force an intra-day auction.

Figure 2.5: Centrica (CNA) – example of a 'fat finger' trade

Used with permission from Bloomberg L.P.

09.30 reversal

I am not a big advocate of technical analysis; however there is one daily trading pattern in UK stocks that occurs more often than simple probability would suggest, particularly for stocks where there has been some pre-market news. I cannot explain why it happens so often; it may be something to do with morning meetings, or when institutions start placing orders. However, very often the high or low for a stock for the day occurs around ninety minutes or so after the beginning of trading. Quite often the opening trend for the stock will be reversed at this point, and will then continue in the reverse direction for the remainder of the day. It is a common chart theme and one that was in evidence and noticed by several of the FTSE 100 Index futures contract traders whom I knew. An example is shown below.

Figure 2.6: Example of the 09.30 reversal – Glaxo (GSK)

Used with permission from Bloomberg L.P.

News from related companies

Key trading figures in European stocks can affect UK stocks; we now operate in a global trading environment. Particular stocks to look out for are influential companies like Nokia, which will affect mobile communication and network stocks and other large European companies that are closely correlated to UK stocks.

For example, results from Sodexho Alliance, the operations management and catering company in France, often influence Compass's shares in the UK, as they have similar business profiles. The multinational German software company SAP, and the US groups Intuit and Oracle, may affect stocks like Sage and LogicaCMG in the UK. News relating to closely correlated UK companies may affect the share price of all the correlated companies, not just the one in the news, such as Electrocomponents and Premier Farnell, although Premier's business profile tends to be more US-orientated (and therefore heavily geared to the key Institute for Supply Management Index (ISM)).

Foreign companies to watch out for that release key figures, which may have an impact on UK companies are:

- Dow Chemical (ICI)
- Engelhard Corp. (Johnson Matthey)
- Electronics Boutique Holdings (Game Group)
- Stryker Corp., Zimmer Holdings (Smith & Nephew)

Credit ratings

Credit rating downgrades and upgrades come out randomly throughout the day but can affect share prices if the change in rating is unexpected, or the company is significantly indebted. Quite often a downgrade or upgrade will have been anticipated by the debt markets and so will not affect the share price as much as anticipated by equity traders.

Broker upgrades and downgrades

Broker upgrades and downgrades can be difficult to get hold of; the best bet is to get in the loop with someone who gets them early. The broker or investment bank will obviously keep the change in rating under wraps as long as possible, but the news agencies will pick up on them sooner or later. Bloomberg and Reuters are particularly good at this. Almost all unexpected early moves can be accounted for by this, unless a large market order early in the day has created an artificial price.

Reporting seasons

Reporting seasons go in cycles; key Christmas retail trading figures come out from the second week in January onwards, with the reporting season winding down in mid-September. The US operates on a quarterly reporting basis with Q1 results coming out in April, led by the big companies such as Yahoo!, Q2 in July, Q3 in October and Q4 in January the following year.

Seasonal effects

Owing to timing issues, a number of sectors can demonstrate seasonal effects.

A simple example is the house-building sector, which often performs strongly in the first quarter. It isn't clear why this is, but it is often attributed to the reporting season which generally takes place from late February to early March providing an update on figures and outlook. It could also be the fact that spring is a popular time of year to move.

Effect of heat waves

Summer heat waves can also change people's habits. People go to the beach, or stay in their gardens, and consumer behaviour changes.

- **Winners** are likely to be: garden equipment suppliers; cold food, barbecue and ice cream suppliers; pubs; and companies such as Hozelock, which supplies hose connections, as well as companies specialising in outdoor pursuits.
- **Losers** are likely to include: chocolate retailers; furniture retailers; department stores; and nightclubs.

Bear in mind that the weather may only have a temporary effect, and it is important to distinguish between items cancelled or just deferred.

The wider stock market also has seasonal effects, not always appreciated by traders, other than the traditional:

"Sell in May and go away, come back on St Leger's day."

Trading volumes and liquidity in the market can dry up over summer, and also in the period between Christmas and New Year. Occasionally, good trading opportunities can occur, particularly in the closing auctions during some of these quiet days, where there is insufficient liquidity to offset a large, clumsily-executed order.

Anecdotal evidence

Often trading opportunities can present themselves from anecdotal evidence, and from taking the initiative of snooping around the internet. It's a wonderful resource. Google is the obvious starting point; don't forget the *News* option on Google for the latest breaking news. Another source is NewsNow, and the excellent finance section on Yahoo!.

Reference

Google: www.google.com

NewsNow: www.newsnow.co.uk

Yahoo UK Finance: uk.finance.yahoo.com

Indirect news

The implication of non-regulatory reported news can also be influential.

On 27 October 2003, reports started hitting the newswires from the publication the *Boston Globe* that Bank of America was set to buy FleetBoston Financial in a $47bn stock transaction. As Barclays had been the subject of feverish speculation for a number of weeks about a possible bid from Bank of America, the sharp-witted quickly sold Barclays Bank short and the price dropped 3% in a matter of minutes.

A similar situation occurred shortly after the market open on 17 February 2004. CNBC reported that Vodafone had lost the bidding war for AT&T Wireless to Cingular Wireless of the US. Vodafone investors have been concerned that the company would overpay for AT&T, and as soon as the reports leaked into the market Vodafone leapt in price. With big liquid stocks there will often be enough liquidity on the order book to take advantage. Smaller stocks may not have sufficient liquidity to make a trade worthwhile.

Key personnel

Key personnel leaving or joining a company can have a dramatic effect on a share price. The chart opposite shows the stock market's reaction to the news that Sir Philip Watts was leaving Shell, after the fiasco of having to restate its known proven reserves – an excellent example of a good intra-day trading opportunity for those traders up to speed with events and able to read the implications of the situation quickly.

Figure 2.7: Shell (SHEL) – key personnel departure

Used with permission from Bloomberg L.P.

For obvious reasons, the finance director is regarded as a key member of the board, and an unexplained departure can often make shareholders nervous.

Using your broker

Cheap dealing comes at a price. Traders using execution-only brokers will not benefit from valuable feedback and market chitchat. Brokers often get to see market flows that an individual will never see. Constantly tap your broker for information as to where the trading activity is, and what the hot stocks of the day are.

Even execution-only brokers can differ. Comdirect will only accept orders electronically, whereas with iDealing it is possible to call the trading desk and ask them to approach the market makers verbally on your behalf when trying to deal inside the market spread in SEAQ stocks. Many traders do not make use of this facility, or are simply not aware of it.

Ex-dividends and corporate actions

In the UK most stocks go ex-dividend on Wednesdays, although there can be occasional special dividends or returns of capital that are effective on other days of the week. Be aware of the major ex-dividends, to avoid being caught out in the opening auction and early trading; many participants still make errors.

Corporate actions are another possible play, but note that the London Stock Exchange automatically deletes any existing orders on the order book after the previous day's close in stocks that are experiencing a corporate action, in an attempt to alert market participants.

Morning meeting notes

Most firms have morning meetings where analysts, salesman and brokers have an opportunity to discuss the day's key company announcements and other figures. Again, it is not always easy to get hold of them, although some firms do include them on their websites.

Placings, program trades and special factors

Large placings or rights issues carried out early in the morning can mop up liquidity and put a dampener on share prices, on what otherwise might appear to be a day when the market was set fair. If a large company comes to the market to raise money suddenly, cash that would otherwise have underpinned the market may be sucked in. Expect a weaker market than might otherwise have been expected in these circumstances.

Program trades (defined as a basket of more than twenty stocks) often influence share prices, although they may not be visible until booked out after the market close. The sudden printing of a line of stock on the trade ticker at a significant premium or discount to the prevailing market price during normal trading will often result in the stock gravitating towards the printed price.

Incidentally, there can also be trading opportunities over the quiet Christmas and New Year period as desks are lightly manned and liquidity dries up. Many proprietary desks are paid annual bonuses based on yearly performance, and after a good year many may be reluctant to establish new positions during December. There can therefore be a dearth of arbitrage capital towards the end of the year, which would normally be deployed in situations such as takeovers (risk arbitrage strategies).

There can also be some odd moves around the end of the tax year (April 5/6) as share trading related to tax issues takes place, where a trader can take advantage of short-term share price weakness resulting from end-of-year selling.

Keeping trading screens logged in

Many online, web-based trading systems automatically time out. An auto refresh plug-in can be easily downloaded into Internet Explorer from sites such as www.download.com, which will automatically refresh the screen at a user-defined interval, ensuring that the dealing screens stay logged in throughout the day without having to continuously log back in.

14.30: US markets open

The US markets usually open at 14.30 UK time, although at certain times of the year, due to daylight saving, it may be an hour earlier or later. As the futures contracts on the US markets trade throughout morning trading in the UK, traders will always have a good idea where the US markets are due to open, subject to the release of economic figures at 13.30 UK time.

16.30-16.35: Closing auction

Since the introduction of SETSmm in November 2003, there are now over 850 stocks which have a pre- and post-market auction process. There can often be opportunities in the closing auction, particularly on the last business day of the month, or when there are index constituent changes. A full explanation of these opportunities is included in a later chapter. The general strategy is to take the other side of a large at-market order that is forcing the uncrossing price away from the day's trading range, in the anticipation that the stock will revert to a more normal trading level on the following day. This strategy involves taking some overnight risk.

After market trade reporting

Trade reporting continues until 17.15. A large number of program trades get booked out after the market close and some of the larger trades can account for inexplicable market moves earlier in the day. Program trades are often booked out with the N and P trade codes appended.

I find it extraordinary how many traders think that the day is finished at 16.30 exactly, and miss both the closing auction and significant news and booking of trades shortly afterwards.

18.30: RNS closes

A number of key announcements can come out after the market close, and although most newspapers will pick up any significant stories, it is worth scanning through the day's late announcements before the start of trading the following day.

News

The regulatory news services open at 07.00 in the UK, which can be described as the start of the UK trading day, although you could argue that a trader's mind should be permanently switched on to interpreting information and assessing possible opportunities. News released throughout the day can be divided into two general categories:

- **Regulatory news** such as scheduled results, contract wins, trading updates and unscheduled statements, which are released by companies in a timely way to meet the obligations of the Listing Rules.
- **Non-regulatory news** reported by news agencies, anecdotal evidence, market gossip, rumours and echoes.

De-regulation of company news

The monopoly on the release of regulatory news was broken on 15 April 2002, with the de-regulation of the *Regulatory News Service* (RNS). The London Stock Exchange's RNS is now no longer the sole provider, so be aware that if you only follow RNS announcements you may now be missing some regulatory news. It was apparent that some regulatory news issued during the trading day in the months after April 2002 by some of the other providers did not result in an immediate price reaction, perhaps suggesting that some traders were not paying full attention to the new providers.

The regulatory news providers are known as *Primary Information Providers* (PIPs), and all listed companies are contracted with at least one PIP to comply with the obligations regarding the release of regulatory news under the Listing Rules. Half-yearly interim reports and preliminary announcements are a regulatory obligation and are the primary means of communicating a company's financial position to the market. The PIPs are listed below with their approximate market share as of early 2003.

Table 2.3: Regulatory news providers

Primary Information Provider	Abbreviation	Market share
RNS Newswire (London Stock Exchange)	RNS	83.10%
PR Newswire	PRN	9.60%
Waymaker Wire News	WKR	3.60%
Business Wire	BUS	2.00%
Pims UK	PIM	0.70%
Newslink Network	NLK	0.50%
Hugin Announce	HUG	0.50%

Source: Knowledge Technology Solutions Quarterly Survey

PIPs in turn issue regulatory announcements to *Secondary Information Providers* (SIPs), like Bloomberg, Reuters, Thomson Financial and Investegate.

As can be seen, the London Stock Exchange's RNS service still has a stranglehold on the release of regulatory news. Companies that have elected to switch to competing providers include Royal & Sun Alliance (PR Newswire), Christian Salvesen (Business Wire) and Northern Rock (Hugin Online).

One of the most comprehensive sources of free UK regulatory company announcements is Investegate (www.investegate.co.uk). The website is easy to use with the release of announcements broken down by the hour as well as an archive feature which can be queried by company name, sector or reporting date. Regulatory announcements are also available on the LSE website at www.londonstockexchange.com/rns. Equality of information does not exist in the UK market, unfortunately, as it is notoriously leaky. Time and again companies are forced to make statements when a share price starts to move sharply for no apparent reason.

If you trade news, pay for a good service

If you are going to trade breaking news it makes sense to pay for the best there is and it is a false economy to rely on a basic news service. Bloomberg and Reuters may be expensive but it is not just the wealth of irrelevant additional bond and currency information that the subscriber is paying for. It is also the 2,000-odd reporters that each service employs who regularly come up with anecdotal background material and comments from press conferences and informal interviews that never appear in regulatory announcements. Although there is a fine line between scoops and privileged information, having a full service like Bloomberg, for instance, with over 400 news feeds from around the world, can soon pay for itself.

Occasionally, regulatory announcements released under one company ticker will affect or refer to other companies that have not attracted an announcement, providing a short-term trading opportunity.

Take the example illustrated below where one-liner headlines from Bloomberg live from Morrison's AGM on 20 May 2004 (from 11.34 onwards) affected the share price long before the regulatory text of the AGM was released on RNS at 11.46.

Figure 2.8: Bloomberg news headlines

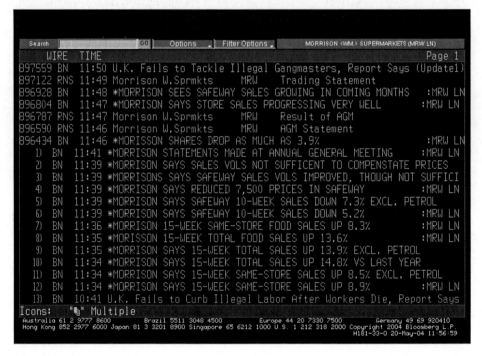

Used with permission from Bloomberg L.P.

Figure 2.9: Morrisons (MRW) – intra-day chart on AGM day

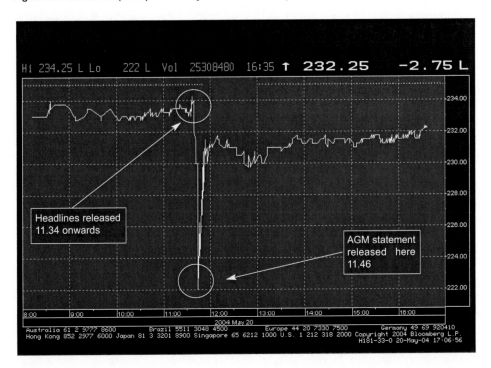

Used with permission from Bloomberg L.P.

News errors

Timing errors over the release of regulatory news do occasionally happen. On 29 October 2003 at 15.59, Cardinal Health of the US confirmed in a regulatory announcement to the UK market that it was launching an agreed 280p cash per share bid for the UK medical products company Intercare worth £233m. Eagle-eyed traders however had already spotted that PR Newswire-First Call had issued the details of the takeover a full five minutes earlier at 15.54.

In another example, on 27 April 2004, Amvescap issued its first quarter earnings, but also inadvertently included an internal document detailing client outflows to analysts and investors on its email distribution list. To maintain equality, the company had to publish the confidential document on its website shortly afterwards, so that all investors had an opportunity to digest it.

We now live in an age where thorough research can often unearth information, particularly on the internet, that is not always fully priced into the share price. So long as the information is in the public domain, it is perfectly legal to trade on it.

Too much news

Companies have to strike a balance between keeping the markets informed and perceived abuse of the regulatory news service by constantly releasing announcements every time a minor contract or agreement is signed (a practice frowned upon by the FSA). A number of companies have been guilty of this in the past in an apparent attempt to swamp the market with commercially insignificant deals.

Trafficmaster appeared to recognise this issue by stating in its AGM statement on 14 June 2004 that, as its Smartnav product was reaching maturity, it would cease making an announcement every time a new partner signed up and would restrict announcements to exceptional new contracts.

An unusual situation arose briefly when Bioprogress announced at its AGM that George Tidy had been appointed as senior vice president at its films subsidiary. However, when the appointment was disputed by rival Stanelco, Bioprogress admitted on its website that it was under advice from its legal advisors and that circumstances had changed. That seems somewhat asymmetrical, and if the appointment was worthy of public mention it would seem appropriate to update the marketplace formally that there had been a change of circumstance; a case of publicising good news but ignoring bad.

Scheduled announcements

Most scheduled announcements come out between 07.00 and 08.00, before the market opens. However, DMA traders should also look out for other scheduled news during continuous trading, such as AGM statements and results from companies that release figures during the trading day (such as Misys). In the UK, trading is not suspended during the release of these announcements, giving a significant advantage to well-prepared direct access traders. The company's website is a good starting point for locating times and dates of future releases and, if in doubt, don't be afraid to call the investor relations department. Other companies that have international interests, such as Colt Telecom and Reckitt Benckiser, also often schedule results during the trading day.

Other market-moving announcements scheduled at specific times on specific days include:

- RAJAR figures (now released pre-market instead of at 11.00);
- airline traffic figures;
- OFT rulings (often on the hour); and
- interest rate announcements.

Key US economic figures often come out at 13.30 and, although these are of more interest to index futures traders, stock traders would be wise to review working orders shortly before their release.

> The key thing to remember above all about company announcements is that no matter how good or how bad the results are, it is the market's expectations that matter.

An unexpected statement may affect other closely correlated stocks, or those in the same sector both negatively or positively. For instance, strong figures from one retailer may not necessarily mean good news for other retailers, as market share may be being increased at the expense of another chain.

Preliminaries and final results

Preliminaries are brief statements that companies are required to release to the market as soon as the annual results are known with any degree of certainty. They can be the most important figures released by a company. They focus on the profit and loss account, and, under London Stock Exchange rules, must contain:

- net turnover;
- profit or loss before taxation and extraordinary items;
- taxation on profits;
- extraordinary items;
- profit or loss attributable to shareholders; and
- earnings per share (in pence).

The statement must also include comparative figures for the previous year, and have been agreed with the company's auditors (although not necessarily based on audited accounts).

Often the release of preliminary figures will be followed later in the morning by analyst presentations where the figures are discussed in more detail. These meetings can have a further significant effect on the share price as feedback starts to leak back into the marketplace.

Some companies issue preliminaries very shortly after the end of the period to which they apply, whereas other companies appear to take a more leisurely approach. The average period is around ten weeks, and the full annual report and accounts usually follow around three weeks later.

Interim results (half-yearly)

The half-yearly report contains information on the company's activities and profit or loss, and must be published within **ninety days** of the end of the period to which it relates (the first six months of the financial year). The interims must also include a profit and loss account, balance sheet and cash flow statement, as well as comparative figures to the corresponding period in the previous year. It is often the case with interims that the statement relating to the current trading outlook is much more important than the results themselves.

Annual General Meetings (AGMs)

AGMs take place all year round, but are heavily concentrated around May and June – a few weeks after many final results are published. AGM statements released to the regulatory news service generally come in two forms:

- routine ones that usually confirm that all resolutions were passed; and
- the more interesting ones from a trader's perspective which comment on the year's trading and sometimes give an insight into more recent trading and the current outlook.

These comments can be important and can be share movers, as can be seen in the following charts when Rank issued a poor AGM statement mid-morning, and Molins warned of the loss of a substantial contract in its AGM statement.

Figure 2.10: Rank (RNK) – effect of a poor AGM statement

Used with permission from Bloomberg L.P.

Figure 2.11: Molins (MLIN) – contract loss in AGM statement

Used with permission from Bloomberg L.P.

Pre-close trading statements

Pre-close trading statements are not a regulatory obligation, but are often released by companies as part of a general policy to update the market prior to entering the company's closed period. The statements can be significant, particularly if there is a sudden change in trading conditions, and although a company may not choose to update the market, that does not in itself imply that trading is exactly in line with expectations. However, a company may choose to update the market to prevent a leakage of price-sensitive information before results day. Also, updating the market prior to the scheduled release of results gives the company an opportunity to focus on the better side if and when poor results are released.

Unscheduled announcements

These are usually market movers and include:

- profit warnings;
- bid approaches;
- the sudden loss of an important contract; or
- news on such regulatory issues as drug approvals (or not).

Just one of many examples featured SkyePharma, which was hit heavily when it was announced during the trading day on 4 March 2005 that the US Food and Drug Administration had halted the production of GlaxoSmithKline's depression medication drug, Paxil CR. This hit SkyePharma as the company had a licensing and royalty deal with Glaxo on Paxil. It is worth noting that the regulatory announcement was released by Glaxo and not by SkyePharma and made no mention of SkyePharma, probably accounting for the relatively slow reaction in SkyePharma's share price. Only those familiar with the deal would have realised the immediate significance on SkyePharma and hence the opportunity.

Figure 2.12: SkyePharma (SKP) – intra-day breaking news

Used with permission from Bloomberg L.P.

Trading The UK Market On Margin

"The most valuable commodity I know of is information.
I look at a hundred deals a day. I pick one."

Gordon Gekko, Wall Street, the movie

After information, the most valuable commodity a margin trader can have is capital. Without capital he cannot participate in the markets. I have seen many novice traders get backed into a corner because of over-gearing and, consequently, having no free equity. Many simply run out of capital while serving their apprenticeship and learning about market basics. The most successful traders I have noted always have firepower in case of an opportunity. You can guarantee that the most attractive trade of the month will come along when the gun has just run out of bullets.

> Just because margined products like CFDs and spread betting offer the ability to gear up, doesn't mean that the facility has to be fully utilised all the time. This is particularly true of opportunistic traders who are trading breaking news and will always want to have firepower available.

I have seen traders try to manage while undercapitalised and it is extremely difficult, not least because costs such as minimum ticket charges make it economically more realistic to trade to a certain scale. All too often there is a slow but gradual conversion of net equity into commission. Trading costs should always be in proportion to the anticipated profits and losses and the risk taken – this applies to accounts of all sizes.

Minimum capital requirements

Capital of around £50,000 is a number that many full-time traders that I know regard as the minimum to trade with, giving access to £500,000 of positions at any one time on typical margin rates of around 10%.

Although I agree that trading on margin is entirely reasonable, the comparison with buying a house with a mortgage is not really valid. With margin trading it is not possible to fall into negative equity and *recover*, due to the mark-to-market nature of the instruments; whereas you can with property – so long as you keep making the payments.

Margin calls

My advice regarding margin calls is not to pay them. The best traders never pay margin calls because they are never on call. That is not to say that all positions should be closed during the day. Some of the best trading opportunities occur during the closing auction or by running positions overnight. Traders who restrict themselves to trading only intra-day, and smugly tell anyone who will listen that they *never* run positions overnight, are simply missing some of the best opportunities.

Short selling risks

"The markets can stay irrational longer than you can stay solvent."
John Maynard Keynes

Although trading long and short are two sides of the same coin, there are additional risks to short selling as discussed earlier. To recap, one of the issues regarding a short position going the wrong way, that is often not appreciated by traders is the outstanding risk.

For example, say a trader is short 100,000 CFDs in Vodafone at 120p, and the stock rises 20% on the day to close at 144p. The mark-to-market loss taken on the day will be £24,000, but the outstanding position is now a short position worth £144,000, up from £120,000. The key point is that the outstanding risk has also gone up – on a losing position. This is the reverse of what happens to long positions that fall sharply. The loss may be painful but the remaining risk relating to the outstanding position is lower. *This is a characteristic not always fully recognised.*

Technical analysis

I am sceptical of the application of technical analysis, particularly to less liquid stocks, although I concede that it becomes self-perpetuating if enough people follow it. A great number of traders that I know, however, do follow basic support and resistance levels, gaps and key moving averages. It's really a question of finding out what works for the individual. Rather than using charts to look for patterns that may or may not play themselves out, or repeat themselves, I find it of more value to see where and how a stock has traded over a recent period of time and how volatile it has been.

Paper trading

"Paper trading isn't worth the paper it's written on."

The quote above is from one of the most successful UK traders I know, who, in the process of a couple of years, turned his CFD trading account from an initial £10,000 balance to over £700,000. He makes a valid point. I have seen numerous aspiring traders paper trade successfully, and then mysteriously start losing money as soon as they trade for real. Human nature being what it is, I suspect it is more to do with the discrepancy in behaviour which occurs when trading with real money instead of imaginary numbers on a piece of paper.

Stop losses

More time is spent debating stop losses than any other trading strategy. Some firms offer guaranteed stop losses and others offer stop losses on a best endeavours basis. The former will come at a premium (typically 0.3-0.75% of the underlying), while the latter may involve some slippage risk in execution.

For someone who is not able to trade full time they offer some insurance from an event happening; and for novice traders they instill good discipline. Even so, I don't believe a standardised stop loss policy exists, or is appropriate for all stocks and instruments.

Stop losses are also susceptible to the vagaries of electronic trading; a *fat finger* can trigger a stop loss after an unrepresentative trade is completed on the order book. It seems to me that stop losses are more suited to automated trading strategies or trades based on technical analysis.

As a special situations and event-driven trader, I find it more appropriate to constantly reappraise situations on an ongoing basis. The most important thing that was drummed into me as a proprietary trader was to estimate the amount that you were prepared to lose on a trade in a worst case scenario, before placing the trade, based on the historic volatility and liquidity of the stock involved, and evaluate the likely possible outcomes and the probability of each scenario. Entering a trade is easy; it's the exit that can be the difficult bit.

Full-time traders can probably afford to adopt a more flexible approach as they can assimilate new information immediately as it becomes available.

Some definitions:

- **Stop loss**: an instruction to sell a share should the price fall to a pre-specified level.
- **Stop buy**: an instruction to buyback a position if the price rises to a certain level.
- **One cancels the other (OCO)**: a combination instruction. If you held a stock at 135p and wanted to take profits at 147p with a stop loss of 129p, you could place an OCO to cancel the other order as soon as the first was executed.

I am also far more comfortable placing stop loss orders with a DMA broker rather than with one that is quote-driven, where the triggering of the stop loss may be more arbitrary. The price at which the stop is executed can also be subject to some slippage when spreads can mysteriously widen.

Stop losses aside, short positions that are going wrong should be carefully managed, as the position is now a much more significant and larger percentage of your net equity than before. Experienced traders are quite comfortable reducing positions to reduce the risk. It isn't necessary to be either all in or all out of a trade. Sometimes it can be easier to close a losing position completely after reducing the position by half, as mentally the admission of being wrong has already been made. I find the same technique also works well for long positions that are making money and hence getting bigger. Taking the profit on half the position allows more room for manoeuvre should the stock retrace, reducing the exposure while retaining an interest.

> It isn't obligatory to have positions all the time. Some of the worst trades are done through boredom. Not having a position is in itself having a position.

Be aware that if there is a sharp move downwards in a stock, or number of stocks, that is popular with margin traders, there may be a knock-on effect in other similarly traded stocks if traders have to reduce other positions to meet margin calls.

In my experience, the most successful traders I know spend most of their time talking about their losing trades; the least successful seem to spend most of their time talking about their few winning trades, and show an obsession with conspiracy theories as to why the market is out to get them.

Where you stand in the UK market

Trading the market is not dissimilar to real life; work out what your competitive advantage is, focus on it and leverage it. The most successful traders I have come across all have an edge which works for them, whether it's:

- in-depth knowledge of a certain sector;
- industry experience;
- an understanding of takeover situations;
- trading breaking news;
- access to placings;
- technical analysis; or
- balance sheet knowledge.

Know where you are on the information curve

I am a great believer in the information curve in terms of trading. If I am the last to hear a tip, it strikes me that there will be no-one else left to buy it anyway. Time and again, novice traders are surprised when stocks fall on good news and rise on bad news because they have failed to factor in the market's expectations. A classic example is broker upgrades and downgrades. These will be released to the general marketplace long after a bank's preferred clients and long after any influence over the stock has passed. However, novice traders continue to ridicule the notes because the stock often moves in the opposite direction after they have seen it. That is the whole point. The average trader is at a competitive disadvantage regarding these upgrades because of the selective release.

One of the best examples of market expectations versus reality occurred in March 2004 in Jarvis, the support services group.

Example: Jarvis

On 3 March 2004, the BBC was due to broadcast a *Money Programme* exclusive on Jarvis which would not be particularly positive, focussing on alleged project over-runs and gripes from a number of sub-contractors that Jarvis was not paying them on time.

This programme was discussed in advance at great detail among most UK trading communities, and sure enough the programme was broadcast on schedule on the evening of 3 March, the stock closing that day at 134.25p.

The performance of the shares over the next two days was startling for many people, but for me completely logical.

Figure 2.13: Jarvis (JRVS) – following a feature on the BBC's *Money Programme*

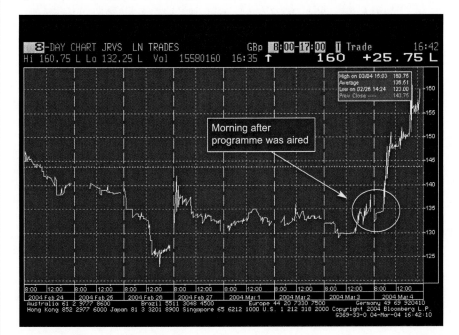

Used with permission from Bloomberg L.P.

Nothing much happened on 4 March (the following day) for the first hour or so of trading, as the stock opened more or less unchanged, much to the annoyance of all those that had either dumped the shares in panic or shorted them in anticipation of a collapse. The situation resembled something like a spaghetti western with everyone watching everyone else out of the corner of his or her eyes,

Example: Jarvis (contd.)

waiting for someone else to make the first move. By 09.30 the stock was on the move, closing that day at 160p and over the next two days a gigantic bear squeeze took place with the stock trading up to 190p at one point; a big move by anyone's standards. There was simply no-one left to sell the stock, and there was a complete capitulation by the bears. If, however, the programme had not been publicised beforehand with the subject remaining secret I am convinced that we would have seen a sharp fall in the share price.

Six weeks later the company released a poor trading update, confirming most of the issues raised in the programme and the stock gave back all its gains (see below).

Figure 2.14: Jarvis (JRVS) – three month chart

Used with permission from Bloomberg L.P.

There was a clear lesson in this episode, not just that timing is everything but that those shorting the stock in anticipation of a downward move were the last to sell it, there was simply no-one left to sell it.

Spotting opportunities

Successful traders will identify and distinguish when a share price is being influenced by a short-term effect, such as a large worked order, or by something more sinister, such as some price-sensitive news leaking into the market. Opportunities will often present themselves when news has been misinterpreted, or the trader has identified stock movements that are only temporary, with the share price likely to revert to a fairer value. Market participants will have different investment styles, different attitudes to risk and different time horizons, all of which may present an opportunity to the alert trader. It may be much more attractive to event trade and go to where the daily action is, than grind away by trading the same stock day after day. It rather depends on the individual trader's skill at interpreting results, statements and breaking news, as well as familiarity with the price action of the stock.

Know your reasons for trading

I have often seen novice traders suddenly start using fundamentals such as current interest rates, price to earnings ratios and dividend yields to justify short-term trades, particularly after they have just started to go wrong.

Between May 2002 and March 2003, Lloyds Bank dropped from over 800p to 290p, almost in a straight line. For the last six months of that fall I had to listen almost daily to people telling me that Lloyds was a buy because the dividend yield was so high (the figure increased every time to almost 12% in the end). The trader should only be concerned with buying something not because it is cheap, but because he thinks someone else will pay more for it shortly; similarly, selling something only because he believes that someone else will take a lower price for it in the near future (sometimes known as the *Greater Fool Theory*).

News sources

Traders in the UK who concentrate on breaking news need the best news source. Bloomberg and Reuters may be expensive but that is for a good reason. With over 2,000 dedicated reporters each, they can often get anecdotal information to the subscriber more quickly, such as unofficial statements and reports from press conferences and company conference calls.

Efficient market hypothesis

I am not a subscriber to the efficient market hypothesis, and every day there are badly handled orders and mistakes, which create opportunities for other traders. Share prices are supposed to represent all that is currently known about a company and embody all available information concerning current and future events, but this takes no account of the laws of supply and demand, which should be of paramount importance to a trader if not an investor.

Comparison with the US

The UK is structurally still more expensive to trade than the US, although that does not make the UK untradeable. Given the choice I would prefer to trade stocks I know and understand a little about for a reasonable cost, than trade stocks that I know nothing about for free.

The term *daytrader* also has different connotations here and in the US. In the US, it usually refers to someone who trades very actively during the day, while running very few, if any, trades overnight. In the UK, it is more commonly associated with a trader who trades the market for a living.

Some traders would argue that by trading for a living they are in effect running their own hedge fund, and there is some truth in this as both adopt strategies requiring the ability to go long and short, utilising leverage, and seeking arbitrage opportunities. Both traders and hedge funds will be attracted to short-term opportunities and trading strategies such as flipping IPOs and seeking volatility – the oxygen of trading. Other shared strategies include market neutral trades, pairs trades and takeover situations, although hedge funds will be better placed to secure an allocation in a new convertible issue, which may come packaged with the short equity hedge.

Significance of large institutional holdings

Disclosure requirements and notifiable interests

The Companies Act requires prompt disclosure of substantial holdings to the company itself within two business days if a share holding:

- reaches 3%;
- above 3%, changes by one whole percentage or more; or
- falls below 3%.

Market makers are exempt from the disclosure requirements to protect their positions from spoiling. In the case of fund managers, the disclosure level is 10%.

212 notices

Enquiry notices can be fired out by the company under section 212 of the Companies Act, requiring disclosure of shareholdings at any point in the previous three years. Shareholders are also required to disclose beneficial ownership. Failure to reply "within a reasonable period of time" can result in the company disenfranchising the shares and removing the associated voting rights and dividends.

Man Financial and Eidos

Large holdings held effectively via CFDs are causing some issues which are likely to result in a change in the disclosure regulations. In early 2004, Man Financial disclosed a large holding in Eidos, the computer games developer, which was almost certainly a hedge against a CFD contract as Man Financial's policy is to hedge all client CFD transactions. This contract was reported to have been with a spread betting firm, where CFD transactions are often used in turn to hedge a spread bet position with a client (reported in the press, in this case, to have been Robert Bonnier).

Eidos is believed to have served Man Financial with a 212 notice. However, as the CFD contract only relays the economic interest in the stock, the beneficial interest would appear to reside with the CFD provider, or Man Financial in this case.

Many of the big holdings over 3% in companies declared by investment banks under the Companies Act relate to proprietary positions and hedge positions in the cash market against synthetic contracts with hedge funds. The press often highlight these but fail to explain their significance.

When a CFD provider like Man Financial, which does not run proprietary positions and hedges all its client CFD transactions in the cash market, appears with a large holding in a company it will generally represent the aggregated net position of the firm in that stock at that time. In any one stock the CFD provider will have a net position, either long or short. Large short positions do not have to be disclosed under the Companies Act, in contrast to long positions over 3%, so it is only the long positions that come to light. A firm that operates a policy of hedging all transactions in the underlying marketplace will have a stock position on its own book that exactly hedges the CFD contracts between itself and its clients.

In summary, when the client buys 100,000 Vodafone CFDs, the CFD provider buys 100,000 Vodafone shares in the market at the same price, places the stock on its own book, and writes the client the CFD contract. The client is long Vodafone CFDs, the firm is short Vodafone CFDs and long Vodafone shares, and the marketplace effectively just sees the provider buying stock in the market, effectively a riskless principal transaction. The client has effectively synthetically utilised the firm's access to the markets and stamp duty exemption to deal cheaply.

Figure 2.15: CFD trade flow

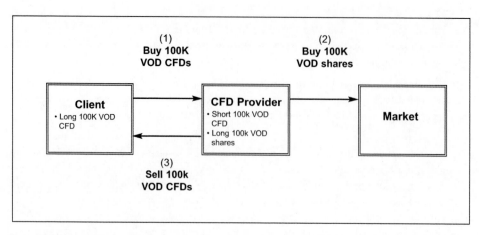

Spread betting companies that are not member firms of the London Stock Exchange will also need a means of hedging, and will often use a CFD provider. For example, if a spread betting firm wishes to hedge a large 'up bet' it will buy a long CFD from the CFD provider, which will simultaneously hedge itself by buying stock in the market. The chain of trades is as follows:

Figure 2.16: Spread bet – CFD trade flow

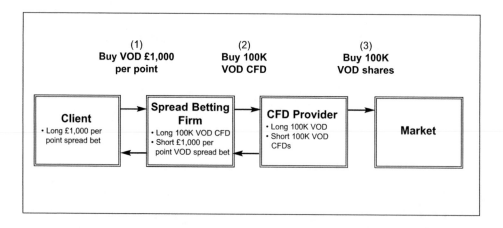

Thus a large holding disclosed by a member firm which is also a provider of CFDs, could in fact represent a large spread bet taken out, or any net combination of CFDs and spread bets. If a number of large positions in a stock are in opposite directions, the net long position may not breach 3% and hence never show up. Some firms operate a policy of not wanting to make these disclosures and so will not take more than a certain percentage stake in any one company, and may subsequently turn business away if the current book position prevents them increasing its stake. IG Markets currently has a limit of 2% on holdings, probably because they do not want to draw attention to their positions or risk going through the 3% declarable level.

CFD providers' shareholdings

Some CFD providers adopt internal guidelines over how large a net position they are prepared to take in a company, as a hedge against a client CFD transaction, before turning business away. This can be demonstrated by the large number of regulatory disclosures that some providers make under Companies Act obligations, whereas others firms rarely make any disclosures.

It is still unclear what would happen if a CFD provider took a position in excess of the bid threshold of 29.9%, triggering a mandatory bid, as this has yet to be tested. Any resulting offer would have to be pitched at a minimum of the highest price paid by a CFD provider for shares within the previous twelve months. A CFD provider could argue that if a separate agreement exists with the client over the voting rights, then its beneficial interest would be less than its registered interest.

> I keep a track of major shareholdings by CFD providers because in the past they have been a good indicator of future corporate activity or share price movement.

If a client is establishing a CFD position, as opposed to a normal stock position, there is usually a good reason.

Although the leverage can be attractive, whereby a large position can be built up on margin without having to finance the total consideration, CFDs are, by their nature, short-term instruments, and often the person establishing the position expects something to happen within a reasonably short time horizon. Because of the nature of the financing of CFDs, it is not normally cost-effective to run long CFD positions for long periods of time, compared to an ordinary share transaction.

Often in risk arbitrage situations the big investment banks, such as UBS, Deutsche Bank, Bear Stearns and Goldman Sachs, will appear with large holdings. These will represent the aggregate stock hedge position against all outstanding hedge fund CFD positions and its own proprietary position. A firm can often be restricted in transactions if it is linked in an advisory role to the takeover situation, as the stock will appear on the firm's internal restricted list. Hedge funds will often have accounts with more than one prime broker in case a stock that they wish to deal in is on the broker's restricted list, perhaps because the corporate finance department of the same firm is advising the client. This can also occasionally create problems if the firm subsequently becomes involved in a takeover situation.

Example: Canary Wharf

During the bitter fight for Canary Wharf in spring 2004, UBS built up a large position in Canary Wharf, partly for its own book and partly as a reflection of hedge fund CFD positions. However, when British Land, one of UBS's clients, joined one of the bidding consortia late in the day, UBS suddenly found itself in the position of not being able to vote its stake, which might have been crucial to the outcome of the bid battle. UBS appealed a Takeover Panel decision that blocked the stake from being voted, and its trading arm was subsequently allowed to vote its stake – a very significant victory as Panel decisions are rarely overturned. However, the case did highlight the potential conflicts that can arise when a bank's trading and advisory arms are both involved in a competitive deal. The Panel had, however, correctly recognised that the reality of the situation was that the trading position was effectively unrelated to the bank's advisory capacity. Although under the letter of the rules the stake could not be voted, the reality was that there had been no deliberate intention to adversely affect the outcome. It is doubtful, in my opinion, whether a court in the US would have ruled the same way, highlighting the strength of the Panel's non-statutory status in allowing an interpretation.

In 2005 the takeover disclosure rules were amended to include the disclosure of CFD positions amounting to more than 1% of a company's total shares in issue. The Companies Act, which imposes the 3% disclosure rule, has however not yet been amended.

Company Watch

Company news

Investor road shows, analyst presentations and briefings

The regulators do not allow selective analyst briefings, but there is evidence that it occasionally occurs, inadvertently or otherwise. FSA guidelines allow companies to discuss information already in the public domain, and restrict the release of *price-sensitive* information, but this type of information is often inadvertently given.

The FSA had to write to all listed football clubs in 2003 reminding them of the rules regarding the release of price-sensitive information, after details of player transfers were posted on websites before any regulatory information was forthcoming.

Under current listing rules, companies should announce without delay any significant developments likely to lead to a substantial share price movement. The Market Abuse Directive has moved public disclosure of price-sensitive information away from the current event-driven scenario to just "possession" of privileged information.

Management can always make personal views known of course, but it is a fuzzy line. For example, shares in GWR rose 10% the day after it hosted a party for several City analysts one evening at the end of August 2003. Although this doesn't prove anything, a simple comment that trading is in line with expectations in a sector which is suffering downgrades, could be interpreted as bullish. It is very difficult to define new information against existing expectations, and interpretation is everything in that what is said, and what is understood, could be entirely different things.

It can be tricky getting regular, reliable advance notice of analyst days, although a good broker may keep you informed. Occasionally, the company will put out a regulatory statement detailing what the teach-in or presentation will cover. Some analysts may be attending for the first time, being new to the company, and upgrades and an initiation of coverage often follow.

Trafficmaster held an analyst trip on 20 May 2004, with a subsequent significant rise in the share price shortly afterwards.

Figure 2.17: Trafficmaster (TFC) – analyst trip

Used with permission from Bloomberg L.P.

Pharmaceutical research and development days often result in analyst upgrades or downgrades with accompanying share price moves; traders should try to be aware of them, even though they are not always publicised. The company website can be a good starting point.

Trade fairs

Trade fairs can be important too, heralding the introduction of new products and launches.

For the IT industry, look out for: the Computer Dealers Expo (Comdex) in Las Vegas in November; the less significant Consumer Electronics Show also in Vegas during January; the CeBIT computer trade fair in Germany; and the interactive entertainment industry's E3 (Electronic Entertainment Exposition) Gaming Conference in Los Angeles in May.

Single product companies

Many companies are heavily dependent on a single product, and news or anecdotal evidence on its success or otherwise can make or break a company. It is not just drug or biotech companies that can be heavily dependent on a single product. Companies such as Transense Technology, Monotub and Torotrak are effectively single product companies.

Example: Monotub

It is interesting to note, in passing, that there was an opportunity in January 2002 when *Which?* magazine reported problems with Monotub's revolutionary Titan washing machine, which it was trialling at the time. The magazine reported that it was experiencing problems and defects but it wasn't until the story was reported in the more widely read *Daily Telegraph* that the stock started to head south in a big way.

Figure 2.18: Monotub – following a report in *Which?* magazine

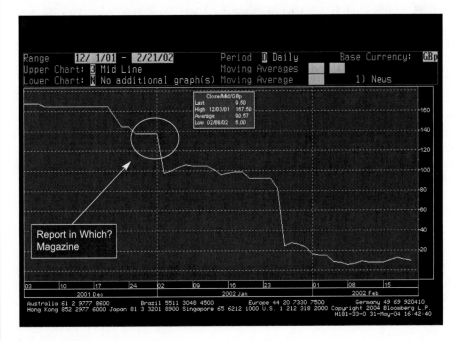

Used with permission from Bloomberg L.P.

Pharmaceutical and biotech companies

With increasing pressure from generic drugs, breaking news regarding the latest court case or an unexpected early end to a patent (usually limited to twenty years) can have a dramatic effect on the prospects for a drug. News can come out at any time of day, and can refer to Phase I, II and III trials.

In the UK, this sector includes companies such as Acambis, Alizyme, Antisoma, Ark Therapeutics, Biocompatibles, BTG, Cambridge Antibody Technology, Cenes, GeneMedix, GW Pharmaceuticals, Phytopharm, Proteome Sciences, Protherics, SkyePharma, Vernalis and Xenova.

Even large drug companies like AstraZeneca can be heavily reliant on a single product, such as its cholesterol-lowering drug, Crestor.

The significance of the outcome to Cambridge Antibody (CAT) of its High Court case against Abbott Laboratories over Humira, its rheumatoid arthritis treatment, was so important that, unusually in the UK, the stock was suspended on the day that the judgement was handed down. Potential revenues were so large, in comparison to the market capitalisation of CAT, that even a small difference in the award of percentage royalties had a large effect on the valuation of the company.

Other companies which are currently heavily reliant on a single product include:

- BTG (Varisolve);
- Vernalis (Frovatriptan);
- Acambis (ACAM2000);
- Elan Corporation (Tysabri); and
- GW Pharmaceuticals (cannabis-based Sativex).

It is tempting for daytraders, who play big moves, to get involved with a stock where there has been a huge move on some news, but it is wise to be familiar with the implications of the news. For example, Antisoma fell over 50% in one day on news that R1549 (pemtumomab), its flagship ovarian cancer drug, was no more effective than placebos. Another good example is that of BTG, looked at in closer detail opposite.

Example: BTG

BTG fell almost 40% intra-day, late on Friday 14 November 2003, on news that the US Food and Drug Administration had placed on hold the Phase II safety study of Varisolve. There were a couple of interesting features to note about this cataclysmic fall:

- Firstly, the stock was **trading on SETSmm**, so those with direct access had a good opportunity to sell the stock quickly. The stock took several key minutes to fall as the order book kept reloading with automatic buy orders that had been left on the order book. Also, market makers will often leave an automated program running that refreshes a quote, and it was reported that a number of market makers lost a considerable amount of money on the day as they were continually hit with stock by other traders as the shares fell.

- Secondly, the **announcement came out just after 15.30 on a Friday afternoon**. Anyone considering trying to catch a falling knife would do well to appreciate that the stock may well get oversold if there are a number of at-market orders, as there is unlikely to be sufficient liquidity in such a short period of time for the stock to revert to a consensual fair value. When considering a trade late on Friday, be prepared to have to run it over the weekend, when there will be a full measured analysis of the news in the weekend press, or be a hostage to the market view on the stock in the short period until market close at 16.30. Similarly the stock may trade lower again on Monday if the implications of the news for the company are not fully appreciated during the short period of trading from 15.30 to 16.30. Once the market has closed there is no opportunity to close the position until the following trading day.

The winning traders were those that understood BTG's exposure and the massive significance of the news for the company's future prospects. The losing traders were those who thought they saw an oversold stock and tried to catch a falling knife.

Example: Acambis

Acambis fell 13% in one trading session on 13 April 2004, when the company announced that it had suspended a clinical trial of its smallpox vaccine ACAM 2000 due to side-effects. Although the US government had not applied the usual rigorous procedures to licensing ACAM 2000, due to the perceived potential risk of bioterrorism there were implications over the adoption of the vaccine on a global basis without a US licence.

Figure 2.19: Acambis (ACM) – after announcing it had suspended a clinical trial

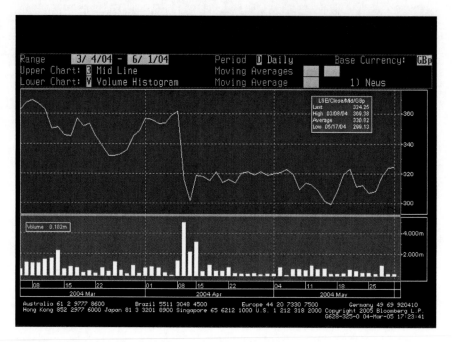

Used with permission from Bloomberg L.P.

Brokers often value drug companies, such as Acambis, by assessing and assigning a probability of success to each product based on the potential commercial outcome, resulting in a theoretical net present fair value (NPV) for the shares. The US Food and Drug Administration (FDA) sets a high hurdle, particularly in the case of cancer drugs which will often need to meet a 99% proof of effectiveness to gain approval, although an extension of life expectancy in the patient is also of high priority. This scenario is not dissimilar to analysing a takeover situation, assessing the possible outcomes and assigning a probability to each. When trading in drug companies, where there is a significant development or item of news, those traders who have a clear understanding of exactly what the implications are for the company will be better placed than those who simply trade the stock as it is where the action currently is.

Clinical trials

Clinical trials, which follow the pre-clinical stage, are studies performed with human patients to test new drugs or combinations of drugs. A principal investigator who leads a research team usually manages clinical trials. There are three stages of clinical trial, namely Phases I, II and III.

Phase I (safety)

After laboratory testing has indicated that a new treatment might be effective, early trials are conducted on small samples of patients, or healthy volunteers (less than thirty), to gauge side-effects and an appropriate dosage. The dosage is gradually increased from the first patient onwards, blood tests taken and side-effects monitored.

Phase II (proof of principle)

Approximately 30% of new treatments make it from Phase I to Phase II. There are a larger number of patients, upwards of fifty, the idea being that a larger sample has a greater chance of showing beneficial effects as different people react differently to different treatments. If the results indicate that the new treatment could be better than receiving no treatment at all (placebo), or better than an existing treatment, it moves to Phase III.

Phase III (pivotal)

At this stage the new treatment is compared with either a placebo or the best existing (standard) treatment. Phase III treatments can involve thousands of people in different hospitals in different countries. Phase III trials are usually randomised so that patients are randomly split into two groups, one getting the new treatment and one the existing treatment or placebo. The new treatment must show that it is significantly better than the placebo or the existing standard.

Information gained from extensive Phase III trials is presented to regulatory authorities when applying for a licence to market and sell the drug. Approximately 50-70% of drugs that reach Phase III clinical trials become saleable.

So the chances of reaching the market are:

- drug in Phase I: **10%**;
- drug in Phase II: **30%**;
- drug in Phase III: **50-70%**.

Radio Joint Audience Research (RAJAR)

RAJAR, which is jointly owned by the BBC and the Commercial Radio Companies Association (CRCA), publishes quarterly figures on the nation's listening habits from a sample of 130,000 volunteers. Over 300 national and regional BBC and commercial stations subscribe to the service. There are, however, often disputes over the figures as the methodology relies on paper-based diaries, and there are currently demands to move to an electronic system of measurement.

Until recently, figures were published on the RAJAR website on Thursdays at 10.30, around five weeks after the end of each fieldwork period, and were followed shortly afterwards by RNS announcements by the major radio companies. However, a recent change in policy means that the releases are now made in the morning pre-market.

Stocks to watch include:

- GCAP Media (GCAP) (95.8 Capital FM, Century FM, Capital Gold, XFM and Classic FM);
- Chrysalis (CHS) (LBC, Heart and Galaxy networks);
- UBC Media (UBC), and
- Emap (EMA) (Kiss 100).

The share of the key London audience between rivals Heart 106.2 and Capital Radio is particularly important, and Chrysalis shares have often moved significantly in the past in response to the figures. A larger market share can allow a radio station to charge a premium for advertising rates.

Figure 2.20: Chrysalis (CHS) – release of RAJAR figures

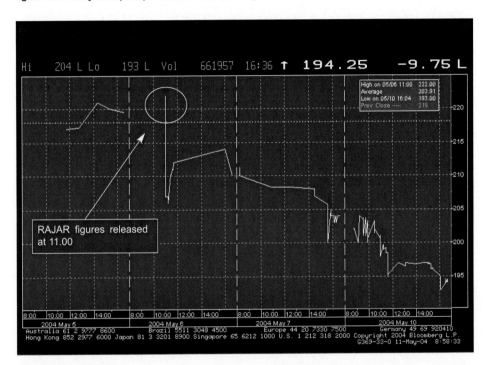

Used with permission from Bloomberg L.P.

Digital television and digital radio are likely to raise the profile of the industry over the next few years.

References

RAJAR: www.rajar.co.uk

Oil exploration

Figures 2.21 and 2.22 starkly illustrate the differing fortunes of oil companies. Both major oil and gas exploration companies, Cairn Energy and Ramco experienced varying degrees of success during 2003 and 2004.

Traders often seek out stocks with high volatility and the ability to move significantly on exploration results. Oil companies certainly fit the bill, although some research needs to be done to accurately translate drilling results into a value per share.

Figure 2.21: Cairn Energy (CNE)

Used with permission from Bloomberg L.P.

Figure 2.22: Ramco (ROS)

Used with permission from Bloomberg L.P.

Generally, surveys are the first stage and if the results of seismic and environmental surveys look good enough the drilling of an exploratory well is considered.

A term often used in oil reports is that of *spudding*. This is the first process, involving drilling a 90cm hole and then putting a wide pipe into the seabed, to guide the drill and drilling fluid, which is lined with a steel pipe casing and cemented in place.

Air traffic figures

Air traffic figures are released monthly by the three main British airlines. Figures often come out during market hours and are of interest to traders, as relatively small changes in the guidance that accompanies the figures can have a dramatic effect on share prices. A couple of examples:

- Ryanair's share price fell 31% in one day in late January 2004, when the company issued its first profits warning since flotation in 1997.
- In early May 2004, easyJet's shares fell 25% in one day when it said that "given the increasingly competitive marketplace it is appropriate now to be cautious about the performance for the full financial year". This was in contrast to a statement three months earlier when the company said it was cautiously optimistic about the outlook for the full year.

British Airways

Traffic figures are released on the third business day of each month, and usually hit the screens between 14.00 and 14.30. These figures can have a dramatic effect on sentiment, as can be seen in the chart below when British Airways subtly changed its wording from "stable" to "some improvement". Note the considerable follow through in the stock the following day from below 230p to above 270p; a huge move for a blue chip stock such as British Airways.

Figure 2.23: British Airways (BAY) – effect when traffic figures are released

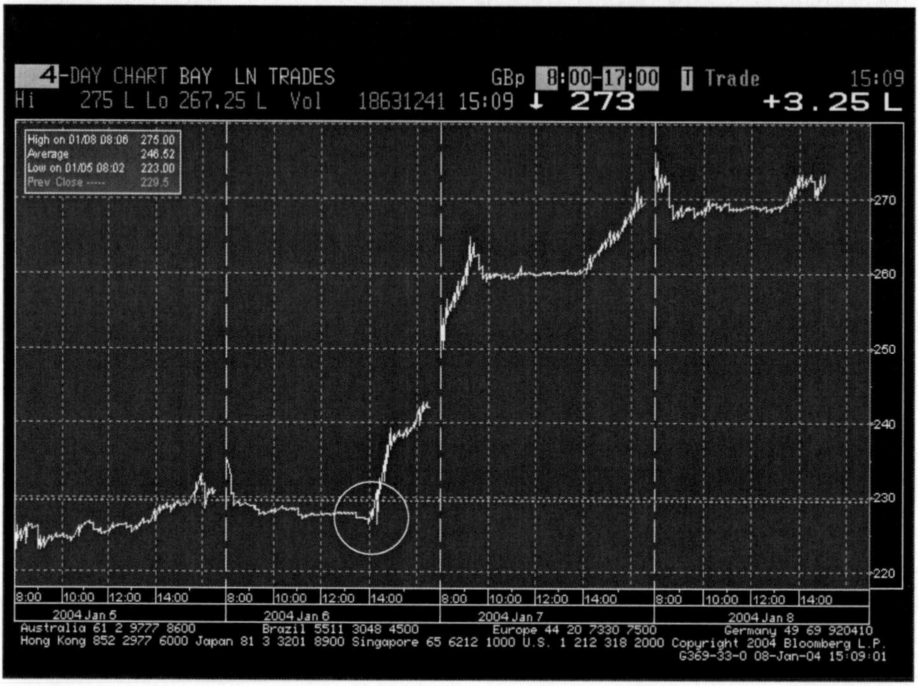

Used with permission from Bloomberg L.P.

easyJet

Passenger numbers and load factors are released on the fifth working day of each month. easyJet profits are seasonal and it tends to generate most of its profits in the second half of its financial year, which runs from April to September.

Ryanair

Load factors and monthly passenger figures are released within the first five working days of each month.

Company statements

Reporting requirements

Unlike the US, where it has been standard practice since the 1940s for companies to report quarterly, UK companies generally report twice yearly; although the EU recently tried unsuccessfully to make quarterly reporting mandatory.

Companies listed on the UK's techMARK, and Germany's now defunct Neuer Markt, are required to report quarterly, as are large European companies with American listings. The argument against more frequent reporting is that it forces companies and the market into short-term thinking.

Not updating the market before the close period can imply that the company has not materially exceeded or fallen short of expectations. Many companies issue trading statements before the close period but it is not mandatory. Analyst meetings after the results come out can provide a clearer clue on prospects and feedback can often influence share prices later in the day.

Sneaking out bad statements on Christmas Eve is another tempting wheeze, as dealing rooms are lightly staffed and newspapers are not published on Christmas Day or Boxing Day, but in practice it doesn't happen very often.

On Christmas Eve 2003, however, Jasmin issued a poor trading update with the stock subsequently falling over 20% on the day. That only delayed matters; four weeks later the stock was suspended when the company's lenders withdrew support.

Reporting timetables and trading statements

Nearly half of the FTSE 350 constituents report on a calendar year basis, and the reporting season in the UK now kicks off in earnest in early February, running through March. Despite having their year-end as 31st January, many retailers issue trading statements relating to Christmas trading in January, as Christmas is such an important part of the year's revenues. Year-ends of 31st March are also common, to coincide with the financial year. The interim results season in the UK is concentrated around September.

Trading statements containing guidance are as important, if not more so, than scheduled interims or preliminaries. There is a lull in company reporting during the summer months, possibly related to the fact that, historically, full-year dividends are paid and reinvested in the first quarter, with no further significant news flow after May until interim results in the autumn.

Most statements are released pre-market, but some companies, such as Reckitt Benckiser, Shire Pharmaceutical and companies listed on other exchanges, release statements during the trading day, which can provide a trading opportunity to those with direct access, as stocks in the UK are not suspended pending results.

> The headline pre-tax figure is rarely as important as the comments regarding outlook and trading since the close of the financial year.

Forward-looking comments are much more relevant than historic figures in the statutory statements which relate to a year-end as long as three months previous. Although the market will often react immediately, there can be a reversal of fortunes when further details are digested, such as cash flow, capital expenditure and the breakdown of businesses.

Additionally analysts' presentations often take place later in the morning and commentary can leak back to the market gradually. One thing to look out for is the early posting of the analyst presentation on the company's website.

Other factors to look for are:

- profits or losses associated with unhedged currency earnings;
- cost of raw materials;
- dividend policy;
- share buy-backs; or
- pension liabilities.

Margins can be as important, if not more important, than sales growth; the market can really take fright at an unexpected squeeze on margins. It will be natural for the company to focus on the strong performing parts of the business, so look out for the use of euphemisms when describing weaker parts of the business.

Exposure to foreign currency

Depending on a company's hedging policy, currency movements can have a beneficial or adverse effect on a company's profitability. Companies that do not hedge their currency risk can be exposed if revenues are in one currency but debt are in another. One solution that some companies adopt is to denominate borrowings in a foreign currency to offset currency losses. A weak dollar can hurt companies who earn most of their revenues in the US, and make US exports more competitive. As oil is denominated in dollars, however, a weak dollar can benefit heavy oil users such as airlines.

Companies that have high dollar earnings include:

- Acambis;
- Enodis;
- BBA;
- Signet; and
- Carnival.

Banking covenants

Loan facilities often contain terms and conditions that may include banking covenants, which the company must abide by or risk the bank calling a default.

Covenants will either be financial or non-financial:

1. **Financial covenants** may dictate conditions such as profit before exceptionals being maintained above a certain multiple of interest payable, net debt remaining below a multiple of EBITDA or a minimum ratio of fixed assets to loan value.
2. **Non-financial covenants** may relate to a change of control, or be conditional on the non-disposal of a key subsidiary.

Other conditions that may come under the auspices of a covenant may relate to the payment of dividends or share buy-backs.

> Expressions in the company statement such as 'challenging environment' can be received very badly, but the real time-bomb can be 'in danger of breaching banking covenants'.

Another wheeze to be aware of is a change in the company's reporting period, which can often be quite legitimate but occasionally suggest something more sinister. Although ostensibly the change may be to "align the reporting period with the seasonality of the revenues of the business", it could be a warning signal that there may be an impending debt expiry, and until the new facility is agreed, the auditors may be reluctant to sign off the accounts without qualifying them.

Holmes Place

I remember quite clearly a number of traders holding on desperately during the time that Holmes Place was in bid talks, while trading deteriorated and the share price sagged almost daily.

Holding a stock in bid talks where the business climate is deteriorating is a risky strategy as the potential buyer will always be in a strong negotiating position. In addition, because the directors may have a personal liability if a firm continues to trade while technically insolvent, the board may be wary about trying to avoid putting the firm into administration. It is much more attractive to hold shares in a company which is in talks where an auction is developing and more than one buyer is keen to acquire a flourishing business, creating some price tension.

Holmes Place was eventually taken over at 25p per share, having been in talks when the shares were 200p at one point. The warning signs were there when Fitness First slid 36% on 2 October 2002 on a profits warning, but the market was slow to realise the implication that the Holmes Place bid could be in trouble, and the stock did not slip until later in the day (another trading opportunity in itself). The real clue came on 10th January 2003, when the company said it was in discussions with its banks to bring its banking covenants into line. That was a major red light.

Figure 2.24: Holmes Place (HOL)

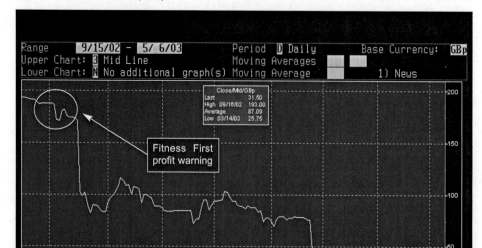

Used with permission from Bloomberg L.P.

Analysing results

The key things to remember when quickly analysing results, are what the market's expectations are and whether there are any surprises. Bad reactions are often a result of a failure to meet expectations, rather than poor results. Exceptional losses are not necessarily bad news, if accompanied with an upbeat statement.

Blaming factors outside a company's control like the weather, political environment, and commodity prices usually fools no-one.

A progressive dividend policy may be positive, but do not fall into the trap of justifying trading based on dividend yield. At one point Lloyds Bank yielded over 10% when markets plunged in March 2003, the stock traded down to 290p and traders were citing 7, 8, 9 and 10% yields all the way down. The dividend payout may not be new information, but the details regarding the earnings and cash flow backing it up may be.

Share buy-backs may appear to give support to a share price, but also begs the question whether the company has a clear strategy for further growth and why it cannot think of anything else to do with the money.

Second half, or more recent, trading may be more important than first half, unless the business is seasonal as is the case with travel companies.

Pre-close period trading statements are not obligatory and, contrary to popular belief, the company can update the market during a close period. (The close period relates to the restriction on dealings in shares by connected parties.) However, a company may feel obliged to update the market before its scheduled reporting date if conditions dictate.

Bear in mind that results may have a greater significance with more room for surprises, when a company has not released a trading statement or issued guidance prior to the close period.

> Before the market opens always check when the company last updated shareholders and when other members of its peer group reported.

Another factor to look out for are statements regarding comments made at the AGM, which often come out intra-day, although not all companies make trading comments in their AGM statements.

Retailers strongly reliant on Christmas trading

A number of retailers are heavily reliant on Christmas trading, and trading statements can be more important than the actual results themselves.

Game Group makes one third of its yearly revenues in November and December and Woolworths makes 40% in the ten weeks leading up to Christmas. Possibly the most heavily reliant are Brown & Jackson with 60% of revenues in the Christmas period, and HMV and WHSmith where over 40% of turnover occurs in the fourth quarter. Other retailers heavily weighted to this period include Marks & Spencer, Great Universal Stores (and its subsidiary Argos) and Dixons. Signet makes up to 70% of its earnings in Q4.

A poor statement from one company may not necessarily be a bad indicator for another in the same sector, particularly if one is winning market share from the other. However, there appears to have been a structural change in the habits of British shoppers in the last few years, with many putting off big-ticket purchases until the January sales, so tales of gloom and doom relating to Christmas trading by the press should perhaps be taken in context.

Note: UK *like-for-like* sales are equivalent to what the US call *same store* sales.

Court cases and Cause Lists

The result of key court cases is often in the public domain before the market is informed by an RNS announcement.

For example, BOC, the UK industrial gases company, opened lower on 29 October 2003 for no apparent reason. It wasn't until 09.30 that a regulatory announcement was released stating that the company had lost a court case in the US the previous day, over the effects of fumes from welding. Traders who had become aware of the publication of the ruling were at an advantage.

Similarly, during the long drawn out regulatory process over the proposed merger of iSoft and Torex in 2004, the results of the court rulings were released in open court before the regulatory announcements were made to the marketplace.

In the UK, the Cause Lists, which detail when and where certain rulings are handed down, can be easily located with a little searching on the internet.

Example: Cambridge Antibody Technology

Cambridge Antibody Technology (CAT) took Abbott Biotechnology, the US healthcare group, to court in late 2004 over royalties on Humira, the arthritis treatment that they had developed together. The case eventually got to the High Court in London in November 2004, and the numbers involved were not inconsiderable. CAT is valued on a combination of its cash pile, tissue growth factor beta program with Genzyme of the US and Humira royalty stream. Sales of Humira were forecast to top $1.2bn in 2005, and analysts believed the drug was worth 250p per share, even if CAT lost the case. Royalties are payable six months in arrears, and CAT then has to pay out some of its royalties to the Medical Research Council, but a relatively small percentage change in royalty payment could have a huge effect on CAT's share price.

Analysts reckoned that a 2% royalty rate was in the price already (equating to a fair value of around 480p per share), whereas a 3% rate would value CAT at 630p and a 5% rate would imply a massive 950p valuation for the shares. The High Court found in CAT's favour, although the ruling went to appeal. As the handing down of the judgement was scheduled for noon, the London Stock Exchange suspended the stock in the morning pending the result, until midday when the announcement was released. This somewhat took away the advantage for those with direct access.

Dividends

Corporate actions can often have a pivotal effect on a share price, setting a short-term high or low for the stock.

The London Stock Exchange deletes all existing orders in a SETS security the night before a corporate action is effective to prevent the execution of orders at inappropriate prices. Even so, there have been numerous examples of orders being placed at an incorrect price, when a participant has forgotten that a stock is trading *ex*.

In the UK most stocks now go ex-dividend on a Wednesday, although some stocks do go *ex* on other days, particularly in the case of special dividends or returns of capital.

It is notoriously difficult to get a reliable source of ex-dividends, although the top providers, Bloomberg and Reuters, are usually very accurate.

Ex dates offer both opportunity and risk.

Buying before the ex-dividend date

One strategy that I have seen novice traders use is to buy stocks in the lead up to an ex-dividend date, particularly a high yielding stock, in the hope that the stock does not fall by the full amount afterwards. I think this is a flawed strategy, incorporating overnight risk with no compensating premium, although the strategy may be more effective in a bull market, where prices are rising anyway. CFD providers generally pay 90% of the dividend on long positions (referred to as a cash adjustment), but debit short positions 100% of the dividend.

Far better to stay alert and look for opportunities and mis-pricings on the actual ex-dividend date.

Examples

In the example below, orders were placed in AWG at the incorrect price on 23 September 2002, when traders forgot that the stock was trading *ex*, and so should, theoretically, drop by the amount of the dividend on the day (31.2p).

Figure 2.25: AWG Plc (AWG) – mistaken orders when the stock went ex-dividend

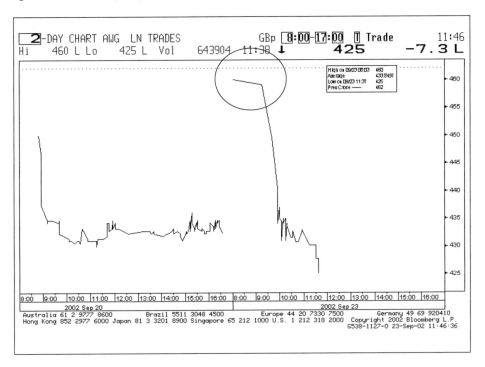

Used with permission from Bloomberg L.P.

Similarly, Granada went *ex* a special 7p dividend on a Monday (25 January 2004), a fact not appreciated by the wider market for a number of crucial minutes.

Figure 2.26: Granada (GAA) – temporary confusion when the stock goes ex-dividend

Used with permission from Bloomberg L.P.

Interestingly, an analysis by Dresdner Kleinwort of 2,000 European dividend events over a five-year period found that trading volumes in high yield stocks were 40% higher on the day prior to trading ex-dividend, and also higher on the ex-dividend date itself. That suggests that the ex-dividend date is of some significance, although it is unclear whether this is because there is a meaningful flow of stock between investors seeking income and those seeking capital gains.

Although investments should never be made on tax considerations alone, the ex-dividend date does mean different things to different investors. In the UK, dividends are paid net with an associated 10% tax credit. Dividends are taxed at 10% basic rate, and 32.5% higher rate, on the gross dividend (i.e. including the tax credit), so the effective rates are 0%, and 22.5% of the gross respectively. There is an annual capital gains tax allowance, after which gains are taxed at the individual marginal rate.

Therefore:

1. a **basic rate tax payer who has already exceeded his CGT limit** will be better placed to sell after the ex-dividend date;

2. a **higher rate tax payer who has not used his CGT allowance** will prefer to sell before; whereas

3. a **higher rate tax payer who is already above his CGT limit** will prefer to sell after.

All this analysis of course ignores the risk in the share price moving during the intervening period.

Some dividend information is available from the websites listed below, but my preference is to rely on the major data providers.

References

Investor Ease: www.investorease.com

itpaysdividends.co.uk: www.itpaysdividends.co.uk

Share capital and share premium account

Company law only allows the payment of dividends from distributable reserves, and prohibits the payment of a dividend while there is a deficit on the profit and loss account.

In the balance sheet the share capital represents the nominal value of the share purchased by the original shareholders. If the original shareholders paid a premium to the nominal value for their shares, the difference appears in the share premium account.

Sometimes a company will need to reduce the share premium account before paying a dividend (requiring an EGM), and use that sum to eliminate the deficit. A reduction in share capital can also sometimes be used to eliminate a deficit on the profit and loss account.

Share splits and consolidations

In a *share split*, or *consolidation*, the nominal value of the shares is changed. For instance, in the Urbium example, fifty 1p shares were exchanged for one new 50p share.

With a *scrip*, or *capitalisation* issue, the company issues free shares to existing shareholders. The resulting increase in shares in issue reduces the share price, but the nominal value of the shares is unchanged and there is effectively just a transfer within the company's reserves.

Difference between UK and US terminology

Note that the UK and US use different terminology. When a company undertakes a 1 for 3 bonus issue in the UK (in other words issues one new share for every three currently held), in the US this would be referred to as a 4 for 3 issue.

I am sceptical whether share splits and share consolidations have any direct effect on share prices at all. Clearly they have no direct effect on the value of a company, however, there is no doubt that companies with very high share prices ('heavy'), or very small share prices ('light') suffer from different adverse factors. I have noticed on occasion that shares can experience some softness in price shortly after a consolidation has become effective.

UK investors appear to be most comfortable with a share price between 100p and 1000p, unlike those in the US or Germany, for instance, where share prices are often the equivalent of £20 or more each. High share prices often have much narrower bid-offer spreads, and penny shares can suffer from illiquidity and wide bid-offer spreads. Human nature being what it is, a 2p spread on a 30p stock doesn't seem as bad as a £2 spread on a 3000p stock – although it is of course exactly the same (6.7%).

Most penny shares trade on SEAQ, and the usual advice about trying to deal inside the spread applies; in my experience investors incorrectly assume that the price displayed on the screen is the only one available.

Example: Urbium

The late-night entertainment group Urbium, which is listed on AIM, is an interesting example. The company had a colossal 520m shares in issue, and the share price was around 6p when it announced on 3 June 2003 that it was to consolidate its shares on the basis of one new share for fifty existing shares. This meant that the new share price would be around 300p, although, of course, the market capitalisation of the company would be unchanged.

Urbium also offered a commission-free dealing service for shareholders with less than 10,000 existing shares to sell. The commission-free dealing offer wasn't completely altruistic as the company wanted to reduce the number of shareholders on its register. 2,733 small shareholders took advantage of the opportunity and sold 116,488 shares as part of a cash-out, which were placed with larger investors at 355p. Urbium shares suffered from having over 15,000 shareholders, partly as a result of the demerger from Chorion a year previously, 13,000 of which held less than 10,000 shares. The share consolidation was effective on 2 July, and was followed shortly by a bullish trading statement on 15 July.

Shares magazine wrote the stock up in late July 2003 and attributed the share price rise to the stock consolidation, but I think it was more to do with the bullish trading statement, even though the stock was on the move before the official release of the statement, as can be seen from the chart.

Figure 2.27: Urbium (URM) – share consolidation

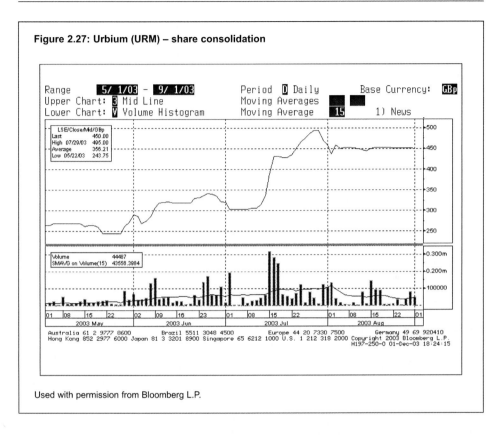

```
Range      5/ 1/03 - 9/ 1/03        Period  D Daily        Base Currency:  GBp
Upper Chart: 3 Mid Line             Moving Averages                        
Lower Chart: V Volume Histogram     Moving Average    15        1) News
```

Used with permission from Bloomberg L.P.

The market always seems to get hold of these things early, but I do believe that share consolidations and splits can exaggerate an existing trend and bring a company into focus.

Urbium sought to reduce the number of shareholders it had because of the costs involved with sending out circulars, but it also made itself more visible to institutional investors and shook off its penny share image. It currently has a typical bid-offer spread of around 10p (3%), whereas before it was more like 0.5p (7%).

Consolidations often coincide with special dividends

Share consolidations often occur in conjunction with special dividends, and are usually effective on the same day as the ex-dividend date. The main purpose of this is to maintain consistency in share price, both for investors and share scheme holders. An appropriate consolidation ratio is chosen so that the share price is roughly the same before and after the corporate action. As the Inland Revenue does not allow adjustments to approved options for special dividends, because there has been no variation in share capital, an EGM has to be called to approve a share consolidation. (There is some slippage risk, however, as the reference price used may be different on the eventual effective date from that used in the calculation for the EGM.)

For example, Mitchells & Butler (MAB) paid a special dividend of 68p, effective 2nd December 2003, with the shares closing the previous day at 235.5p. The stock should therefore theoretically open at 167.5p the next day, but the company simultaneously effected a share consolidation on a 12 for 17 basis, so in fact the theoretical *ex* price was:

```
167.5 x 17/12 (there are now less shares in issue) = 237p
```

The sole purpose of this exercise is to maintain a comparable share price, although, of course, the market capitalisation is lower as there are fewer shares in issue.

Stock buy-backs

Companies cannot usually buy-back their own shares while in a closed period, and so may have to suspend operations until the publication of results. Under the Model Code, a company generally cannot buy its shares back when the directors are prevented from dealing, although there are exceptions. For instance the Model Code allows an exemption if:

> *"The company is purchasing or redeeming a security in accordance within an agreement where the date, amount and price of the securities to be bought back was fixed, and was entered into at a time when the director of the company would have been free to deal."*

This exemption therefore allows some companies to buy back their shares subject to certain preset parameters and this will often be declared in RNS announcements.

If the buy-back has been providing support for the shares and liquidity for natural sellers of the stock, then the stock may experience some weakness when the buy-back is suspended, although it is of course as always, subject to other influences. Traders should keep a track of buy-backs anyway, even if they are not trying to anticipate a share price move, so that they are not caught out if the operation stops or recommences suddenly.

Buying during the close period

A strategy that shrewd investor Jack Petchey has employed in the past (for instance in A&J Mucklow) is to buy shares in a company during the close period when the company is itself unable to buy them, and then feed them out when the buy-back recommences after the close period. The strategy behind this is to take advantage of potential share price weakness during a period when the company cannot deal in its own shares. Clearly you need to be comfortable with the prospects for the company and that it is not going to surprise adversely on results day, but it could work well for value investors looking to gain a good entry price in a company valued cheaply compared to net asset value.

Vodafone sale of put options

In a novel development in the summer of 2004, Vodafone found a way round the problem of being prohibited from buying its own shares back during its close period. Vodafone asked shareholders to approve a scheme whereby it was able to sell put options over 60m of its own shares to investment banks in return for a small premium. This allowed the company to buy-back its shares in the close period at a price determined before the period commenced.

- If the shares traded **above the strike** on expiry, the banks would not exercise the option and Vodafone would get to keep the premium.
- If the shares trade **below the strike** at expiry, Vodafone would get to buy its shares back.

The banks are happy as they have almost certainly bought an attractively priced option, which they can delta hedge in the cash market (extracting some gamma), so long as the volatility of the stock exceeds the implied volatility paid.

Treasury shares

Previously, companies had to cancel shares they had bought back, however, new rules introduced in December 2003 allow companies to buy back shares to be held in treasury for future re-issue, if they feel that they are currently undervalued by the market. There are restrictions on the sale or transfer of treasury shares while the company is in a close period or in possession of price-sensitive information, and a limit on the discount to the market price at which shares can be subsequently sold for cash by the company non pre-emptively.

Useful for investment trusts

Investment trusts now have an alternative to buying back shares and cancelling them, or launching a tender offer to buy out shareholders (often arbitrageurs). By buying back shares at a discount to NAV and holding shares in treasury instead, companies can later re-issue them when sentiment improves (stamp duty does not apply to shares that have been held in treasury). However, there is opposition to this as some institutions believe buying back the shares and cancelling them, resulting in an uplift in NAV for the residual shareholders, is better than re-issuing the shares at a later date, after being held in treasury, at a discount to NAV.

Stock buy-backs can have another unintentional side effect. A large minority shareholder can run into problems if stock buy-backs reduce the number of shares in issue to an extent that an existing large stake goes above 50%.

Example: Caledonia Investments

This is what happened to Caledonia Investments when 37.8% shareholder Cayzer Trust, together with family members holding a further 12%, needed a *whitewash agreement*, or Rule 9 waiver, from the independent shareholders. Major shareholder Hermes Focus Fund suddenly found itself in a position where it could have some influence over the board and would only support the buy-back if Caledonia instituted a boardroom shake-up.

Rule 9 waivers are so called because normally under Rule 9 of the Takeover Code, the shareholder or concert party concerned with the significant stake would be obliged to make a mandatory offer should it increase its voting rights to above the highest percentage of voting rights held in the previous twelve months or by more than 1% over the previous twelve months.

Hermes said:

"We can only back Rule 9 waivers when we know that the boards live up to the standards of independence required by the Association of Investment Trust Companies and the Combined Code on Corporate Governance."

75% approval needed for buy-backs at AGMs

Incidentally, at the AGM a 75% majority is required to approve share buy-back schemes – something that minority shareholder Lawdene, with a 24.4% holding in Beale, the department store chain, has exercised by using its holding to block buy-back motions.

IPOs and conditional dealings

New issues are one of the best indicators of market sentiment. In a bull market they are over-subscribed many times over, and invariably open at a premium to the issue price. But when there is market volatility and uncertainty, nobody wants them. A successful allocation will often depend on a strong relationship with a broker, and by scaling the issue down or limiting the money raised, the company can play on scarcity value.

Grey market dealing

Generally a stock will trade on a *when issued* basis (known as conditional dealings or a *grey market*) for a period of time before unconditional dealings commence. A CFD account can be useful in these instances, as it will often be possible to trade both long and short CFDs from the first day of conditional dealings, whereas many stockbrokers will not allow ordinary shareholders to sell their allocation until unconditional dealings have commenced.

Spread betting firms often offer a two-way price even before conditional dealings have commenced.

Greenshoe option

A term often used in the context of IPOs is the *Greenshoe option*. This is when the underwriter of an IPO is granted an option to sell additional shares if demand warrants it, or buy-back additional shares to provide stabilisation for a limited period after trading commences. The name comes from The Green Shoe Company, which was the first to use this type of option. It can give the issuer an opportunity for price arbitrage during the stabilisation period.

Accelerated Initial Public Offering (AIPO)

Collins Stewart, led by CEO Terry Smith, pioneered accelerated IPOs when it floated Northumbrian Water on AIM in 2003, closely followed by the accelerated IPO of Center Parcs.

The technique is likely to be increasingly used as institutional investors have become frustrated at the number of companies that have gone private, only to reappear after only a few months, earning their venture capitalist partners a considerable profit on their investment and leaving the institutions feeling undersold.

In an AIPO the broker forms a new company to acquire the assets and then invites a small number of institutions to bid for shares in the new vehicle, rather than carrying out a more usual book building exercise. The acquisition vehicle is then floated on AIM, with a move to the main market later retained as an option.

In effect, companies pre-sell their shares to institutions. By committing to the accelerated IPO option, institutional investors back the management directly and cut out the venture capitalists, who will also demand a higher rate of return from their investment. This means that management will often end up sharing a higher stake in the business than they would have done with VCs as backers.

Both trade buyers and private equity houses are likely to find increasing competition from institutional investors prepared to use AIPOs to back companies coming to market.

Reference

Digital Look: companyresearch.digitallook.com

An excellent guide to forthcoming new issues and IPOs in its IPO Centre.

Public offers, placings and rights issues

Companies generally raise money through three routes:

1. public offers;
2. placings; and
3. rights issues.

Companies have an obligation under the Companies Act to give pre-emptive rights to existing shareholders, although shareholders may choose to disapply these rights in special circumstances.

Public offers

Two thirds of new issues are raised by public offer which, in theory, are open to everyone, but a good business relationship with your broker may ensure you are higher up the queue. Public offers can also be carried out in conjunction with a placing.

Placings

A placing, where a company issues new shares to a closed list of institutions, can be an attractive means of raising financing for a company as it does not have to offer shares to existing shareholders, get shareholder consent, or prepare listing particulars.

As placings cannot generally exceed 10% of the number of shares already in issue, there is usually a ready supply of buyers, and the new shares can usually be placed at a narrow discount to the prevailing share price. Recent rule changes have allowed the 10% limit to be waived at an EGM, but still must not be executed at more than a 10% discount to the prevailing mid-market price. AIM-listed companies are not bound by these restrictions and can place new shares at any price.

The company will often make an open offer at the same time, so that existing shareholders not included in the placing are not diluted. However, you have to be an existing shareholder on the register to qualify. You don't qualify if you buy shares on the day, or subsequent to the announcement.

Shareholders are not obliged to take up all, or any, of their entitlement. The offer is normally open for around three weeks, with the new shares commencing trading shortly after it has closed. The take-up rate is announced three days later. If the offer is underwritten, the underwriters will place any shares that have not been taken up. Sometimes an excess entitlement is available where shareholders can apply for shares not taken up by others, above their existing entitlement. You can sell your shares after the announcement, ex-open offer, and retain the entitlement to buy the open offer shares.

Watch out for the appointment of a new broker

One thing to look out for is the appointment of a new broker, which can presage a future corporate action. When Imagination Technologies announced on 2 April 2004 that it had appointed Cazenove & Co. as corporate broker and financial adviser in conjunction with the release of a trading statement, there was speculation that the new broker would take the opportunity to raise capital. This was subsequently the case when two months later, on 17 June, Imagination announced a fully underwritten placing (by Cazenove) of 8.5m new shares at 85p to raise £7.2m.

Rights issues

A rights issue is an offer to existing shareholders of the right to subscribe to further securities in proportion to their existing holdings. All shareholders have the right to participate, and the rights will trade separately (as nil-paid rights) for a period, allowing shareholders to sell some, or all of them, and other investors to buy them.

Unlike an open offer, shareholders can sell their entitlement after the rights start to trade separately. Effectively, shareholders have four choices:

1. take up the rights in full;
2. sell all the rights;
3. sell some of the rights to finance taking up the remainder; or
4. do nothing. If you do nothing, the company will sell the rump (unsubscribed rights) to the underwriters and send the cash proceeds to you.

Under the pre-emption rights of the Companies Act, listed companies are restricted in their issues to new shareholders of 5% of the existing share capital in any one year, or 7.5% over three years (shareholders can waive these rules with a 75% majority). Although if it does not wish to use the existing 5% authority, or wants to issue more than 5% (limited to 10%), the company may decide on a placing. This can create problems for companies that need to raise cash in a hurry. The BioIndustry Association is currently lobbying for a change in the rules to allow more flexibility for life science companies capitalised at under £1bn, to raise up to 20% of their share capital over a three-year period on a non-pre-emptive basis. This would probably suit the investment banks as well, as the underwriting fees from rights issues tend to be far less than the fees associated with normal fundraisings in the UK.

Once the offer is made, it must be open for acceptance for at least twenty-one days, commencing on the day after the posting of documents. A fully underwritten rights issue is where a bank has agreed to buy any shares not taken up by investors at the proposed issue price.

The new shares are offered at a discount to existing shares and the discount may be substantial, depending on current market conditions and the reason for the raising of new funds. Rescue rights issues may not be as well received as those that are pitched to take advantage of what the company convinces shareholders may be a unique opportunity. Rights issues are more easily executed from a position of strength rather than weakness. Often the broker running the rights issue will test the water by contacting key institutional shareholders beforehand to gauge sentiment.

The London Clubs rights issue in early 2004, for example, was leaked in advance and was, therefore, not a surprise to the market when finalised. There was also a good story to sell with the forthcoming de-regulation of the gaming industry. Highly discounted offers save on underwriting fees, but may adversely affect the prevailing share price.

The shares and nil-paid rights will trade separately for a period of time, providing an arbitrage opportunity best demonstrated with a couple of examples.

Example: London Clubs

On 5 March 2004, London Clubs announced a fully underwritten 1 for 2 rights issue at 70p, a discount of around 40% to the previous day's closing price of 116.75p, in order to raise money to invest in casinos, and settle all outstanding matters related to its ill-fated investment in Aladdin in Las Vegas. The issue of 73.69m new shares raised around £49m net of expenses, and as the company already had around 147m shares in issue, the total number in issue rose to 221m.

The EGM to ratify the rights issue was set for 29 March, with the shares due to trade ex-rights the following day, 30 March, and the final deadline for acceptance and payment set as 19 April.

Calculating the theoretical ex-rights price

Once the shares and nil-paid rights trade separately, the shares will fall in price effective from the ex-rights date. The theoretical ex-rights price can only be calculated from the closing price the previous day, and bears no relation to the price on the day the issue was announced.

On 29 March, the last day before trading ex-rights, London Clubs shares closed at 122.5p. The theoretical ex-rights price can therefore be calculated as:

```
((2 x 122.5p) + (1 x 70p))/3 = 105p
```

The rights meanwhile, which are effectively a deep in-the-money call option, granting the right to subscribe at 70p, will trade at around:

```
105-70 = 35p
```

As can be seen below, the shares and the rights will trade in lock step for the duration of the period that the nil-paids are traded separately (until 15 April in this case). This is because the nil-paids are kept in line with the shares by an arbitrage opportunity.

Figure 2.28: London Clubs (LCI) – shares and nil-paid rights track each other closely

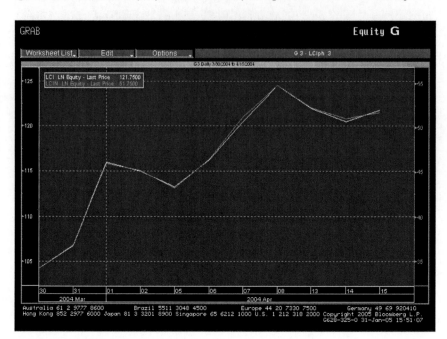

Used with permission from Bloomberg L.P.

Nil-paids are kept in line through arbitrage activity

If I can buy the nil-paids for 45p, and short an equal number of the ordinary shares for 116p, I can later tender my nil-paids, pay 70p, and deliver the new shares against my short position – pocketing the 1p difference. The trade is positively funded as the value of the short position is bigger than the long position, generating a cash position on which interest is receivable.

Market makers are best placed to execute this arbitrage, as it is capital intensive and they have the ability, with flow, to buy the rights cheap and sell the stock at the offer price (right-hand side of the spread). Also, as LCI was quoted on SEAQ (LCI has since moved to SETSmm), it was very hard for the individual to participate in the screen franchise. However, with stocks quoted on SETS there is a much better opportunity, as long as dealing costs can be kept low.

Synthetic put option

There is one further feature of buying the nil-paids (rights) and short selling the stocks. Option traders will recognise that this trade in effect creates a synthetic put option, as the trader has bought call options and shorted stock. This is not significant unless the stock trades down towards the price of the rights issue, when the put option at the strike price of 70p will start to pick up some premium. Hence, if the stock was trading at 100p, one would expect the nil-paids to trade at 30p. However if the stock trades down to, say, 72p, the nil-paids might trade at a premium to the theoretical value of 2p, because a trader buying the rights and shorting the stock creates a put option that has a value.

To demonstrate this, consider what happens if the rights issue runs into trouble and trades below 70p. The nil-paids cannot trade below zero, but the short position continues to work for the trader.

This is a popular trade for hedge funds. If they can put the straddle on for minimum cost (i.e. buy the rights and sell the stock for no net cost), they have created a cheap put option. This can either be utilised by:

- simultaneously selling option premia elsewhere (with a similar strike and expiry in the same stock, capturing some premium income); or
- held in the event that there is a sudden downwards move in the stock below the subscription price, perhaps due to a general market sell-off, resulting in the rights issue failing and the shares being left with the underwriters.

Figure 2.29: London Clubs (LCI) – adjustment of historic prices following a rights issue

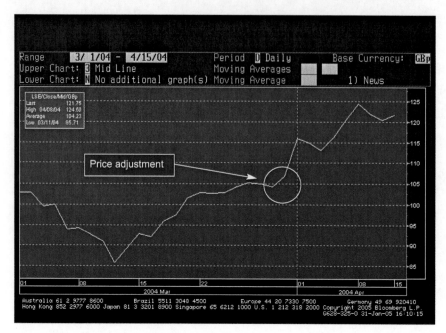

Used with permission from Bloomberg L.P.

Subsequent adjustment of historic share prices

After a stock trades ex-rights, and the price falls to the known theoretical ex-rights price, data vendors need to adjust the historic share prices to make the charts consistent. As can be seen above, although LCI closed at 122.5p on 29 March, the chart has been adjusted to show a closing price of 105p. The ratio used (the adjustment factor) in this case is 0.857143, and is the ratio of the theoretical ex-rights price to the closing price on the previous day.

Example: Royal and Sun Alliance

On 4 September 2003, Royal and Sun Alliance announced a fully underwritten 1 for 1 rights issue at 70p. The shares traded ex-rights from 23 September with the nil-paids trading separately until 13 October.

Summary

- Announced: 04/09/2003
- Ex-rights date: 23/09/2003
- Total amount raised: £960m
- Terms: 1:1
- Issue price: 70p

Figure 2.30: Royal and Sun Alliance (RSA) – rights issue

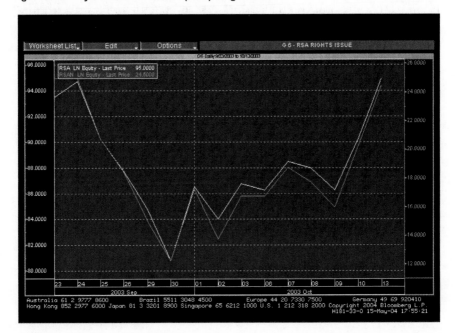

Used with permission from Bloomberg L.P.

As can be seen above, the shares and nil-paids traded in line, and as both were quoted on SETS, it was much easier to arbitrage.

Example: Royal and Sun Alliance (contd.)

The closing price on the day prior to trading ex-rights (22 September) was 113.75p, so the theoretical ex-rights price was:

`((1 x 113.75) + (1 x 70))/2 = 91.88p`

giving an adjustment ratio of:

`91.88/113.75 = 0.8077`

Hedge funds often short the shares of companies if they are getting wind of a potential rights issue, in the hope of buying the stock back cheaper at a later date, after the fundraising is publicly confirmed. It can be difficult keeping a rights issue under wraps as the key shareholders will normally be consulted first and, therefore, made insiders. However, the rules surrounding 'pre-marketing' of a new share issue, such as a convertible bond, are a grey area and the regulations probably need some clarification. There have been occasions in the past where a stock has clearly been heavily sold short before an issue came to market. Surprise rights issues can also often backfire, as Prudential found to its cost in 2004 when a poor reception from the market led to a huge sell-off in the shares; the company had previously indicated that it would not be tapping the market for cash.

The unwanted option – Ciga Hotels

The unexpected can sometimes happen and I learnt a great lesson in 1994, when some nil-paid rights, that the market in Italy assigned little value to suddenly raced into the money.

In March 1994, as part of a rescue plan for the highly indebted Italian hotels chain Ciga Hotels, creditor banks agreed to convert their debts into 943m new Ciga shares, with a nominal value of 1,000 lire. ITT Sheraton would then buy these from the banks at between 725 and 742 lire, a discount to the price at which the rights issue had been set, but around where they were trading at in the real market. Sheraton would then make an offer for the remaining shares.

The share issue was designed to clear the company of its debts and deliberately pitched at a high level so as to be unattractive to shareholders, although there was an outside chance that shareholders might subscribe to the issue.

The rights issue was a 10 for 1 (that's 10 for 1, not 1 for 10) at 1,000 lire, and the nil-paid rights traded separately for a period of time during early April. Not surprisingly, these rights, which were effectively call options a long way out of the money, traded at just a handful of lire. It struck me that due to the highly geared nature of the rights I might buy a few, so I bought $40,000 of rights – an amount I could afford to lose for the bank I then worked for. I thought no more of them, and went on holiday to Courchevel for four days on 15 April.

While I was away I got an excited call from my broker telling me that, in the meantime, the Ciga stock had started to take off and was now above 1,000 lire. In fact, over the next few days it traded as high as 1,300 lire. There was some speculation that Sheraton would pay more for Ciga, and the rise in the stock price now meant that the banks would not be able to deliver Ciga to Sheraton.

The rights that I had bought for a few lire, which the market had attributed almost no value to, had now exploded in value. In addition, it became apparent that the new shares that I would receive when exercising the rights would be delivered in time to satisfy short sales for the current trading account. That allowed me to not just start selling my rights, but also short sell stock to hedge myself.

When the dust had settled, I had cleared over $6m on the trade, the equivalent of a 150-1 shot coming in.

Equity lines of credit

GEM Global Yield Fund

Sometimes you may notice an announcement revealing that a company, such as the US-based private investment group GEM, has signed an equity line of credit agreement with another company. Several UK companies, including Tadpole Technology, have entered into these agreements, which usually involve GEM agreeing to subscribe to equity at around 90% of the average closing bid price for the fifteen days prior to the draw down.

There is a limit on the draw down of shares, typically a multiple of the average daily trading volume in the fifteen-day period. GEM acquires shares at a 10% discount to the market price, the company secures funding and times the exercise to coincide with a period of heavy trading in the shares and when the share price is as high as possible, thereby maximising the subscription amount.

GEM simultaneously borrows a large line of stock (loan shares) from major shareholders, often directors, which can be sold short in the market to hedge themselves.

Directors' dealings

A great deal has been written about the significance of directors' dealings in UK companies, and many studies have been carried out on the performance of share prices subsequent to significant share purchases and sales. I have always been somewhat sceptical of linking share price performance with dealings by directors, because there are so many other influences on a company share price, but it is certainly worth being aware of what the rules are regarding directors' dealings, and hence which deals may be more significant than others.

Directors' dealings are closely followed by investors in the US, although be aware that they are referred to there as *insider dealing*, which has a completely different connotation in the UK.

The rules governing directors' dealings

Dealings by directors in their own company's shares are restricted under the listing rules by the *Model Code for Securities Transactions by Directors of Listed Companies*, as set out in the Yellow Book, and these rules go beyond those restrictions imposed by law. There are also further obligations detailed in the Companies Act, the Company Securities (Insider Dealing) Act, and the Takeover Code. The Model Code is seen as setting a minimum standard of good practice. It is important to remember that the Companies Act governs disclosures by directors, whereas restrictions on dealings are covered by the Listing Rules.

The director has five days in which to notify the company of a share transaction, and the company must notify the London Stock Exchange by the end of the following day.

The rules governing directors' dealings include:

> *"Directors, connected persons and certain employees are prohibited from dealing on considerations of a short-term nature, during the closed period, when in possession of 'unpublished price sensitive information', and must seek clearance from the Chairman of the company."*

This statement is particularly interesting in that it states that 'a director must not deal in any of the securities of the listed company on considerations of a short-term nature'. That implies that dealings should be of an investment nature rather than a trading nature. That rather makes dealings of less significance to a short-term trader as an indicator, but nevertheless can still provide a useful vote of confidence to an investor.

The rules no longer just govern share dealing: in 2003 the net was widened to include modern derivative instruments, including spread bets and CFDs.

The closed period

Directors are also prohibited from dealing during the closed period. There is often some confusion over the closed period, which is often assumed to be the two months leading up to the publication of the interim or preliminary results (if the company reports on a half-yearly basis). However, this closed period can be truncated if the time between the close of the financial year and the publication of results is shorter, and it is this period that counts as the *closed period*. If a company reports quarterly (common practice in the US), the closed period is one month, or the period from financial year-end until publication if shorter.

This is an important point, as companies in the UK report results at varying intervals after the end of the accounting period; the intervening time period can typically be anything from six to twelve weeks. If a company reports four weeks after the end of its financial year, the closed period is only four weeks. The intention is to allow dealing up until year-end and after, if the company takes more than two months to publish results.

The closed period framework therefore imposes extra significance on dealings just prior to the closed period and after results publication, as it presents the last and first opportunities to deal around results respectively.

Unpublished price-sensitive information

'Unpublished price-sensitive information', although appearing clear-cut, can be subjective. Directors have been known to buy shares in their own company shortly before a routine company briefing or company visit, which may in itself result in an unanticipated price movement, as analysts update their forecasts, or issue a revised note.

Despite all the debates about what is or what isn't price-sensitive information, I'm still firmly of the opinion that the marketplace itself is the best judge of what is price-sensitive information, although that doesn't resolve the issue.

The sale of £13.5m worth of shares in Iceland, the frozen food retailer, in December 2000 by founder Malcolm Walker a month before a profits warning, resulted in a public outcry, aggravated by the press, but such examples are few and far between.

Nevertheless, directors remain inevitably better placed to appreciate the current business climate, future prospects, signing of new contracts and changes in personnel, than the ordinary investor.

Which are the most important factors when assessing directors' dealings?

- Size of transaction (in relation to an existing holding)
- The number of directors who are dealing
- Which directors are dealing
- The timing of transactions; and
- Frequency can send different signals

In general, I look for clusters of share dealings by several directors, rather than one individual. Also, the monetary value of the transaction should be of significance; I tend to disregard anything below £20,000 in value, unless it is part of a larger number of transactions. Similarly, a director buying or selling a modest number of shares in relation to a large existing holding may also be unimportant. Not all directors are equal; I would attach a greater significance to the finance director (who should be very well placed) and the chief executive, and possibly the chairman, particularly if he was previously the CEO. If they do not have their finger on the pulse, I don't know who does.

Interpreting directors' dealings

Cluster dealing – Manpower Software

An example of cluster dealing caught my eye in April 2003. Although the amount spent by directors was a relatively modest total consideration of only £50,000, the deals assumed a greater significance as the company concerned, the IT developer Manpower Software, only had a market capitalisation of £1.7m. The timing was interesting as well, with interim results for the six months to 30 November 2002 having been recently released on 28 February 2003. The following directors' purchases were then made on 22 April 2003 at 4p.

Table 2.4: Directors' dealing example – Manpower Software

Director	Number	Consideration	Total holding
Robert Drummond (Ch.)	750,000	£30,000	2,840,352
Paul Scandrett (MD)	50,000	£2,000	65,312
Simon Thorne (FD)	200,000	£8,000	685,083
Philip Morgan	100,000	£4,000	147,468
John Archibald	75,000	£3,000	102,562
Ian Lang	200,000	£8,000	595,625

Following the company announcing a major contract win worth £3.2m over five years on 1 May, the shares subsequently traded up 28% in two days. Simon Thorne bought a further 30,000 shares at 7.7p on that day as soon as the news was out, and a further 42,000 shares at 8.75p on 9 May. Robert Drummond bought 1m shares at 10.75p on 12 June.

Final results for the year ended 31 May were released on 15 September 2003, the shares continuing to trade higher before reaching a peak of 48p on the release of interim results in March 2004.

Figure 2.31: Manpower Software (MNS) – clustered directors' dealings

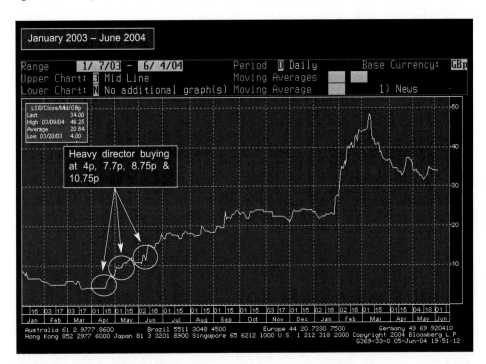

Used with permission from Bloomberg L.P.

A good example of an under-researched, smaller capitalisation company winning a number of important contracts, which few people will have been keeping track of; but the directors' transactions would have alerted an investor to a potential investment opportunity.

Demergers

Demergers can often be pivotal points for the fortunes of the two companies that subsequently trade separately. The consumer electronics company Kesa Electricals was demerged from Kingfisher in July 2003, and although a number of brokers were cautious about the prospects of Kesa, the directors' share dealings proved to be a better guide. David Newland (Chairman) and Martin Reavley (Finance Director) bought over 100,000 shares on 10 July, shortly after the demerger was effective on 7 July.

Figure 2.32: Kesa Electricals (KESA) – demerger

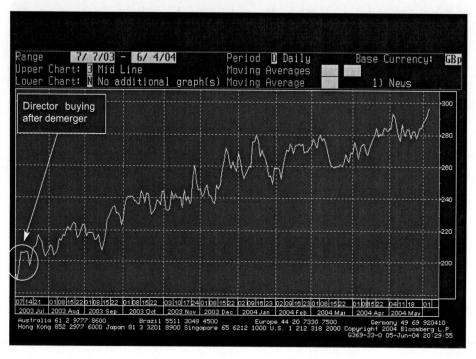

Used with permission from Bloomberg L.P.

As mentioned earlier, Countrywide had a run after a write-up in the influential *Barron's* weekly in June 2004, but it also coincided with Chairman Harry Hill buying a substantial number of shares (in excess of 700,000) in April and May 2004, shortly before the demerger of Countrywide Assured into Chesnara and Countrywide became effective.

Figure 2.33: Countrywide (CWD) – strong run after demerger

Used with permission from Bloomberg L.P.

Highly respected non-executives

Dealings by non-executives can also be of significance, if they are highly respected or industry experts.

Sir Tom Farmer, founder of Kwik-Fit Holdings, bought significant amounts of MyTravel shares, nearly 5m in total, during the course of February and March 2003, at prices between 13p and 19p (when its future was in jeopardy), which some investors saw as a big vote in confidence. As the chart shows, the share price climbed to over 35p at one point, and although it has since collapsed and gone through a debt for equity restructuring, it does demonstrate that the buying may have had a short-term influence on the shares.

Figure 2.34: MyTravel (MT) – non-executive buying

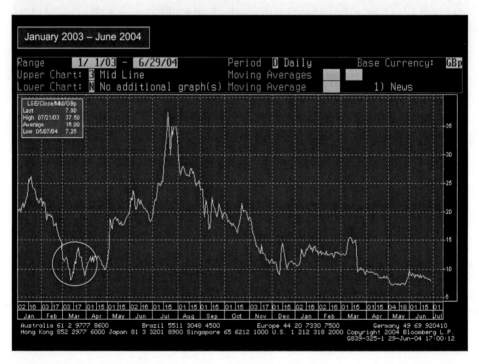

Used with permission from Bloomberg L.P.

What really caught my eye here was heavy buying while the company was going through a major restructuring, which can make it difficult for small investors to assess future prospects. MyTravel was particularly interesting in that it was seen as a high-risk recovery stock – almost 'option money'. There was a general feeling that the company would either go under or offer an exciting recovery play. The press was sceptical, and many investors preferred to steer clear, but those who followed the lead of Tom Farmer did well – for a period.

It doesn't always work out, as Marconi shareholders can testify.

The directors of Marconi demonstrated poor judgement when a clutch of them bought substantial amounts of shares while the stock was in freefall in the summer of 2001: Chief Executive Lord Simpson buying 166,000 shares at 104p; Director Derek Bonham buying 100,000 shares at 105p, and Finance Director John Mayo buying 200,000 shares at 111p. But this attracted little press at the time. Although it would seem logical that the directors are better placed than anyone else, it would appear that they are not infallible either.

Purchases by new board members should be viewed with caution; companies often encourage a new board member to show commitment by making a modest purchase of shares, so there may be a different motive.

In general though, purchases are of more interest than sales, as they show an increase in risk exposure to what may also be one's employer, whereas sales can be made for all manner of reasons including a divorce settlement, tax, school fees or a new conservatory. These reasons also act as handy excuses, including the old favourite 'to satisfy institutional demand'.

'Satisfying institutional demand'

I am sceptical of the euphemism 'satisfying institutional demand', which often accompanies the disclosure that a director has sold a significant amount of stock, and is used to assure shareholders that the shares are being sold out of the goodness of their own heart to improve liquidity and increase institutional holdings. I never knew directors could be so philanthropic.

It strikes me that holding onto the shares instead would be more likely to increase their rarity value, and if the institutions buying the stock are long-term holders then they are unlikely to increase the liquidity of the shares by buying and sitting on them anyway.

On 5 March 2004, Chairman Colin Halpern sold 2m shares in Domino's Pizza at 220p, at a small discount to the prevailing market price of 230p, seeking to satisfy institutional demand. The trade can be identified by the volume spike in the chart below, and appears well timed. It appears that the institutional demand does indeed seem to have been well and truly sated; six months later the shares had gone nowhere. I would have been more impressed if the shares were placed at a premium rather than a discount to the prevailing market price, confirming genuine demand.

Figure 2.35: Domino's Pizza (DOM) – 'satisfying institutional demand'

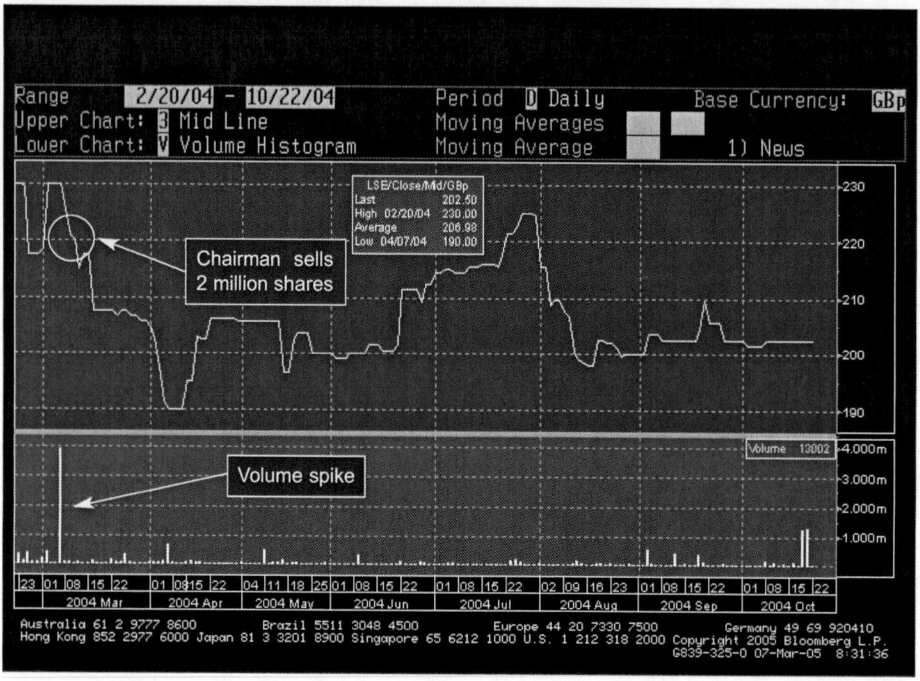

Used with permission from Bloomberg L.P.

Top-slicing, or significant sales after a substantial stock market rise, should be no surprise to anyone, whereas extensive purchases when all is gloom and doom shows a very positive vote of confidence. As such, the implications over the prospects of the wider market should be taken in context, although I think that actions do often speak louder than words. It seems less likely to me that a director would sell a large block of shares if the company were set to exceed analysts' forecasts, unless personal circumstances dictated it.

Selling prior to the end of the tax year

There can also be a swathe of selling just before the end of the tax year (sometimes accompanied by repurchases in the new financial year) to crystallise tax losses that may have more to do with the director's financial arrangements than his view of the future prospects of the company. The rules are now much tighter regarding share sales and buy-backs, although *bed and spousing* and *bed and ISAing* still allow for some manoeuvrings.

The share prices of large, blue-chip companies are subject to a number of influences not least of which are extensive analyst coverage from people far better qualified than myself. However, mid-cap and smaller companies, which have less coverage and are less well researched, seem to offer a better potential opportunity. In these companies, directors' dealings are of more significance and can offer a degree of comfort to the fellow investor.

Dealing around the closed period

One of the most bullish indicators is a cluster of buying just before the commencement of the closed period, which will be the last opportunity that directors will have to deal for a number of weeks, or immediately after the release of results. In the latter case, due to the delay between the end of the accounting period and publication of results, directors may have a good insight into trading in the new financial period subsequent to the one that the results relate to. Buying by directors immediately after the release of well-received results, and especially subsequent to an early positive price reaction on the day, is a very bullish signal.

Expiry of share options

The expiry of share options can dictate when a director exercises and sells shares, and so may not necessarily be indicative of his view of the future prospects of the company. Directors may exercise and sell one set of shares as they are about to qualify for more options at a more favourable price. If the stock is illiquid the director may decide to place the shares, rather than feed stock into the market, depressing the price over a period of time.

Timing of directors' transactions

The timing of directors' transactions can also be significant: for instance, buying after a successful trade fair, which may have coincided with the launch of a new product or the signing of new orders.

Decent buying of shares by directors out of the blue can also be intriguing.

In January 2004, a number of directors bought shares in Indigo Vision, which specialises in a full motion real time video product, including a purchase of 289,000 shares by CEO Oliver Vellacott. By buying at this stage in the cycle, this would appear to assume more significance and demonstrate a real confidence in the product, rather than simply attempting to prop up a flagging share price in a market led by a falling NASDAQ, as was seen in 2000 and 2001. One to watch.

Dealings on results day

Dealings announcements are also happening much more promptly, with dealings by directors often reported to the marketplace within hours of taking place. Particularly important are dealings on results day itself. Traders will be looking for guidance and direction among the wealth of conflicting views and analysis, and a director buying or selling on results day assumes a greater significance and sends a real signal to the market, as it will have been the first opportunity for the director to deal for perhaps two months.

On 15 April 2004, Jarvis, the facilities management business, issued a poor trading statement, but a director bought 17,000 shares in the morning at 137.5p, and the release of the announcement at 15.58 in the afternoon detailing the transaction was enough to temporarily boost the share price. The share price move may look modest, but a 10p move equates to around 8%.

Figure 2.36: Jarvis (JRVS) – a director's dealing on results day

Used with permission from Bloomberg L.P.

Similarly, JJB Sports, the sportswear retailer, issued final results on 14 April, and by 10.30 that day the announcement that a director had sold 34,000 shares a couple of hours earlier at 290p was already out, and accounted for an immediate 7p drop in the share price.

Figure 2.37: JJB Sports (JJB) – a director's dealing on results day

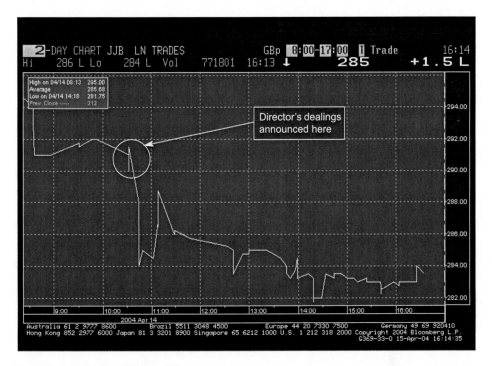

Used with permission from Bloomberg L.P.

Mid-cap companies

Mothercare is an excellent example of how a medium-sized company was turned around, and where solid buying by directors over a period of weeks preceded a significant upturn in the share price, far outpacing the performance of the relevant sector.

The frenzy of buying is summarised below:

Table 2.5: Directors' dealing example – Mothercare

Director	Date (2003)	Number	Price	Consideration
Steven Glew (FD)	28-Mar	20,000	102.75p	£20,550
Ben Gordon (CEO)	28-Mar	19,412	102p	£19,800
Steven Glew	23-May	35,000	144p	£50,400
Ben Gordon	27-May	34,427	144p	£49,575
Ben Gordon	21-Jul	7,000	162p	£11,340
Steven Glew	21-Jul	5,000	162p	£8,100
Bernard Cragg	21-Jul	20,000	161p	£32,200
Maurice Minzly*	31-Jul	5,000	185p	£9,250
Ian Peacock (Ch)	31-Jul	7,665	194p	£14,870
Karren Brady	13-Aug	1,500	200p	£3,000
*Husband of non-executive director Angela Heylin				

Figure 2.38: Mothercare (MTC) – directors' buying precedes significant upturn

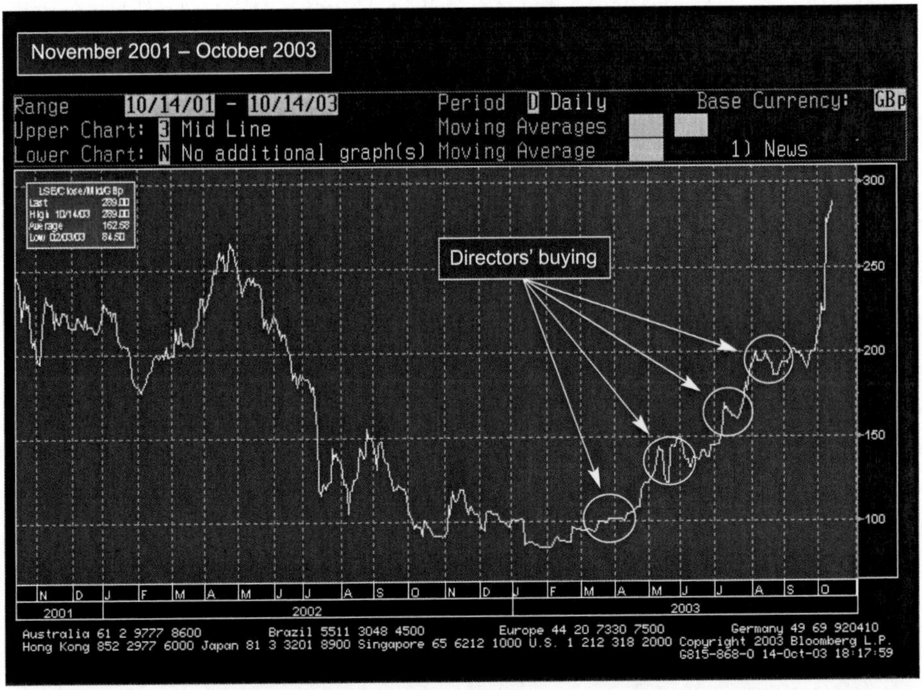

Used with permission from Bloomberg L.P.

There are numerous examples of well timed directors' sales, and it seems unfair to focus on two examples; however they do seem to be exceptionally well timed.

On 13 April 2004, Clive Thompson, chairman of Rentokil, the business services company, sold 5m shares at 183.5p, and there was something of a furore in the press when, in a trading statement just four weeks later on 19 May the company issued a downbeat earnings forecast. The shares fell 14% from 175.5p to 151.5p in one day, with Thompson simultaneously stepping down as chairman.

Figure 2.39: Rentokil (RTO) – chairman sells before a downbeat trading statement

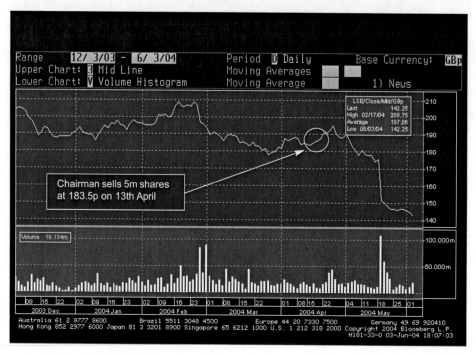

Used with permission from Bloomberg L.P.

First quarter results from Bookham on 5 May 2004 were poorly received, but the stock had already been falling fast leading up to the release of figures at the end of April, subsequent to some significant directors' sales during March.

Table 2.6: Directors' dealing example – Bookham

Director	Date (2004)	Number	Price	Consideration
Robert Rickman	10-Mar	-60,000	122p	£73,200
David Simpson (Dep Ch)	10-Mar	-150,000	121p	£181,500
Andrew Rickman (Ch)	12-Mar	-772,130	118p	£911,113
Dr. Peter Bordui	19-Mar	-48,061	114p	£54,790

Figure 2.40: Bookham (BHM) – directors' sales precede share price decline

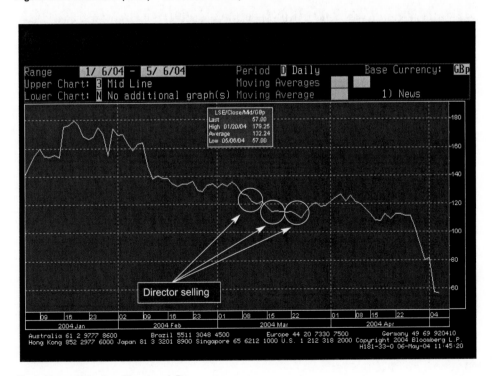

Used with permission from Bloomberg L.P.

Finance director

Although a change of finance director is not always significant, the position is one of the most important for a company and its shareholders.

On 11 June 2004, Filtronic, the mobile phone base station and aerials group, announced that John Samuel, Finance Director for over thirteen years, was leaving the company with immediate effect to join Zetex as Chief Financial Officer. On 23 June, less than two weeks later, Filtronic issued a poor trading statement blaming, among other things, the impact of the weak dollar. Over the course of the following three days the stock slumped by almost a third from over 300p to nearly 200p. Although the two events may be unconnected, the fact remains that the dealings and appointment or loss of a finance director can be perceived as significant events for a company.

Figure 2.41: Filtronic (FTC) – poor trading statement

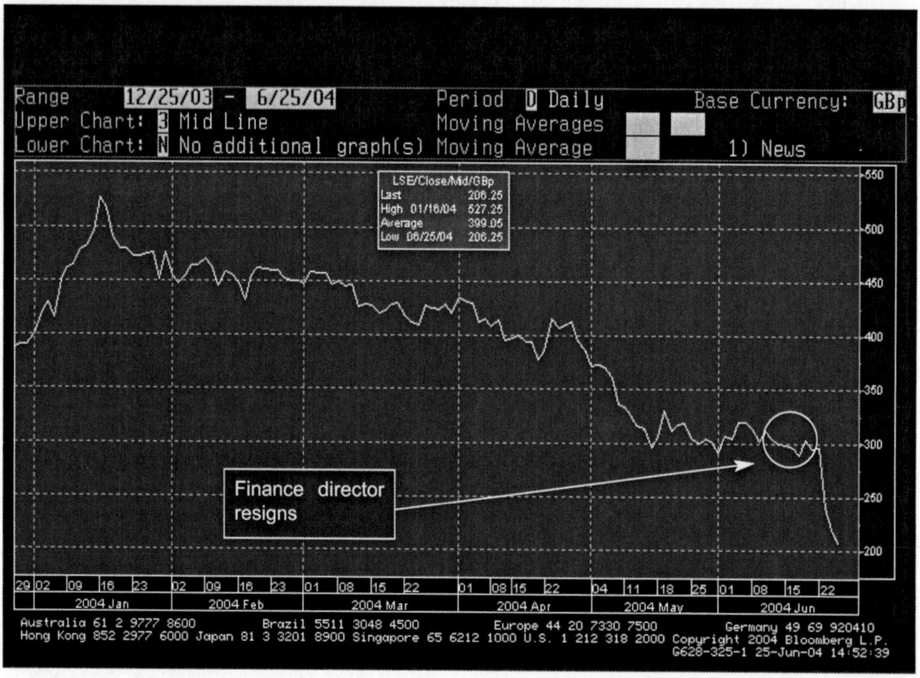

Used with permission from Bloomberg L.P.

Buying after a substantial rise

It takes a certain confidence to buy shares in your own company when they have already risen three-fold, but that is what the directors of Cairn Energy did in June 2004, and the significance of this transaction was not lost on investors.

Table 2.7: Directors' dealing example – Cairn Energy

Director	Date (2004)	Number	Price	Consideration
Norman Murray (Ch)	17-Jun	10,000	1185p	£118,500
Mike Watts (Exploration)	18-Jun	16,543	1200p	£198,516
Hamish Grossart (Dep Ch)	22-Jun	50,000	1248p	£624,000

These announcements were made between 18 and 22 June, and by the end of that week the stock was already trading up through 1400p. Traders who noted the significance not just of the size of investment involved, but also of the vote of confidence in the company's prospects, and moved quickly to follow the directors' lead, did particularly well as the purchases received considerable press coverage over the following days, including the influential weekend press, fuelling the share price rise further.

Figure 2.42: Cairn Energy (CNE) – directors' buying after a strong rise

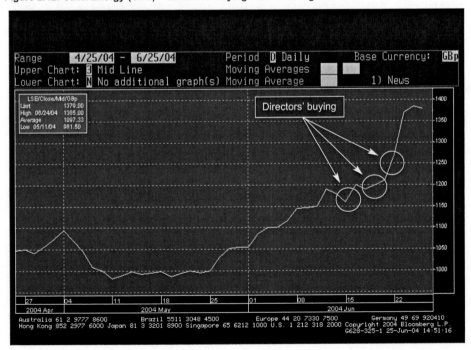

Used with permission from Bloomberg L.P.

Sifting dealings data

The standard regulatory announcement on directors' dealings is not particularly user-friendly, and I have often spent time wading through a dealings announcement to find that somebody's wife bought seventy-seven shares for her ISA. It would be a lot more useful if the announcement were released with a summary in the subject line, or at the beginning of the body of the text, stating when, who, buy or sell and how many shares. Many companies use the standard regulatory template, which runs to around twenty paragraphs with the key information often hidden away and inaccessible. At least some companies have adopted a more helpful approach to shareholding announcements, e.g. Bodycote giving more detail in the subject line such as "Fidelity's interest now at 4.98%".

Fortunately, there are a number of good websites that take the sweat out of it. Two of my favourites that cover directors' dealings in different ways are Citywire and Digital Look. Both approaches have their attributes.

The Citywire site has a comprehensive value-added approach, which incorporates a write-up and commentary, and extends the net from just directors to secret buying and acknowledged shrewd investors.

Digital Look has a daily editorial round up on Sharecast, and also a useful feature that allows you to scan down dealings in the last few days, either by transaction size or by name, filtering all deals below, say, £10,000 automatically for a particular company. In addition you can query its database to display a market-wide list of the biggest buys and sells over any period of time, say, in descending order of consideration. There is a further feature that allows you to chart the share price with director dealings annotated as shown opposite.

Figure 2.43: Directors' dealings for Mothercare (MTC) (Digital Look)

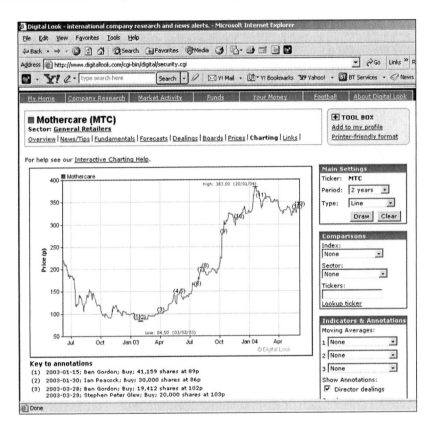

Source: Digital Look

Another excellent site if you simply wish to skim through dealings in one particular stock, is Investegate, the regulatory news specialist. This is a good resource if you are investigating company by company. Investegate now also has a new search facility, allowing the user the ability to pull up only the most important RNS statements, such as AGMs, interims and finals over a selected period of years, saving hours of searching through several pages of irrelevant RNS statements.

Reference

Citywire: www.citywire.co.uk

Digital Look: www.digitallook.com

Investegate: www.investegate.co.uk

Summary

Overall, I think dealings should be taken in context and in combination with other factors. They should certainly be on the checklist before making an investment, as well as how much equity in total the management has in their own company, but trading around directors' dealings in isolation seems unreliable.

There is no doubt that investors and traders alike are watching directors' dealings, particularly in small companies, as share prices often move shortly after the obligatory regulatory announcement is published. The days of a share price moving on Monday morning, after a write-up highlighting dealings by directors in the *Weekend FT* are long gone, as the marketplace now follows such dealings more closely, and they are often highlighted and written up on financial websites on the same day. Unfortunately, many of these companies have low liquidity and wide dealing spreads, making any short-term trade unattractive.

Broker upgrades and downgrades

It can be difficult to obtain a list of daily broker upgrades and downgrades, by which I mean a change of recommendation or price target. An inexplicable price move, often immediately from the opening bell in the morning, is usually explained later in the day by an upgrade or downgrade becoming public knowledge.

Obviously the investment banks are going to make sure their best clients get their research first, but there are a number of services that do collate this information, including Citywire and Yahoo!. Best of all is to use your broker and hear directly from the desk, as word of mouth is often quicker.

Usefulness of brokers' notes depends on your position on the information curve

Many novice traders like to mock brokers' notes as contrary indicators, but fail to realise that by the time they have got to hear about it, the move has already happened. Investment banks spend millions on research and it is unrealistic to expect to have an early take on that research before the bank's preferred clients who pay the most commission. It is a good example of the sole trader being badly placed on the information curve.

Some broker research is available on the internet, for instance some excellent smaller company reports can be accessed free at the Evolution Securities website (www.evosecurities.com).

But this is where having a Bloomberg or Reuters terminal comes into its own, as they will invariably put out upgrades and downgrades as soon as they hear of them. Regulatory releases will not cover them and, although some traders begrudge paying for a premium news service, it can pay for itself very quickly.

The rating of the analyst in the sector will also be important, as the star analyst will inevitably have a greater influence than a lesser rated one. Brokers that are specialists and well regarded, such as Numis in retail stocks, may be more influential.

There are often unaccountable stock moves first thing in the morning, or late in the previous day's trading session, later explained by a new analyst note. Some big firms are much more proprietary trading-orientated than others, and despite regulatory attempts to restrict the early release of rating changes internally, stocks still seem to experience mysterious moves beforehand. Once the information is in the public domain the move has usually already happened. Notes from more client-orientated firms, such as Merrill Lynch, which are much less focussed on proprietary equity trading, are rarely leaked in advance, and traders can often benefit from a continued follow-through in the stock well after the information is in the public domain. Some American houses also have huge retail distribution in the US, so follow-through can continue late into the afternoon of UK trading hours.

The importance of the house broker

The most important broker of all is the house broker, in other words, the broker retained by the company as its advisor. Their recommendations can be the most influential, particularly if the analyst is highly rated in the sector, as they are often closest to the company.

I try to maintain a list of major companies and their associated house brokers and keep it to hand; you can find a list sorted by investment bank at Hemscott.

Interestingly, there is no such thing as a 'corporate broker' on Wall Street – it is a very British tradition. In the UK, the blue-chip client lists are dominated by Cazenove (now part of a joint venture with J.P. Morgan Chase) with around thirty-nine clients, Hoare Govett (part of ABN-AMRO) with twenty-five, and Merrill Lynch with around thirty. The corporate broker acts as an intermediary between the company and the markets, whereas in the US, companies tend to use multi-purpose integrated investment banks.

The house broker is usually in the loop, and is often one way of getting information to the market. The Listing Rules place a general obligation on companies to:

> *"disclose certain information which is not public knowledge and which may lead to a substantial movement in the price of its securities. Such information will include major new developments, changes in the company's financial condition or business performance or changes in the company's expectations of its performance."*

It isn't clear what "substantial" means, and although 10% appears a good rule of thumb and has become almost an unofficial guideline, perpetuated by the media, the FSA has made it clear that there is no '10% rule'. However, companies have fallen foul of selective briefings in the past, despite it being specifically unacceptable.

For example, Brown & Jackson briefed analysts in November 2003, which resulted in forecasts being cut, but there was no RNS until the next day, and there was outrage among ordinary shareholders who felt that there was a lack of equality of information.

Events which are deemed by the Listing Rules to be price-sensitive are:

- dividend announcements;
- board appointments or departures;
- profit warnings;
- share dealings by directors or substantial shareholders;
- acquisitions or disposals above a certain size;
- annual and interim results;
- preliminary results;
- changes in the business model or trading strategy;
- rights issues; and
- other offers of securities.

Companies and advisers should be aware of the market expectations built into the share price.

Closed period relates to a period before any regular reporting event and places restrictions on directors' dealings. Although many companies adopt a policy that they will not communicate with the market during this period **it is not a regulatory requirement**, contrary to popular belief.

Reference
Citywire: www.citywire.co.uk

Yahoo UK Finance: uk.finance.yahoo.com

Evolution Securities: www.evosecurities.com

Hemscott: www.hemscott.com

Market Watch

Auction imbalances

The SETS and SETSmm auction process has been described in a previous chapter. Traders who are not availing themselves of participation in the auctions are missing some of the best trading prices and opportunities of the day.

Auctions are used by market participants for guaranteed stock execution for a number of reasons:

- **An order that is worked throughout the day** may be completed in the auction. If there is insufficient liquidity in the closing auction, an imbalance may occur, pushing the uncrossing price away from previous levels of trading, providing an opportunity for a trader (prepared to take some overnight risk) to take the other side.
- **VWAP orders**, where a broker has divided a large order into tranches to execute throughout the day to guarantee a price to his client close to the day's VWAP, may seek to complete the order in the auction and is dependent on sufficient liquidity.
- **Tracking funds** also make extensive use of auctions, as the uncrossing price is usually used as the official closing price. If the constituents of an index, such as the FTSE 100, are being re-shuffled, tracking funds will often seek to trade in the auction, to guarantee their correct stock weighting at the price that the stocks enter and leave the index at. Other influential events, such as the MSCI re-shuffles, can result in huge volume. A record 176.5m shares traded in the closing auction on 31 May 2002, as funds manoeuvred new and old holdings, and more than 10% of the total FTSE 100 volume for the day took place in the closing auction. In certain stocks there is often higher volume in the closing auction than during the normal trading day.

Best opportunities at the end of month/quarter

Some of the best opportunities, accompanied by larger volumes, often occur in the auction on the last business day of the month and quarter. There is no concrete evidence why this is so but I suspect that it is related to either expiry of OTC derivative instruments, index tracking funds executing minor re-weightings, or even someone deliberately moving a closing price in favour of their book.

UK traders who do not have access to the pre- and post-market auction processes are denying themselves the full daily trading range for a given stock. The following three-day charts in Next and Imperial Tobacco clearly show the substantial opportunities available to traders prepared to accept some overnight risk, when an at-market seller in the closing auction forced the price down several percentage points from the day's established range. Both stocks recovered their respective falls almost immediately after the open the following day.

Figure 2.44: Next (NXT) – large seller in closing auction

Used with permission from Bloomberg L.P.

Figure 2.45: Imperial Tobacco (IMT) – large seller in closing auction

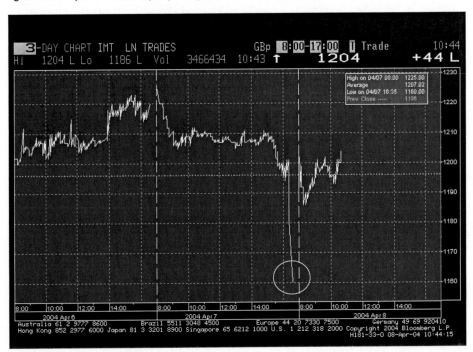

Used with permission from Bloomberg L.P.

Following the clever money

Some of the best investing and trading results I have had in recent years have been from riding on the coat-tails of investors far brighter than myself, who have done more research on a company than I will ever be inclined to.

It can be a tedious process following all the dealings that get reported through the RNS announcements, but I try to maintain a list of major stakes and holdings in nearly three hundred UK companies. This allows me to keep track of who is increasing or decreasing their stakes in certain key companies.

Companies Act disclosure requirements allow private investors to keep track of the activities of shrewd investors who have a proven track record of successful investing. Websites, such as Citywire, also dig around below the surface by accessing shareholder registers, to discover early stake building below the reportable 3% level. Proven successful investors often have a wealth of experience, and are much better placed to make successful investment decisions in less-researched smaller companies than private investors will ever be.

A couple of things are worth noting:

- Firstly, small investors who follow bigger stake builders have an advantage in that they can nimbly move in and out of positions quickly. A large shareholding, however, can be hard to both establish and later exit, and so dictates a degree of commitment. Smaller investors can follow but enter and exit at will.
- Secondly, because takeover rules limit stakes to 29.9% without making a mandatory takeover offer, some share price weakness can ensue after the stake builder increases their stake rapidly to that level, and then stops without bidding. Stake building in a company that starts to approach 29.9% can be both bullish and bearish for the share price in the short term.

Shrewd investors

Listed below are some of the shrewd investors and shareholder activists who invariably seem to spot value in companies at an early stage.

Jack Petchey (Trefick)

Property entrepreneur Jack Petchey acquires stakes in listed real-estate companies trading at significant discounts to NAV through his Isle of Man investment vehicle, Trefick. He also has considerable experience in the motor distributor sector, and has had a great deal of success investing in the sector. He takes large stakes in companies, and puts pressure on management to restructure in order to maximise shareholder value.

Time and again, companies that Petchey invests in become takeover targets shortly afterwards, as his target is brought into focus. Examples include property company Estates & General, which was bid for by Winten, shortly after Petchey accumulated a 29% holding.

A common strategy he uses is to launch tender offers for his target, which can be a good barometer for gauging how loose or 'sticky' shareholders are, as well as demonstrating how undervalued the company is.

Saville Gordon eventually agreed to buy Trefick's 29% stake in December 2000, to get him off the shareholder register (in what was effectively greenmail), and was eventually taken off the market in an MBO in May 2002. Petchey is a classic facilitator. Petcheys current holdings include Aston Villa (20%), Bizspace (23.7%), Brixton (5.4%), De Vere (13.7%), Euro Motor Holdings (14%), HR Owen (17.5%), JS Real Estate (29%), Mallett (7.6%), Mucklow (14%), Rugby Estates (3%) Warner Estates (14%).

Peter Gyllenhammar

Swedish activist investor Peter Gyllenhammar specialises in companies trading at substantial discounts to net asset value or in need of restructuring, often through his investment vehicles, Erudite, Förvaltnings AB, Nakterhuset, Bronsstadet and Silverslaggen. He often seeks board representation and works closely with management. Gyllenhammar has a background as an analyst and corporate finance advisor to several major Swedish corporations. He has interests in a number of UK public companies, and is Chairman of British Mohair Holdings, and a director of Browallia International. Current significant holdings include Aortech International (10%), Berkeley Technology (6.4%), Densitron Technologies (24.3%), European Colour (20.9%), Hartest Holdings (16.4%), Jarvis Porter Group (26.6%) and Sherwood Group (13%).

Bob Morton

Arthur Leonard 'Bob' Morton is well known as a serial and entrepreneurial West Midlands investor, who often utilises his investment vehicle, Southwind, to make strategic investments. He returned several times his investment when he took a 15% stake in Tenon, the accountancy and professional services firm in February 2003. He is believed to be worth more than £100m, has investments in over twenty quoted companies and is chairman of numerous companies, including Armour Group (16%), Clarity Commerce Solutions (5.6%), Harrier Group (30%) and Systems Union. Mortons holdings include DCS Group (8%), IS Solutions (19%) and Lorien (21%).

Figure 2.46: Tenon (TNO)

Used with permission from Bloomberg L.P.

Jon Moulton (Alchemy Partners)

Jon Moulton is best known for founding Alchemy Partners in 1997, a private equity advisory business that specialises in buy-outs, buy-ins and the provision of later stage development capital. He's estimated to have made more than £10m from a modest investment in Bookham Technology.

Martin Hughes (Toscafund)

A former deputy CEO and head of research at Credit Lyonnais Lang, and Number 1 rated banking analyst in the mid-1990s. Before setting up his own hedge fund, Toscafund, he was head of global financials at Julian Robertson's hedge fund Tiger Management. Toscafund uses a bottom-up approach to selecting equity securities and takes both long and short positions. Toscafund currently has significant holdings in AMEC and Manganese Bronze.

Dermot Desmond

Financier Dermot Desmond is a billionaire shareholder in Celtic and Manchester United, and also jointly owns the Sandy Lane Hotel in Barbados with John McManus. Investment vehicles include International Insurance & Underwriting (IIU) and Crossbill, which held 5% of TBI, the airports operator, before it was taken over.

In February 2004, Desmond's investment vehicle, Bottin International Investments, bought heavily into Barlo, the Irish radiators and plastics maker, while it was subject to an MBO at €40c per share led by CEO Tony Mullins. A few weeks later, Quinn Group trumped the proposed MBO with a successful €48c per share offer and Desmond cleared an estimated €2m.

Hanover Investors

Hanover Investors is a turnaround investment specialist that combines the injection of fresh capital with hands-on operational management involvement by its principals.

Hanover principals, Edward Bramson and Matthew Peacock, have extensive buy-out and corporate finance expertise as well as in-depth practical experience of operational management.

I first noticed Edward Bramson appear on the shareholder list of 4Imprint on 28 July 2003, and he continued to increase his stake with Hanover, accounting for 26.6% of the shares at one point. I followed their lead, invested in 4Imprint, and sold out after a reasonable return some months later. Hanover eventually reduced its holding on the release of final results on 29 March 2004, the first opportunity that they had as the directors were restricted during the closed period. Hanover popped up in early 2005 with a 10.3% stake in Elementis. One to keep an eye on.

Figure 2.47: 4Imprint (FOUR)

Used with permission from Bloomberg L.P.

Lansdowne Partners

Lansdowne is a secretive West End-based hedge fund boutique run by ex-Mercury fund managers Stuart Roden and Peter Davies since 2001. Recent successes have resulted from substantial holdings in Arcadia, Burtonwood, Harvey Nichols, Waste Recycling and Manchester United, all of which have received takeover approaches or been taken over. Landsdowne's current significant holdings include Aberdeen Asset Management (10%), Evolution Group (4.5%), Inmarsat (8%), Manganese Bronze (9.4%), Pinewood Shepperton (9.6%) and Soco International (6%).

Taube Hodson Stonex

THS is run by legendary investor Nils Taube, assisted by fellow partners Cato Stonex and John Hodson.

THS first came to my attention when the fund bought a substantial holding in Burford, the property company, shortly before it was taken over. Although focussed on longer-term strategies, the fund is not immune to taking short-term positions where it senses an opportunity. THS made a very useful turn buying into, and selling out of, Safeway during its takeover by Morrisons. It also immediately sold its entire holding on the day that WHSmith announced that it had had an approach from Permira, almost at the high watermark.

Shareholder activists

Guinness Peat Group (GPG)

A classic *deus ex machina*, GPG is an activist investment group founded by New Zealander, Sir Ron Brierley, and assisted by Blake Nixon who runs the UK arm. A common theme adopted by GPG is to target companies with good tangible assets, often cash-rich, which are perceived to be poorly run.

However, GPG appears to have met its match with its investment in the family run Young & Co's Brewery. Although there is no dispute that Young's trades at a significant discount to net asset value, so far the company has fought off the unwanted attention of GPG, mainly because of the unusual share class structure allowing a minority holding to wield a majority of the votes. A good example of why publicly listed, family companies often trade at a discount.

GPG has also had successes in the motor distributor sector, where a 20% stake in Quicks, the motor dealer, paid off when CD Bramall subsequently launched a bid in March 2002.

Laxey Partners Limited

Laxey is an Isle of Man based active value company, led by investment trust busters, Andrew Pegge and Colin Kingsnorth. Laxey's investment strategy is to take active positions in companies which are trading at a discount to their underlying assets, including closed-end funds and cash-rich companies. Laxey Partners also runs the Value Catalyst Fund, an offshore closed-end investment company. Laxey has taken advantage of bombed-out internet and technology companies trading below the value of cash on their balance sheet. For value investors it is well worth taking a look at companies where Laxey appears on the shareholder's register.

Laxey also hit the headlines when it targeted British Land, and borrowed a line of British Land stock for the sole purpose of utilising the associated votes to increase their influence at an AGM.

JO Hambro Capital Management

JO Hambro is an activist UK fund manager, run by Chris Mills, that specialises in accumulating large majority stakes in listed companies, particularly those trading at discounts to net asset value, cash on the balance sheet, or just trading on a low rating. Mills, who is chief investment office for Hambro and CEO for North Atlantic Value, then puts pressure on the company to realise value for shareholders, sometimes through initiating corporate activity. In 2003, JO Hambro diversified its investment management activities into four entities, and the active value and private equity investment business is now incorporated into North Atlantic Value LLP.

Dawnay, Day Group

Dawnay, Day is a property investment and financial services group of companies with combined gross assets of more than £1.5bn, owned and run by Guy Naggar and Peter Klimt. They took control of cash shell Amberley, which is likely to be used for a future deal. The group's two major property holding companies are Dawnay, Day Properties Ltd and Starlight Investments.

Both men look for undervalued public companies with strong assets which are cash flow positive, and, although they are not asset strippers, they have made a number of shrewd moves in the last few years and are worth following.

Naggar and Klimt have two private investment companies, ForwardIssue and Totalassist respectively, which often take stakes in companies through CFDs. Naggar is also Chairman of Paramount, which owns the Chez Gerard restaurant chain. Dawnay, Day backed the floating of Volvere, chaired by former Dixons Chairman Sir Stanley Kalms, an activist and value-seeking investment vehicle on AIM in December 2002.

Judges Capital is another activist vehicle backed by Dawnay, Day that listed on AIM in January 2003, activist David Cicurel is Chief Executive. Judges seeks to acquire strategic stakes in undervalued quoted companies where it can initiate a break up or cash distribution.

Acquisitor Holdings

Acquisitor Holdings is a Bermuda-based activist shareholder that listed on AIM in October 2002, after being spun out of Acquisitor (which has now been reversed into Tinopolis), with the simultaneous transfer of 90% of the assets of Acquisitor. Acquisitor Holdings specialises in cash-rich situations and shell companies, such as Baltimore and Nettec, where it has substantial holdings. Directors include entrepreneur Luke Johnson and Chris Mills of JO Hambro.

According to Managing Director, Duncan Soukup:

> *Acquisitor fills a gap in the market – it bridges the gap between private equity and public equity. We look at the public market with private equity eyes, but take decisions in the public market based on business analysis rather than stock analysis. Then we try and unlock or create value to narrow the discount between the private market value and public market value.*

Active Value

Active Value is probably the best-known shareholder activist and its principals, Brian Myerson and Julian Treger, are now often referred to as veterans. Large current holdings include Communisis (7%), Corporate Services Group (46%), Marylebone Warwick Balfour (22%) and Novar (17%). At the end of 2004, Myerson and Treger announced that they were going their separate ways and would gradually wind down their existing strategic holdings.

Steel Partners II

Warren Lichtenstein's Steel Partners is a New York based hedge fund that came to my attention during 2004, when it appeared with an 8.12% holding in the UK company API Group, which was going through a restructuring to concentrate on its core foils and laminates products. Steel Partners continued to increase its stake to 15% in November, 20% in December and then very quickly took it to the maximum 29.99% possible without bidding, in January 2005. Meanwhile the share price had run up from 80p to 120p. To aggressively take this stake to the permitted maximum is a very bullish signal in my eyes, and I quickly bought some shares at around 120p. The company subsequently announced that it had received a bid approach on 11 February and I took my profits at around 148p, although needless to say the stock continued to run up to 175p. Steel Partners also has holdings in Delta (6.5%), Lavendon (7.4%), London Scottish Bank (4%), Netteck (21.4%), Renold (7%) and UNIQ (12%).

Figure 2.48: API Group (API)

Used with permission from Bloomberg L.P.

Paul Scott

One of the real gems on the internet is Paul Scott's little known board on Motley Fool named *Paulypilot's Pub*. The board attracts a unique collection of individuals, many with a proven investment track record. Scott himself is an ex-finance director for a retail chain and has had many recent successes both in smaller companies and cash-rich situations where he has, on occasion, become an activist. His site can be found at:

boards.fool.co.uk/Messages.asp?bid=51144

Meetings and resolutions

It is worth noting in this section, and in the context of increased shareholder activism, the notice periods around company meetings.

The three types of resolution are: Ordinary, Special and Extraordinary. Ordinary resolutions require a simple majority of the votes (over 50%); while Special and Extraordinary resolutions require 75% of the votes to be passed.

Note: Directors can only be removed through a resolution at a board meeting.

AGMs

AGMs require twenty-one calendar days' notice, must be held each calendar year, and there must be a maximum period of fifteen months between AGMs.

EGMs

EGMs require fourteen calendar days' notice, although if the event requires a Special Resolution (requiring 75% approval) the notice period is twenty-one days.

EGMs are usually called by the board for the approval of a specific event, but can also be requisitioned by shareholders representing 10% or more of the votes. If requisitioned by shareholders, notice of the EGM must be sent to shareholders within twenty-one days of the directors receiving the request.

Volatility and VIX

Volatility is one of the most important concepts in options pricing, and yet it is often ignored or misunderstood by investors of both options and warrants.

Historic volatility

Historic volatility is a backward-looking measure, and can be calculated precisely for any share or index over a given time frame via statistical analysis. One standard deviation either side of a share price trend represents a band inside which the share price would be expected to remain 66% of the time.

For example, a historic volatility of 25% would imply that the share has a one in three chance of trading outside a band of 25% away from the current share price. A 50% implied volatility implies a one in six chance that an instrument will halve over the year.

Implied volatility

Implied volatility can be calculated for an option and represents what the market thinks future volatility will be for the underlying stock or index.

A theoretical value for an option can be calculated from:

- strike price of the option;
- underlying stock or index price;
- period to option expiry;
- risk-free interest rate;
- stock dividends; and
- underlying stock or index volatility.

But given an actual price that an option is trading at in the market, the calculation can be reversed, whereby a volatility can be found such that the calculated theoretical option value is the same as its actual current trading price. This back-calculated volatility is called the *implied volatility*.

Implied volatility can be viewed as the market's perception of future risk (volatility), *not* market direction.

However, although volatility should be independent of market direction, this isn't always the case. In a falling market, implied volatilities can increase, reflecting the strong demand for buying put options. (Fear would seem to be more powerful than greed!)

VIX Index

The Chicago Board Options Exchange (CBOE) SPX Volatility Index (VIX) reflects a market estimate of future volatility over the next thirty calendar days, based on the weighted average of the implied volatilities for a wide range of strikes for options based on the S&P 500.

Many commentators believe there is an inverse link between the VIX (a commonly used measure of risk aversion), and subsequent market moves.

- **High levels of VIX** happen near market lows, when there is a high demand for option protection and can be a bullish signal, as they can be interpreted as evidence of panic in the market.
- Conversely, a **low VIX** implies market complacency and often precedes a sell-off.

As seen in the following charts, lows in the VIX regularly precede a market sell-off; whereas high levels precede stability and a rising trend. As such, VIX is often quoted as a measure of current market sentiment, and a possible inverse indicator to future market direction. There is, however, no empirical evidence that volatility is either a good contra-indicator or accurate barometer of future stock market moves.

Figure 2.49: Six year VIX chart

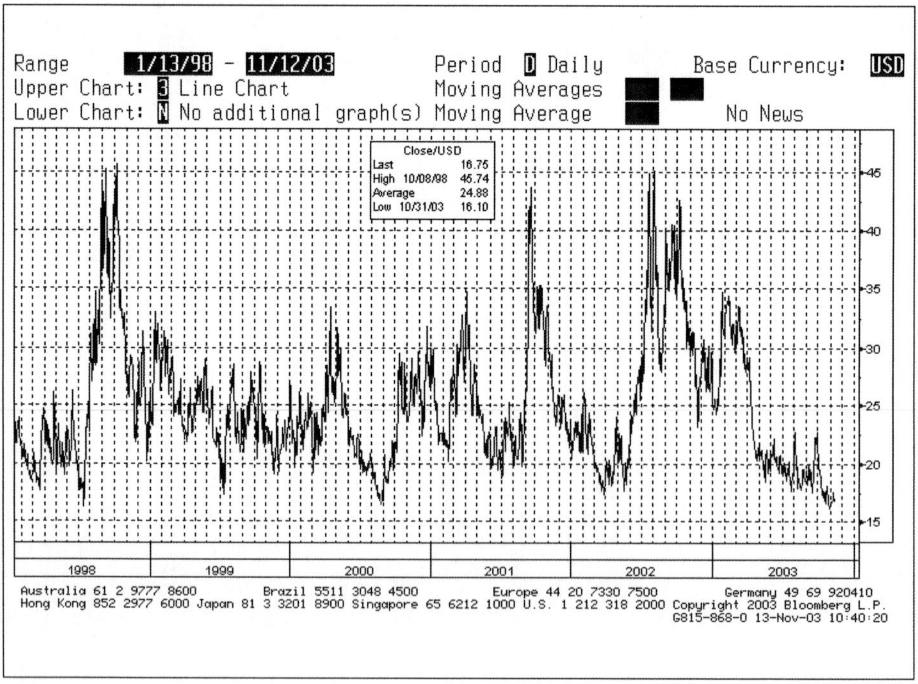

Used with permission from Bloomberg L.P.

Figure 2.50: Six year S&P 500 chart

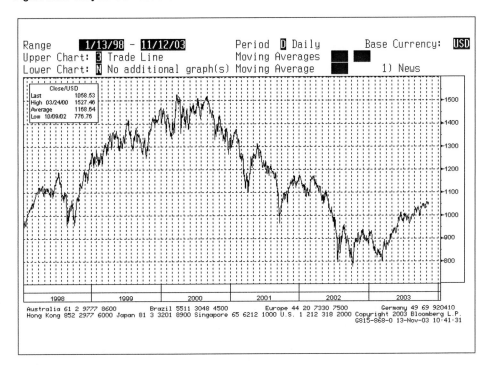

Used with permission from Bloomberg L.P.

In September 2003, the CBOE changed the definition of VIX from one of being based on options on the S&P 100 to options based on the S&P 500. The old VIX now goes under the ticker VXO.

As VIX is now based on a broader index, VIX will tend to be lower than VXO. For the same reason, implied volatilities on individual stocks are almost always higher than on indices.

As a general measure, implied volatilities of 15% or below are seen as low, with spikes above 40% regarded as high.

Implied volatilities can stay low or high for long periods, however, and go through structural changes. For example, in the early 1990s volatility was low for many years.

Reference
VIX Index: www.cboe.com

Event Opportunities

Lock-up expiries

When a company lists one of its subsidiaries on the market but retains a large interest (such as GUS did when it sold its stake in Burberry), it is common for there to be a lock-up arrangement over the remaining stake in an attempt to reassure potential investors that the market is not about to be flooded with cheap stock. A similar arrangement takes place in IPOs, where the original private equity backers undertake not to sell further stock for a period of time.

Lock-ups generally run for 180 days from the IPO and prohibit existing shareholders from selling, but specific details can often be found in the listing prospectus.

However, despite the existence of such lock-up agreements, it was increasingly becoming routine strategy for market participants to take advantage of the provisions by short-selling stock (often using CFDs), ahead of the lock-up expiry. In an attempt to pre-empt this, some investment banks have sought to thwart this short selling by releasing the private equity backers from their commitment early.

Lock-ups can be waived at any time

Lock-up arrangements are only a contractual agreement between a bank and a selling shareholder, which can be made void at any time.

For example, in late 2003, the market was out-foxed when a lock-up in Yell was brought forward with the agreement of the banks, and the placing in Yell by Goldman Sachs and Merrill Lynch ahead of the lock-up wrong-footed market participants expecting a flood of shares. A similar situation occurred with the waiving of Telecom Italia's lock-up on its Telekom Austria's stake by J.P. Morgan and Merrill Lynch.

Share price performance around lock-up expiries will often be determined by the market's perception of where the stock has gone. Full removal of an overhang can be more beneficial to the shares than a partial removal, as there will always be uncertainty about the placing of the residual. Similarly, if the overhang is simply passed along to another short-term holder, or a failed placing leaves stock on an investment bank's books, the share price can suffer badly.

Example: Acambis

A good example of the effect on a share price of the expiry of a lock-up took place in December 2003, when a lock-up arrangement that Baxter, the US healthcare company, had over 21% of Acambis, the smallpox vaccine manufacturer, expired.

Baxter sought to place its 21% stake almost immediately on expiry of the lock-up at the beginning of December, but the market got wind of the placing after potential investors were sounded out by the investment banks involved. The stock was sold down savagely and the placing was temporarily abandoned.

A successful placing was carried out later in the month on 18 December at 245p – an 11% discount to the prevailing market price – but the chart below clearly demonstrates that the effective discount was actually much bigger, as the stock had weakened considerably during November in anticipation.

As soon as the placing was complete and the overhang cleared, the stock recovered a substantial amount of the lost ground. As is so often the case, a spike in the traded volume coincided with a turning point for the stock.

Figure 2.51: Acambis (ACM) – effect of the expiry of a lock-up

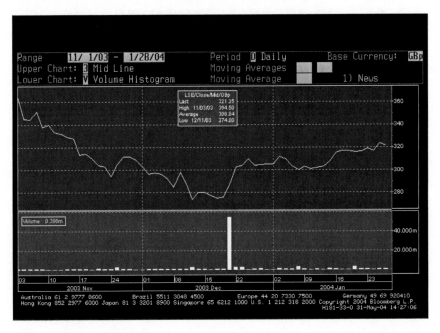

Used with permission from Bloomberg L.P.

Note: Stock placed as a result of a lock-up expiry will often be executed as a block trade or 'bought deal'.

Index reviews, re-weightings and investability changes

Substantial stock flows can often be observed around the dates when index constituent changes are made effective.

One of the most popular strategies adopted by traders is to buy stocks that are due to enter an index and sell those that face deletion, in anticipation of buying and selling by index tracking funds on or around the date of implementation. This strategy had a great deal of success a few years ago, but has become a victim of its own success, with the arbitrage capital drawn to the trade more than compensating for any influences from tracking funds.

All trading strategies that rely on future stock flows to influence prices are reliant on limited liquidity being available on the day of implementation. If too much arbitrage capital is drawn to the situation, there will be more than sufficient liquidity to soak up any flows.

FTSE indices

In the UK, the main indices are managed by FTSE Group, an independent company that originated as a joint venture between the *Financial Times* and the London Stock Exchange. It has since evolved globally with more than 600 indices calculated in real time, and over $2.5tn of assets are estimated to be under management using FTSE indices.

Figure 2.52: FTSE indices

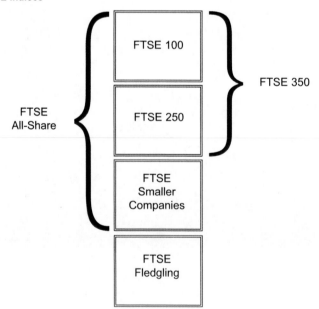

FTSE 100 & 250 Indices

A company becomes eligible for inclusion in the FTSE 100 if it rises to 90th or above in the ranking of all companies by market capitalisation. Similarly, an existing FTSE 100 company will be deleted if it falls to 111th or below at the time of the review.

In the FTSE 250, the levels are 325th and 376th respectively.

FTSE All-Share Index

The FTSE All-Share Index consists of the aggregate constituents of the FTSE 100, FTSE 250 and FTSE Small Cap Index – a total of around 687 companies. The Index aims to represent 98-99% of the full capital value of all eligible UK companies, subject to investability weightings. Securities becoming eligible for addition to the FTSE All-Share Index at the quarterly reviews must turn over a minimum of 0.5% of the shares in issue per month, in at least five of the six months prior to the review, after the application of free float restrictions. New issues need to satisfy the above criteria, as well as possessing a trading record of at least twenty days. There is also a minimum market capitalisation with a 15% band set for promotions/deletions between the Small Cap and Fledgling Indices.

FTSE Fledgling Index

The FTSE Fledgling Index consists of those companies which are too small to be included in the FTSE All-Share, but would otherwise be eligible.

In the UK most tracking funds follow either the FTSE 100 or FTSE All-Share Indices, so changes to other indices, such as the FTSE 250, are of less significance. If a company is entering all the major indices for the first time, the effect of tracking fund purchases is likely to have a greater impact than a move between indices.

Index reviews

The rules and mechanisms of constituent changes are completely transparent, and press releases regarding changes can be accessed at the FTSE website (www.ftse.com).

Index constituents are usually reviewed quarterly by the FTSE Steering Committee, which meets on the Wednesday after the first Friday in March, June, September and December, using the closing prices from the previous Tuesday.

FTSE Group publishes a *Reserve List* of companies, which is used in the event of an ad-hoc change occurring between scheduled index reviews, such as the result of a takeover or merger. The highest capitalised company on the reserve list when the takeover is declared wholly unconditional will then be included in the index.

The All-Share Index is fully reviewed in December. The constituent changes are implemented on the next trading day following futures and options expiry in the UK (usually the third Friday of the same month).

Understanding the effect of the reviews

A comprehensive analysis of stock price performance and volumes compared to average daily volumes around the effective dates is beyond the scope of this book, but I believe it is important for traders and investors alike to be aware of index changes that may affect stocks that they are interested in, so that they can account for unusual, if albeit temporary, price moves.

The one-day chart of Capita below, shows a clear run up in the share price leading up to the closing auction on the day before the inclusion of the company in the FTSE 100 was made effective.

Figure 2.53: Capita (CPI) – run up to inclusion in FTSE 100

Used with permission from Bloomberg L.P.

As the closing price of a stock is used to determine at what price a company enters or leaves an index, and the closing auction process in the UK usually determines the closing price, institutions can guarantee that they will track an index by dealing in the closing auction.

Unfortunately, leaving at-market orders to execute trades in the closing auction with investment banks, who also have their own internal proprietary trading desks, has been subject to some abuse. The most egregious example was the inclusion of Dimension Data in the FTSE 100 in September 2000, a few months after the SETS auction process was introduced in the UK in May 2000. The stock, which had been trading at around 670p throughout the day, was pushed up 49% to 1000p in the closing auction on the Friday before the stock was due to enter the Index, and a number of traders and hedge funds made a great deal of money shorting the stock to buying it back the following Monday at around 700p. The losers were the tracking funds. The auction process has since been refined to allow time extensions, so more liquidity can be provided by the marketplace, and the situation is unlikely to occur again.

The following charts clearly identify the influence of flows from tracking funds on two stocks around implementation of the changes in the FTSE 100 Index constituents after the June 2001 index review. Here, Railtrack was removed from the FTSE 100 and Next added, with effect from the closing auction on 15 June.

Figure 2.54: Railtrack (RTK) – effect of removal from FTSE 100

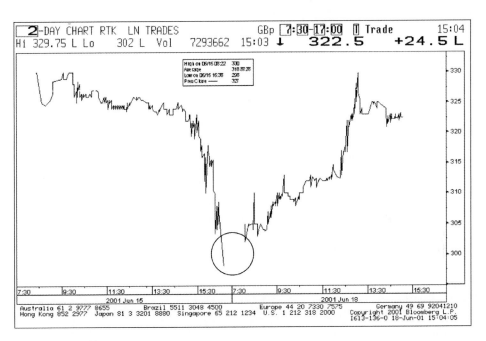

Used with permission from Bloomberg L.P.

Figure 2.55: Next (NXT) – effect of addition to FTSE 100

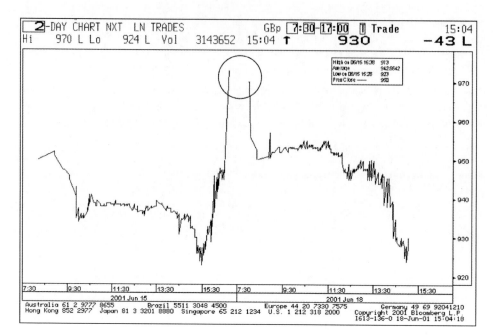

Used with permission from Bloomberg L.P.

Investability changes

Companies with a limited free float may be included in indices, but not with their full weighting, so index funds only have to maintain a weighting proportional to the free float. Investability weightings are banded according to free float, such as 25%, 50% and 75%.

FTSE downgraded Liberty International's investability weighting from 100% to 75% in September 2003, and the flow created by tracking funds was evident in the unusually heavy trading activity in the week leading up to the change taking effect. Average daily trading volume in the week was 3.4m shares against a long-term daily average of 1m shares. Tracking funds would have had to sell a quarter of their holdings to maintain the correct weighting.

Investability weightings are banded and to qualify for a full weighting, not less than 75% of the shares must be free float, i.e. not owned by founders, family and/or directors. The decision was reversed after an appeal by the company, and the shares appreciated significantly in the lead up to the 100% band being reinstated on 22 December.

Figure 2.56: Liberty International (LII) – investability weighting change

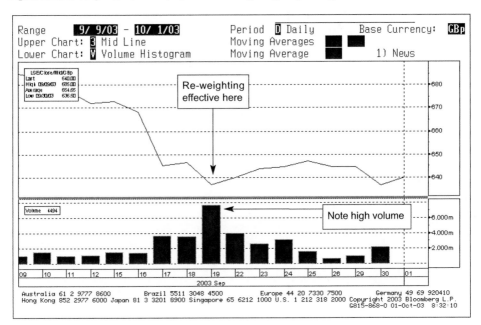

Used with permission from Bloomberg L.P.

MSCI changes

Morgan Stanley Capital International is the leading provider of equity, fixed income and hedge fund indices. Over $3tn of funds are believed to be benchmarked against MSCI's global indices, with MSCI's Europe Index consisting of around 530 companies.

Membership decisions are based on a combination of factors, including:

- the free float of a company's shares in issue;
- the average daily volume;
- market capitalisation; and
- the existing representation of the company's industry group and home country in the MSCI indices.

The MSCI full country index review occurs once per year around May, and is a systematic re-assessment of the various dimensions of the equity universe.

On 11 May 2004, MSCI announced that fourteen stocks would be added to the MSCI United Kingdom Index. The performance between the announcement and implementation (28 May) is detailed in the table following, with the FTSE 100 and FTSE All-Share included for comparison.

Table 2.8: MSCI UK Index changes – May 2004

	11-May	28-May	Change
Arriva	379	389.5	2.70%
Bellway	718	755	5.20%
Cookson Group	41.25	43.25	4.80%
HMV Group	229	235.5	2.80%
ICAP	266.5	283.5	6.40%
Inchcape	1500	1575	5.00%
Intertek Group	509	541	6.30%
London Stock Exchange	355.25	376.5	6.00%
Marconi	550	651.5	18.50%
Meggitt	246	251.25	2.10%
National Express Group	684	696.5	1.80%
Premier Farnell	250.5	242	-3.40%
Punch Taverns	469.5	513	9.30%
Trinity Mirror	608.5	620	1.90%
FTSE 100 Index	4455	4431	-0.50%
FTSE All-Share	2210	2202	-0.40%

A similar theme was evident in 2003, when the five largest additions to the UK MSCI Index (with performances over the relevant period included in brackets) were:

- Alliance Unichem (+11%)
- EMAP (+8.6%)
- Friends Provident (+18%)
- Liberty International (+11.3%)
- Tomkins (+17%)

All of the additions outperformed the FTSE 100, which rose 3% during the same period between announcement and implementation (29 April to 30 May).

Figure 2.57: Relative performance of new additions to the MSCI UK Index

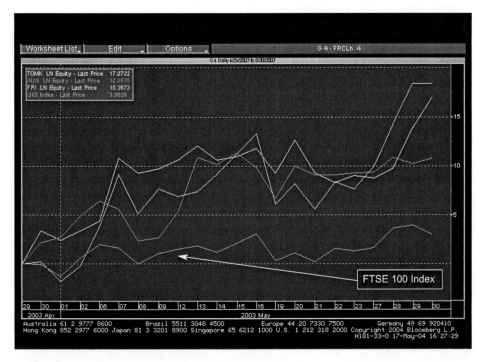

Used with permission from Bloomberg L.P.

Hedge fund strategy

A strategy utilised by hedge funds and traders in the UK is to buy a basket of the stocks that are due to enter the indices a few days before the changes are effective, and to sell an appropriate number of FTSE 100 futures against the basket as a hedge. Each FTSE 100 future hedges a value equivalent to ten times the index (as the multiplier on the contract is £10), so one future sold at 4700 is equivalent to hedging £47,000 in stock. The strategy will be successful if the basket of stocks (which can be equally weighted) outperforms the relevant index over the time period. The position is usually unwound close to the effective date.

As with most strategies that involve anticipating stock moves based on significant flow from index changes, the more arbitrage capital that chases the situation, the lower the returns are likely to be. Companies reporting in that period should also be avoided. (When I put the trade on, I avoided taking a position in Premier Farnell, which was due to report the day before the final effective date, and I also delayed establishing the basket until after ICAP had reported its scheduled results.)

The performance of EMAP in 2003 between the announcement of its entry to the MSCI Indices and its actual inclusion can be clearly seen in the chart.

Figure 2.58: EMAP (EMA) – enters MSCI UK Index

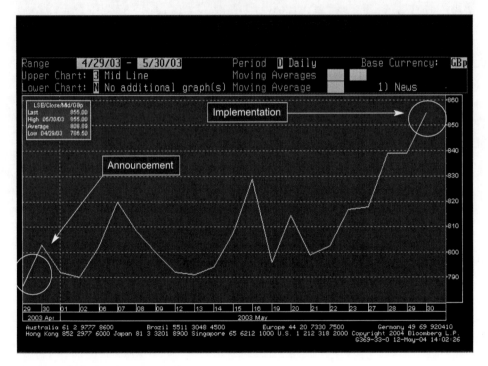

Used with permission from Bloomberg L.P.

Sector switches and re-ratings

Stocks can sometimes be re-rated when reclassified to another sector, as different sectors generally trade on different multiples. Such reclassifications may follow disposals by the company of subsidiaries or a demerger.

Similarly, a move in a primary listing from a smaller country to a major economy, or more liquid market such as the US, where the market or sector trades on a higher multiple, may result in an upward revaluation, and where there is access to more specialist investors. Gaining a higher profile, or exiting a heavily regulated or highly taxed jurisdiction, may be another reason, although changes in primary listing may crystallise tax liabilities and induce selling by domestic funds, as they are unable to invest overseas.

In 2004 the management of News Corp, Australia's largest company, proposed to move its domicile and primary listing to the US. Generally, a non dual-listed company cannot be double counted in indices in two markets, and the move resulted in significant stock flows as Australian tracking funds sold out and US funds bought in. Indeed, News Corp's shares fell nearly 5% in June 2004 when Standard and Poor's confirmed that it would exclude News Corp from its local indices, despite lobbying from investors and the Australian Stock Exchange.

In the UK, moving down to AIM may result in lower listing fees, but may incur forced selling by funds and individuals who cannot invest in AIM stocks. (Note: AIM stocks cannot be held in an ISA.)

Credit rating changes

Long-term debt is divided into *investment grade* and *non-investment grade* (junk); the differentiation between the two levels is significant.

Rating changes from the agencies are released at all times of the day and can have an effect on a share price, particularly if the company is heavily geared or the rating change has not been anticipated by the equity or bond markets. Downgrades can result in companies having to pay more interest as a result of bond covenants; upgrades may result in a reduction in the effective interest rate bill. In addition the ability of insurance companies to write certain types of general insurance is dependent on the maintenance of appropriate credit ratings from the rating agencies (one reason why RSA had a rights issue).

One measure of a company's likely credit rating is its net debt/EBITDA ratio. Companies with a ratio higher than around 3.5 risk being downgraded to non-investment grade, although simply reducing the ratio below this level will not necessarily restore the rating; an improvement to as much as 2.5 may be needed to reverse the downgrade.

Rating changes will often be anticipated by the market

This stickiness means that the market will often be ahead of the agencies, and a change in rating may not have a dramatic effect when announced, as it has already been anticipated.

BSkyB fell to junk bond status in 2000, and although it only regained its investment grade status late in 2003, the tradeable debt spent most of that year priced as though it had already been upgraded.

Upgrades may make the debt accessible to a new pool of capital and wider range of investors, as not all investment grade managers are allowed to hold junk bonds. When a company is upgraded, it may be included in investment grade indices used as benchmarks, creating additional demand for the debt.

Moving from junk to investment grade, or the reverse, leads to the term *cross-over credit*. Debt fund managers will often try to anticipate the future rating of a company which is changing its capital structure. If a company is under-geared it may seek to boost shareholder returns and optimise its capital structure by taking on more debt, simultaneously moving down the credit curve and incurring a lower credit rating.

Companies may also be put on Creditwatch (S&P) or Review (Moody's), with a negative outlook adopted (for example, previously stable) and be under review.

Rating agencies

The three most influential rating agencies are:

- Fitch Ratings
- Moody's Investor Services
- Standard & Poor's Creditwire

Investment grade

With reference to Moody's rating system, investment grade is rated Aaa, Aa, A or Baa. Each generic rating has a numerical modifier 1, 2, 3 for all classes from Aa though Caa: 1 ranks the debt at the higher end; 2, mid-range; and 3, lower end.

Table 2.9: Comparison of investment grade credit ratings

Moody's	Standard & Poor's	Fitch
Aaa	AAA	AAA
Aa1	AA+	AA+
Aa2	AA	AA
Aa3	AA-	AA-
A1	A+	A+
A2	A	A
A3	A-	A-
Baa1	BBB+	BBB+
Baa2	BBB	BBB
Baa3	BBB-	BBB-

Table 2.10: Investment grade definitions

Aaa	Rated best quality with the smallest degree of investment risk
Aa	High quality by all standards, and together with the Aaa group, comprise what are generally known as high-grade bonds
A	Possess many favourable investment attributes and are regarded as upper-medium grade
Baa	Medium grade, neither highly protected nor poorly secured

Non-investment grade

Non-investment grade (junk) ranges through Ba, B, Caa, Ca and C as follows:

Table 2.11: Comparison of non-investment grade credit ratings

Moody's	Standard & Poor's	Fitch
Ba1	BB+	BB+
Ba2	BB	BB
Ba3	BB-	BB-
B1	B+	B+
B2	B	B
B3	B-	B-
Caa1	CCC+	CCC+
Caa2	CCC	CCC
Caa3	CCC-	CCC-
Ca	CC	CC
C	C	C

Table 2.12: Non-investment grade definitions

Ba	Speculative elements and not well safeguarded
B	Generally lacking characteristics of desirable investment
Caa	Poor standing and in danger of default
Ca	Speculative in a high degree and vulnerable to non-payment
C	Lowest rated with poor prospects of attaining investment standing

Futures and options expiries

Expiry and triple witching

In the UK, index futures expire on the third Friday of March, June, September and December, with index options expiring monthly on the same day. Now that stock options, which have an expiry every month (although different stocks are on different cycles), have been moved from Wednesday to the following Friday as well (although stock option expiry is based on closing prices), the expiry is now a *triple witching* rather than a double witching. In the US, where single stock futures and options expire on the same day as index options and futures, the expiry is known as *quadruple witching*.

Calculation of the EDSP

The FTSE 100 Index futures contracts expire at the exchange delivery settlement price (EDSP), which, until recently, was based on the average value of the FTSE 100 Index every fifteen seconds between 10.10 and 10.30 on expiry day, which is always the third Friday of the delivery month.

In November 2004, the London Stock Exchange introduced a new procedure whereby the final EDSP was calculated using an intra-day auction, using the same concept as the closing auction, except that there is no volume check. Expiry now starts at 10.10, with the uncrossing taking place at 10.15, plus a random start time. This new procedure was introduced to concentrate expiry liquidity into a shorter period of time, and to avoid the wild swings that have occurred in the index during previous expiries.

If large index arbitrage positions exist, because the futures contracts have not been rolled over until the next quarterly month, there can be some significant moves during this expiry period.

Large positions may have built up if:

- The futures contract has traded at a substantial **premium** to fair value during the life of the contract. There is then likely to be a large long stock position against short futures in the market.
- Similarly, if the futures contract has traded at a **discount**, the arbitrage position is likely to be long futures, short stock.

Whichever way the position, the futures leg will cease to exist on expiry if it has not been rolled forward (which may have been difficult if the next month is not trading at an attractive level), so the arbitrageurs will need to unwind the cash position during expiry, hence the heavy level of trading.

September 2002 expiry

The 20 September 2002 expiry saw extraordinary moves rarely seen before, with the index moving in a 309 point range in twenty minutes. Some stocks had even bigger percentage moves.

There have been a number of versions of what actually happened on this day by various commentators, but what appears most likely is that an automated system to execute the stock transactions was incorrectly programmed, and accidentally submitted a basket of stocks to the SETS platform twice without any limits on the price paid. In attempting to correct the situation the program was then reversed, creating a sharp spike back downwards.

A great deal of money was both made and lost on the day by the various market participants. The investment bank that submitted the basket in error lost hundreds of millions of pounds, buying high and selling low. The winners were other member firms that bought low and sold high, sometimes several times over in the same stock within minutes; also benefiting were individual traders with direct access.

As one can imagine, this unnatural market created problems for spread betting and CFD firms over the triggering of stop loss orders left by clients.

Figure 2.59: Gyrations during September 2002 index futures expiry

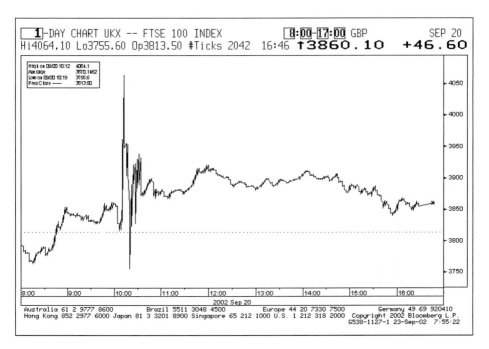

Used with permission from Bloomberg L.P.

Market Neutral Strategies

Market neutral trading is one of the most popular classes of hedge fund strategy, often utilising CFDs and other derivatives to buy one stock and short another simultaneously, as well as using leverage.

Typically, a hedge fund may run a significant portfolio of long and short positions, maintaining a broadly market neutral approach, which is almost self-financing. Average holding time and turnover of stock will depend on the model or black box used by the fund, which is often based on historical statistical analysis of share prices. Longs and shorts may not be limited to one country, with a long position being established in, say, a German insurance company against a short position in a UK insurance company, while simultaneously hedging the currency risk. The strategy works particularly well where there is a good historic correlation between stocks, but a significantly wide enough arbitrage channel or stock volatility, to take advantage of short-term price discrepancies; or where there is plenty of volatility between stocks but not necessarily any market direction. It doesn't work well when stocks are subject to company specific events like takeovers or corporate actions.

Pairs trading

In its simplest form a relative asset allocation play involves buying one stock and selling another; or maybe buying a stock and selling futures on an equity index against it to reduce directional market risk. Pairs trades such as this can be attractive to traders who prefer to run positions less sensitive to the general direction of the market.

If the two assets are quoted in different currencies, a currency transaction hedge is usually undertaken, which involves selling the currency where the short sale has generated a cash balance to fund the long position.

Pairs trade performance can be monitored in terms of the ratio between the two shares.

Example: Pairs trading, Land Securities vs British Land

Take the example of Land Securities trading at 1169p, and British Land trading at 685p. A chart of the two companies' share price performance is shown below.

Figure 2.60: Land Securities and British Land – example of pairs trading

Used with permission from Bloomberg L.P.

Dividing one share price by the other to obtain a ratio is an effective way of monitoring the performance of the trade.

Figure 2.61: Land Securities and British Land ratio chart

Used with permission from Bloomberg L.P.

The ratio here is 1.707 (1169/685), and it can be seen that over the ten month period covered, the ratio ranged between 1.78 and 1.64 – around an 8% range. The ratio is currently right in the middle of this range but, as it drifts down towards 1.64, Land Securities is trading cheap against British Land, whereas at the top of the range, Land Securities starts to look expensive against British Land.

The sharp fall in Land Securities' performance against British Land in late November, and subsequent recovery in early December, can be attributed to the sharp rise in British Land (partly as a result of a Morgan Stanley upgrade ahead of results), which was not reflected in the Land Securities price until early December.

Dividends should always be monitored for both stocks as this will distort the ratio, and may skew the apparent performance. Most CFD providers deduct 100% of the dividend for short positions, but only pay 90% for long positions, so there may be an additional loss of performance over the dividend date.

Most hedge funds will exclude stocks where a special situation exists or a corporate action is pending, and a great deal of research and analysis involving back-testing goes into identifying suitable stocks to trade.

Case study

30th January

- Sell 4985 Land Securities @ 1003p
- Buy 8636 British Land @ 579p

Trade established at a ratio of 1.73, value £50,000 per leg

12th February

- Buy 4985 Land Securities @ 1045
- Sell 8636 British Land @ 622p

Trade closed with a ratio of 1.68

P/L

- Loss on Land Securities: 4985 * 42p = £2,094
- Profit on British Land: 8636 * 43p = £3,713
- Overall profit: **£1,619**

Although both stocks have moved up during the period, British Land has outperformed Land Securities, so the loss on buying back Land Securities has been outweighed by the higher profit on the British Land leg. Throughout the trade, the trader can easily monitor the performance of the trade by monitoring the ratio. So if Land Securities is trading at 1030p and British Land at 609p, the current ratio is 1.69, and the trade is around 2.4% in profit. Since the position was established with a value of £50,000 each leg, the profit as of that moment will be approximately 2.4% on £50,000 = £1,200.

Similarly, the P/L at any one time will be the difference between the current size of the long position and the short position:

```
Size of short position: -£4,985 * £1,030 = -£51,346


Size of long position: £8,636 * £609 = £52,593


Profit & loss: -£51,346 + £52,593 = £1,247
```

Pairs trading Schroders shares

One of the most popular spread trades in the UK is the arbitrage between the two classes of Schroders share: the ordinaries and the non-voting shares. As can be seen from the chart below, the ordinary shares have traded at a premium to the non-voting shares of between 9% and 15% over the nine-month period selected from September 2003 to May 2004.

Here a trader might sell the ordinaries and buy the non-voting shares when the discount gets to the top of the range, around 14%. Trades are often put on in incremental percentages (13%, 14%, 15%, 16%, etc.) to allow some flexibility in unwinding the position on reversal. Establishing the position in reverse, i.e. shorting the cheaper share and buying the more expensive when the premium nears the bottom of its range, is often referred to as *chinesing the spread*.

Liquidity in the non-voting shares can be limited, and therefore it can be difficult to establish a reasonable size position. This is not a trade where the trader will get rich quickly and, as the potential return is limited, it will only be suited to traders who have direct market access and low execution costs. Nevertheless, it is an excellent situation on which traders can cut their teeth, learn the nuances of direct market access, manage contingent orders and appreciate the importance of liquidity matching.

Figure 2.62: Schroders (SDR) – historical premium of voting shares over non-voting shares

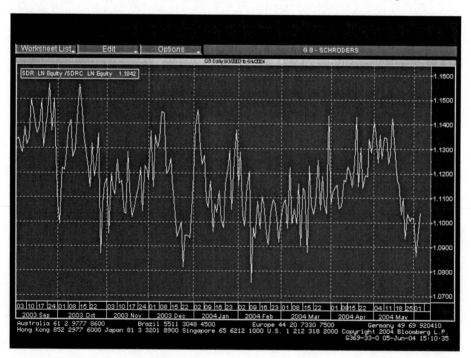

Used with permission from Bloomberg L.P.

It is an unfortunate characteristic of pairs trading that the further the divergence between the two stocks, the more attractive the trade becomes. It can be good discipline to establish a pairs trade at certain incremental levels to allow some flexibility in unwinding the trade. However, there has to be a point at which defeat must be acknowledged when an historically correlated pair breaks down.

The strategy is very capital intensive and sensitive to cost, as one pairs trade involves four transactions to both establish and unwind the position. The lower the difference in funding costs between what is paid on long positions and what is received on short positions, the closer the position will be to self-financing. Regular traders should seek margin relief from their CFD provider.

Use of ratio charts

Using ratios and ratio charts is an extremely effective way of identifying and monitoring pairs trades. In contrast, charts which track relative performance are usually normalised at some random point in the past. A ratio chart gives the trader an instant feel for the volatility within the ratio, the arbitrage channel and whether the ratio is trending one way or another. Ideally a ratio chart should trend sideways with no measurable outperformance of one stock over another but enough variation in the share price differential to be able to trade. It can also be important to look at longer time frames as well as shorter ones. An ideal pairs trade ratio might resemble a mathematical sine wave; with no out performance of one stock over the other in the long-term, but sufficient amplitude to generate an arbitrage channel.

Other popular pairs trades in the UK include:

- HSBC-Standard Chartered
- Aviva-Prudential
- BATS-Imperial Tobacco
- Unilever-Reckitt Benckiser
- BP-Shell
- Reed-Pearson

Regression charts can also be used to monitor the current relative positions of the two stocks and identify opportunities, and are a key component is assessing past performance.

Figure 2.63: Regression chart for pairs trading

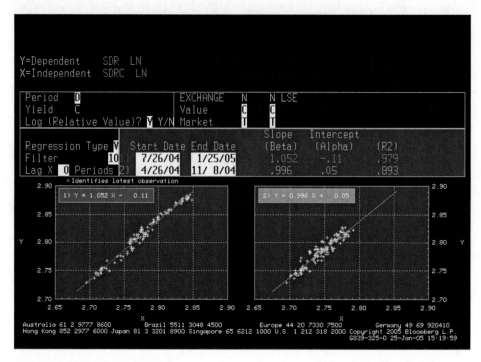

Used with permission from Bloomberg L.P.

Balance sheet arbitrage

When one quoted company holds a significant stake in another, there can be a loose arbitrage opportunity if the valuation of one dramatically exceeds the other.

Examples in the UK are rare, but during 2000 and 2001, Dixons' stake in Freeserve far exceeded its own market value. These discrepancies can last for some time, and there can be other issues such as tax considerations and the debt held in one of the entities.

In Europe there are several examples of companies that trade at a variable discount to their quoted constituent parts. The opportunity can come in trading the channel that this discount ranges in, by buying the holding company and short selling the constituent assets as a simultaneous basket trade hedge in the appropriate ratios. The trade is then unwound when the discount narrows, and even *chinesed* by shorting the holding company and buying the underlying assets, if the discount narrows to such an extent that it may be expected to widen again.

Popular European holding company trades against the corresponding constituents include:

- Investor (Sweden);
- Dior (France); and
- Heineken.

Investment trust discounts

Similar opportunities can present themselves by trading investment trust discounts.

When the trust trades at a wide discount to its constituents, the trust's shares are bought and the constituents, or proxy hedge, are sold. When the discount narrows the trade is unwound. Similarly, if the trust trades at a premium, or the discount is expected to widen, the investment trust shares can be shorted (if borrowable), and the constituents bought as a basket.

Convertible bond arbitrage

As explained previously, if all variables for an option are known, including the price, the one remaining variable, the (implied) volatility, for that option can be calculated. This can then be compared with the historic statistical volatility of the underlying instrument. If the implied is lower, it suggests the option is cheap, or if the implied is higher, it suggests the option is expensive.

Convertible bonds and callable bonds can be regarded as comprising:

- a **fixed interest** element; together with
- an **option** to convert into the underlying.

The option part will have a value that can be calculated by taking the price of the convertible bond and stripping out the fixed interest component (which will be priced according to the company's credit rating).

Callable bonds are repackaged bonds issued by investment banks, generally yielding more than the underlying, with an embedded option giving the issuer the right of repurchase if triggered by certain events.

Isolating volatility

Traders can isolate volatility embedded in a convertible by shorting the stock and delta hedging against a long convertible bond position. However, if the volatility of the stock turns out to be lower than anticipated, the convertible bond trader who is long of premium will lose out.

Convertible bonds are usually initially sold with the implied volatility priced at a discount to the historical volatility of the stock in order to make them attractive. Convertible bond issues are particularly attractive with hedge funds that will look to extract the volatility embedded in them. They will buy the convertible and hedge the position by short-selling stock against it in the appropriate ratio. This is why a stock can sometimes be hard to borrow and experience some weakness in its share price, at the time of issue of a convertible. The investment bank will frequently package together the convertible and borrowing facility in the stock before offering it to hedge funds and proprietary traders.

It should also be remembered that the fact that the company has issued a convertible bond in itself might alter the volatility of the stock, depressing it more than anticipated. This is because as the stock rises, the hedgers will sell stock and as the stock falls they will buy it, improving liquidity and dampening volatility. The lesson, therefore, is to expect share price weakness when a convertible bond is issued.

If the convertible trades expensive, the trade can *chinese* the spread by shorting the bond and buying the underlying stock in the cash market at the appropriate ratio.

Example: United Business Media

United Business Media launched a $400m offering of five-year convertible bonds due in 2006 with a conversion price of 577p and interest rate of 2.375% on 14 December 2001.

Figure 2.64: United Business Media (UBM) – convertible issue

Used with permission from Bloomberg L.P.

Dual listed shares and cross border arbitrage

A number of companies have dual listed shares. In other words, the stock is quoted in different jurisdictions and in different currencies. These are generally not fungible (deliverable against each other), so a strict arbitrage does not exist, and although the prices will be closely aligned they will fluctuate with local supply and demand.

The best known and well established of these is the dual listed Anglo-Dutch shares of Royal Dutch Shell, Unilever and Reed Elsevier.

Royal Dutch/Shell arbitrage

For years the Royal Dutch shares listed in Holland traded at a premium to its counterpart Shell shares in the UK, partly due to different taxation rules regarding dividends, and Royal Dutch being a member of the main US indices; this premium has ranged as wide as 20%. The strategy of buying one and short selling the other, as well as transacting the currency hedge, thereby makes the trade circular, is capital intensive, and its one of those pairs transactions that unfortunately get more attractive the wider out they get.

Neither are they risk free, as the Long-Term Capital Management (LTCM) hedge fund found out in 1998 when it bought Shell and sold Royal Dutch short in huge numbers, as the spread continued to widen. This was just one of a number of trades that theoretically have a low risk, but, when the sixteen banks that had extended margin credit to LTCM decided that they wanted their money back, LTCM ended up having to be rescued to avoid a crisis in the entire financial industry.

This scenario is often associated with *noise trade risk*, where the unpredictability of noise trader's beliefs deters arbitrageurs from trading against them. In other words, the fact that the mispricing exists can cause it to increase.

Some arbitrages, however, exist purely because the cost of the arbitrage is prohibitive. That's to say, the high cost of borrowing the overpriced asset to short sell is reflected in the spread itself.

Other dual listed shares where there is an arbitrage opportunity are listed in the table below.

Table 2.13: Dual listing arbitrage opportunities

Domestic	Foreign
Billiton (UK)	BHP (AU)
Brambles (UK)	Brambles Industries (AU)
Carnival (UK)	Carnival (US)
Corus (UK)	Corus (NL)
Rio Tinto (UK)	Rio Tinto (AU)

Brambles has been dual listed in the UK and Australia since June 2001, although the Australian quote has historically traded at a premium, as illustrated below.

Figure 2.65: Brambles (BI) – percentage premium of Australian quote over UK

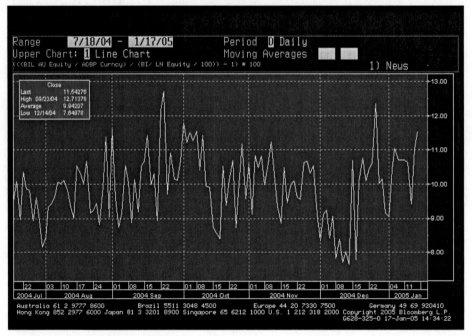

Used with permission from Bloomberg L.P.

It is frightening how many novice UK traders are unaware of closing prices quoted in other jurisdictions in stocks that they trade. The percentage move on the day is irrelevant, especially if the two markets overlap trading hours (like the US and UK). What matters is the closing price adjusted for the currency – which can of course itself move overnight.

UK quoted companies with active quotations in South Africa include: Anglo American; BHP Billiton; Investec;

> If you are trading a stock, it is essential that you are aware if it has a dual listed quotation (and what the closing price of the other share is when converted from the local currency), so you are not caught out by an unexpected overnight move in the other market.

Liberty International; Old Mutual; Randgold Resources; and SAB Miller. If you are trading these stocks without access to live prices for the other markets you may as well be driving blind.

Stocks like Bookham, where the number of shares traded on NASDAQ in the US exceeds the number of domestic shares traded in the UK by over 50%, are effectively driven by the US quote. One reason why Bookham sought to cancel its UK listing and move to the US, was that it felt technology stocks were better understood in the US, with higher representations in the benchmark indices.

Takeovers

A company is worth what a buyer is willing to pay.
There is no such thing as a merger of equals.
Wall Street mantras

Takeover situations can generate some of the most exciting trading opportunities in the UK stock market, and the cost-effectiveness and flexibility of CFDs has allowed individuals access to strategies that have traditionally only been available to well-capitalised funds and proprietary desks. *Risk* (or *merger*) *arbitrage* can be a complex strategy and an in-depth analysis is beyond the scope of this book. (A number of good books already exist including *Risk Arbitrage – An Investor's Guide* by Keith Moore.) What I have attempted in this book is to give an overview of the regulation of takeovers in the UK, and how the timetable that applies to all bids is structured. The European directive, which is likely to come into force in 2006, will probably bring the Code under a statutory umbrella.

Two types of takeover

Bids for companies generally fall into two categories:

- **Agreed**: the boards of both companies believe that the offer is in the best interests of both sets of shareholders, and the acquiring firm secures a recommendation from the target company's board that shareholders accept the offer.
- **Hostile**: the predator appeals directly to the target company's shareholders, bypassing the target's board, usually because the existing management does not want to be taken over.

The Takeover Code

The Panel on Takeovers and Mergers (POTAM), which oversees conduct and enforces the non-statutory Takeover Code applied during takeover situations in the UK, is respected throughout the world, despite lacking the force of law.

The system of adherence to the ten general principles of the City Code on Takeovers and Mergers has generally worked extremely well, with the Panel's only power of enforcement being the threat of withdrawal of market facilities from a transgressor.

Despite the lack of legal backing, the Code has historically been highly effective and admired throughout the world's financial markets, and has successfully avoided tactical litigation and the unsatisfactory situation so common in the US, where bitterly contested takeover bids end up being dragged through the courts over technicalities. One of the main principles of the Code is that primary regard should be given to the underlying purposes involved, so that parties to a takeover do not have their legitimate expectations frustrated by a technical application of the Code.

The Code applies to offers for all listed and unlisted public companies resident in the UK, and some private companies. The takeover code does not, however, apply to preference shares.

There is a strict timetable to actual bids, although this is not applied to pre-conditional bids.

Principles and Rules

The ten *General Principles* that comprise the Takeover Code (listed in the Blue Book) are expressed in broad terms, and are effectively statements of standards of behaviour, to ensure fair and equal treatment of all shareholders in relation to takeovers. In addition to the General Principles, there are a series of *Rules* that govern specific aspects of takeover behaviour. Occasionally the Rules are modified to incorporate new developments, such as the use of contracts for difference in a takeover situation by related parties for the first time in the mid 1990s. The Panel has recently released a consultative document regarding introducing greater disclosure over CFD and derivative transactions in takeover situations; a direct result of the current lack of visibility involving investment bank holdings in stocks held as a hedge against CFD transactions, primarily between the banks and hedge funds. Under the new proposals, greater visibility will be required regarding who holds not just the beneficial interest, but also the economic interest in a company through structured products like CFDs and equity swaps, even if the total interest is below the current disclosable level of 1%.

The most important of the Principles relate to the announcement of an offer being made only after the most careful consideration, and that the offeror should have every reason to believe that it can implement the offer, including securing the necessary funding. In other words, a firm offer should not be made without fully committed funding. Negotiations should remain secret so as to avoid a false market in the shares of the target, and, even in a hostile situation, the target's board should be notified, even though it may be just minutes before the launch of a bid. The Panel will seek to avoid a false market in a company's shares by forcing potential bidders into the open where appropriate. Recently we have seen the increasing prevalence of the *indicative offer*, where a company expresses an interest in bidding without a full commitment to make a bid.

Shareholders must be treated equally

Takeover rules require that all shareholders in the same class of equity be treated equally in a bid situation, although there are exemptions for stakes held by management, without which proposed MBOs could not occur. However, there have recently been suspicions that large existing shareholders are benefiting from an ongoing equity interest by claiming to be joint offerors, although they are not involved with the day-to-day running of the business, allowing them not to offer other investors a chance to participate. The Takeover Panel has sought to rectify this by putting pressure on bidders to offer outside shareholders the chance to invest in the bidding vehicle on the same terms as management.

Concert party

A *concert party* is where an agreement exists between two parties to acquire and act collectively in regard to their shareholdings. Holdings by individuals in a concert party must be disclosed in aggregate.

Offer period

The Takeover Panel publishes a Disclosure Table on its website and via the Regulatory News Service daily. The Table lists which companies are currently in an offer period, and is updated and re-released as soon as a company announces that it is in bid talks, or when bid talks have been terminated.

Reference
The Takeover Panel: www.thetakeoverpanel.org.uk

When an announcement is required

The Code lists six circumstances when an announcement is required, the four most common being:

1. when a firm intention to make an offer is notified to the target board;
2. following an approach, the target is subject to rumour and speculation and there is an untoward movement in the share price;
3. when the target is subject to rumour, or there is an untoward movement in the share price and there are grounds for concluding that it is the action of the potential offeror, before the approach has been made; and
4. when negotiations are about to be extended to include more than a restricted number of people.

There used to be a 10% rule for 'untoward movement', but that has now been replaced with a more flexible approach. However, the Takeover Rules stipulate that if an approach has been made to a company, the Panel should be consulted at the latest if the offeree company is the subject of rumour and speculation, or if there is a price movement of 10% or more above the lowest share price since the time of the approach. Even a smaller abrupt price rise of, say, 5% should result in the Panel being consulted by the board of the company subject to the bid. The Panel will then take into account all relevant facts, and decide whether a public announcement is appropriate.

Note that the Takeover Panel and Listing Authority take different approaches to public statements regarding rumours and speculation.

- Under the **Takeover Code**, a company need not deny a baseless report or rumour, although the Panel encourages a continuing dialogue between itself and financial advisers so it can monitor share price movements and trading patterns. In addition, share prices can move during negotiations, but for unrelated reasons such as updated research notes. Though if a story appears in the Sunday papers with a basis in fact, a statement is likely if it is true, whereas silence can mean something, although the company is not obliged to deny it.
- The **Listing Rules,** however, say that "a company need not notify to a Regulatory Information Service information about impending developments or matters in the course of negotiation". This implies that corporate activity, including finalising a rights issue, can be kept under wraps, and the UKLA is less likely to be consulted.

Types of announcement

There are generally four types of announcement:

1. **Pre-conditional offer**: the statement must make it clear if the pre-conditions must be satisfied, or if they are waivable.
2. **Firm intention** to make an offer.
3. **'Talks' announcement:** usually because there has been a leak. There is no obligation to name the potential bidder, but the Panel will require the offeror to clarify its intentions at some point and not allow the process to extend indefinitely.
4. **Denial of bid intention**: the offeror is then precluded from bidding for six months, unless there is a material change in circumstances, such as a third party entering the fray.

Bid timetable

All bids in the UK run to a strict timetable, as defined under the Code, and the dates in the timetable are particularly important in the context of hostile bids.

When a firm offer has been announced, the offeror has a maximum of twenty-eight days in which to post full details of its offer. The clock starts ticking on posting day (Day 0) in what is a fixed time framework. Generally the deal must complete by Day 60 or lapse, subject to regulatory issues or time extensions at the discretion of the Panel. This is to ensure a balance is achieved between shareholders having sufficient time to consider the offer and limiting the time frame to minimise disruption to the target company. The bid timetable is summarised below.

Figure 2.66: Takeover time line

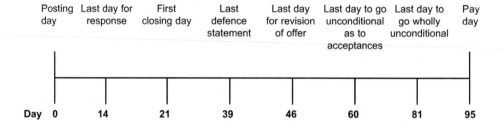

Certain events have to happen by certain times, while other events cannot happen before certain periods of time have elapsed.

The key dates in the bid timetable are shown in the table below (calendar days such as weekends and bank holidays are included for the purpose of the timetable).

Table 2.14: Bid timetable

Day 0	**Posting day**
	This is the key date and the baseline against which all later dates are referenced. Documents are often posted quickly; in the case of a hostile offer, to increase the time pressure on the target company or reduce the risk of a competing offer in the case of a recommended offer.
Day 14	**Last day for response**
	This is the last day for the company to advise shareholders of its views of the offer, either by recommending acceptance or issuing a defence document.
Day 21	**First closing day**
	An offer must remain open for at least twenty-one days from posting, as this is deemed to be a sufficient time for shareholders to consider the proposal, so this is normally the first closing date. If the offer has achieved the level of acceptances stated in the offer document, the offer will be declared 'unconditional as to acceptances' and the tendered stock can be taken up by the offeror. The offer will then remain open for at least a further fourteen days. If the offer has not achieved the required number of acceptances, the offeror may, at its discretion, revise the bid and extend the offer period.
Day 35	If the offer was declared unconditional as to acceptances on the first closing day (Day 21), Day 35 is the first day on which the offer may close. This allows undecided shareholders a further fourteen days beyond the date when the offer would otherwise have expired to accept the offer. If the offer became wholly unconditional on Day 21, Day 35 will be the last day for payment of consideration.
Day 39	**Last defence statement**
	This is the last day that the defending company can issue information relevant to the bid such as trading results, asset valuations or dividend forecasts.
Day 42	Day 42 can be significant as an accepting shareholder has a right of withdrawal after the expiry of twenty-one days from the first closing date, unless the offer has become unconditional to acceptances. If the situation has become competitive, this allows the accepting shareholder to recast his vote and, in addition, the offeror cannot be sure that the acceptances of the offer are irrevocable after Day 42.

Day 46	This is the last day that the offeror company may revise its offer for the final time, as the offer must be kept open for at least fourteen days and the offer must become unconditional as to acceptances by Day 60 or lapse. For the same reason it is the last day that the offeror can make an announcement regarding trading results or profits, as in the case of a share offer rather than cash offer; this news could have the effect of increasing the value of the offeror's shares.
Day 60	**Final day 13.00 hours** Day 60 is the final day for an offer to be declared unconditional as to acceptances or to lapse. If the bid lapses the offeror is prohibited from launching another offer for twelve months, to prevent the company being under a permanent state of siege. The level of acceptances is often set at 90% but is waivable down to 50% – this can be used as a get out.
Day 81	If the offer had been declared unconditional as to acceptances on Day 60, then this is the last day for all other conditions to be fulfilled and for the deal to go wholly unconditional.
Day 95	**Pay day** Settlement must be made no later than fourteen days after the offer goes wholly unconditional, so this is the last date for settlement.

If a competing offer for the target emerges, the clock is reset and the timetable automatically moves to the bid timetable relating to the new bid, so bid battles can be considerably extended.

Regulatory issues

If the competition issues have not been dealt with by Day 39, the Panel will usually freeze the bid timetable until the appropriate regulators have made a decision. If the bid is referred to the Office of Fair Trading, the timetable is usually frozen and re-started at Day 37. If the bid is then further referred to the Competition Commission, the bid will lapse and the offeror can launch a new bid after the regulator's investigation is complete, recommencing at Day 0 if they so wish.

It is not really necessary for investors to make up their minds by the first closing date, as, even if the offer reaches sufficient acceptances to become unconditional, it has to remain open for at least a further fourteen days, during which time the bidder will still accept the shares. Even if the investor has already accepted an offer when a better deal comes along, it's possible to reverse the decision. If the offer hasn't been declared unconditional, acceptances can normally be withdrawn from Day 42 onwards.

'Unconditional as to acceptances' means that the acceptance condition has been met (often 90% initially, but this can be waived down to as low as 50%), but that other conditions must still be met. Any shares tendered may still be returned if the offer lapses.

If shares were tendered prior to the offer being declared wholly unconditional, consideration is remitted within fourteen days of going wholly unconditional. If shares are tendered after this date, the consideration is posted within fourteen days of the acceptance form being received by the registrar.

Once a bidder has reached 90% acceptances and the deal is wholly unconditional, it can send out compulsory acquisition notices under Section 429 of the Companies Act, which become effective after a period of six weeks; this is otherwise known as a *squeeze-out*.

Mandatory offers

Although, legally, control is achieved when a shareholder reaches 50%, in the eyes of the Panel effective control is achieved at 30%, and if the stake is taken through that level then a mandatory bid is required. A mandatory offer must be launched at not less than the highest price paid by the bidder in the preceding twelve months and be for cash, or carry a cash alternative. Unlike an ordinary offer, where the bidder can set the acceptance level, a mandatory offer must be conditional upon acceptances received which results in the offeror carrying more than 50% of the votes.

Dealings and transactions

Once a company is in an offer period, additional disclosures are required over and above those required by the Companies Act; these are so-called *Rule 8 disclosures*. Since June 1996, dealings in derivatives by related parties, including CFDs, now fall within the disclosure requirements which will also show up in the Rule 8 disclosures.

Any shareholder owning more than 1% of the share capital must disclose all transactions (sales or purchases) by noon on the next business day. In the case of a large company, there can be many Rule 8 disclosures every day, most of which are insignificant, but it can be of interest if a broker is actively accumulating a position as a hedge against a client CFD or swap position. In addition, the market's risk arbitrage position can often be gauged by the positions adopted by some of the big investment houses.

It can be significant if a party or parties suddenly starts to accumulate a stake after an agreed deal has been announced. This often means that someone expects further developments. Heavy buying by a number of individuals in QXL Ricardo in late 2004 after an agreed MBO had been announced at 700p per share alerted me to the fact that there may be further developments, and sure enough a frenzied bid battle ensued with the company later subject to an aggressive counterbid.

EMM Disclosure regulatory announcements are not particularly significant, and are simply summaries under Rule 38.5, of trading in companies in an offer period by market makers who have exemption from dealing restrictions normally placed on related parties to the proposed transaction (usually part of the investment bank advising one of the parties but separated by a Chinese Wall).

Stock lending and borrowing dealings are not reportable as, although there is a transfer of title, the beneficial interest resides with the lender, but linked transactions to the underlying physical stock via derivatives and CFDs *are* reportable.

Once a company is in an offer period, certain restrictions come into force including dealings in shares by directors.

Extra cost for company when in an offer period

There is also the expense and time involved with making additional disclosures to the marketplace by the company's secretary. For this reason being in an offer period can sometimes be a nuisance and place additional administrative costs on a company.

Malcolm Glazer made a general comment regarding his shareholding in Manchester United on 16 February 2004 and the Takeover Panel immediately put the company into an offer period. The extra disclosures then required produced a stream of tedious regulatory announcements, and six weeks later Glazer confirmed that he had no current intention of bidding for the company, after pressure, I suspect, from the rather jaded company secretary.

Schemes of arrangement

An alternative means of taking over a company to that of a standard public offer is via a *scheme of arrangement* (under section 425 of the Companies Act). The scheme structure, which is becoming increasingly commonplace, can be an attractive vehicle for a number of reasons:

- Full ownership can be gained by squeezing out minority shareholders without attaining the normal 90% acceptances required to send out a compulsory acquisition notice.
- WPP utilised a scheme of arrangement in its acrimonious takeover of Cordiant Communications in July 2003, as it would have been tempting for some Cordiant shareholders to retain their minority interests, knowing that WPP would have taken care of all the debts.
- The acquirer can assume full control by gaining approval from 50% of the target's shareholders holding 75% of the shares.
- The company itself, rather than the bidder, writes to shareholders and arranges an Extraordinary General Meeting (EGM).
- A Court Meeting is also set, and the scheme is exempt from the conventional conditions imposed by the Securities & Exchange Commission (SEC) in the US, if an offer includes US shareholders. WPP utilised a scheme as, once it had taken on Cordiant's debt, this was the only way it could be sure of taking control.
- Schemes of arrangement are also exempt from stamp duty and are therefore popular in the UK, where there is a punitive 0.5% tax on share purchases.

Other situations where a scheme may be preferable are:

- in the case of two companies merging to form a new holding company;
- where a group is demerging a subsidiary; or
- where a company is moving to a new jurisdiction.

A scheme is often used when the bidder is confident of the deal going through and the certainty of getting to 100% outweighs other issues, such as timing and flexibility. However, a straightforward offer, where the bidder wants to reach 50% acceptances faster, may be more appropriate in other situations.

Schemes are usually used in recommended offers as they require the co-operation of the directors of the target company and they are vulnerable to a competing bid. Purchases of shares in the market will not assist the bidder as shareholders connected with the bidder are precluded from voting.

Schemes can be much quicker then general offers

At the EGM, the company decides whether to sell itself to the bidder, rather than its shareholders entering into a contract with the bidder. If the Court then confirms the scheme, 100% control of the target company is immediately and compulsorily transferred to the bidder. The whole process can be a lot quicker than with a general offer, thereby avoiding any additional destabilising of the underlying business.

It is also possible for the scheme to provide for the target company, to give financial assistance in connection with the offer. (This is generally not possible under takeover rules without invoking the Companies Act whitewash exemption, after achieving 90% acceptances and sending out compulsory acquisition notices.) That means that the debt in the bidding vehicle can be assimilated more quickly with the assets of the target company.

The use of schemes is set to increase in the UK, although they are not always popular with retail investors or minority shareholders as they can be squeezed out.

Schemes don't always work

For all their advantages, schemes of arrangement don't always work out.

Example: Harvey Nichols

On 18th September 2002, Hong Kong billionaire Dickson Poon's vehicle, Broad Gain, which already held a 50.1% stake in Harvey Nichols, launched a recommended cash proposal to buy out the remaining 49.9% free float, via a scheme of arrangement at 250p per share, valuing the whole company at £138m. The Court Meeting and EGM were set for 11 November 2002, and, as is usual in a scheme, approval was required from a majority by number (over 50%) of public shareholders representing 75% of the free flows in issue. Despite protestations from shareholders that the bid undervalued the company, on 1 November Poon declared that the offer was final and would not be raised.

Deutsche Asset Management, which held 14.9% of the shares in issue, equivalent to nearly 30% of the free float, made it clear that it would vote against the scheme, therefore blocking the deal. Staring defeat in the face, Poon announced on 8 November that he would instead make a conventional general offer if the scheme was defeated in a vote. DAM voted against the scheme and duly defeated it (the total vote was actually 55.2% in favour and 44.8% against), and Poon posted a new general offer on 14 November. Twenty-one days later, on 4 December, Poon was able to announce the offer was wholly unconditional with acceptances from 53.49% of the free float (26.69% of the total). DAM ultimately sold its holding as it didn't want to remain as a minority shareholder in an unlisted company.

A trading opportunity arose towards the end of October when the stock fell sharply as the market realised that the scheme would fail, but failed to fully appreciate that Broad Gain may well launch a general offer to get the deal through anyway, requiring only 50% acceptances of the free float. A point worth remembering if a similar situation occurs again.

Figure 2.67: Harvey Nichols (HVY) – trading opportunity

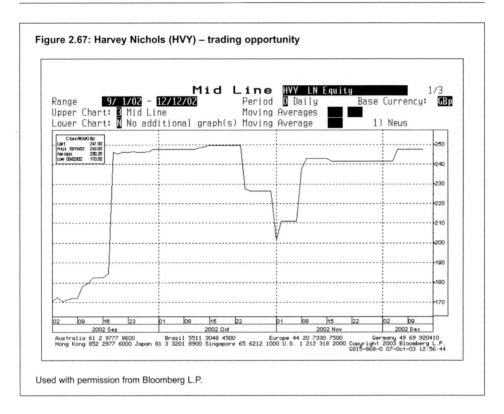

Used with permission from Bloomberg L.P.

Examples: Fitness First and Pizza Express

During 2003, two other situations developed as a result of resistance from institutional shareholders who believed that agreed bids were undervaluing companies in which they had shareholdings. As previously mentioned, if the offeror receives over 90% acceptances, the successful bidder is able to compulsorily acquire the remaining shares at the bid price. Takeover rules, designed to ensure equal treatment for all shareholders, mean the bidder cannot offer any remaining minority shareholders an increased offer for a period of six months from the deal going wholly unconditional.

Both Fitness First and Pizza Express had to de-list with minority shareholders in tow. DAM increased its stake in Fitness First from 7.2% to 10.29% after a management buy-out, backed by Cinven, at a price of 175p per share went unconditional. Nevertheless it will be interesting to see if the strategy pays off for those prepared to risk investing in an unlisted company as a minority shareholder. There is nothing stopping other investors jumping on the bandwagon, as they too cannot be squeezed out once 90% has failed to be reached – perhaps accounting for the squeeze in the share price at the end of June. DAM may have decided to stick with Fitness First as Cinven has a strong reputation and a typical investment time horizon of three to five years.

Figure 2.68: Fitness First (FTF) – minority shareholders

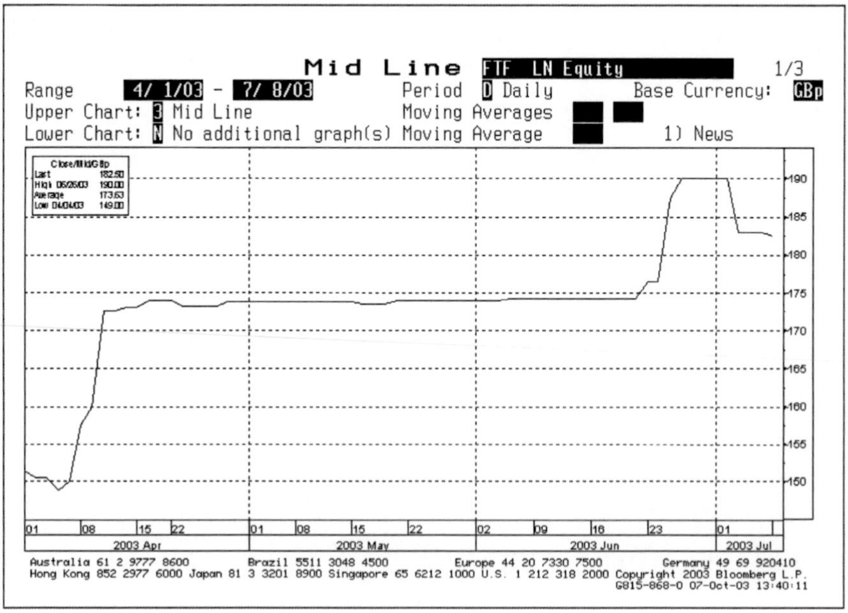

Used with permission from Bloomberg L.P.

With Harvey Nichols, there was less chance of a timely exit.

Some fund managers are not permitted to hold shares in unquoted companies and will therefore be forced to sell out. Minority shareholders are also solely reliant on company law for protection, as the listing rules for a public company will no longer apply. Failing to reach the 90% acceptances specified in the offer document is not necessarily a deal breaker, as the acceptance level can be waived down, at the bidder's discretion, to as low as 50%. However, the banks financing the deal generally regard 75% as a key level to get security, although 90% is preferable, and the arbitrageur should always be aware that it may cause minor disruption to a deal, particularly in a public to private transaction, if there is trouble in reaching an overwhelming level of acceptances.

In the second case, during Gondola Express' takeover of Pizza Express, the original acceptance level of 90% was waived down to 75% when the deal reached 75.28% acceptances, to allow Gondola (a TDR Capital and Capricorn Ventures vehicle) to declare the offer unconditional as to acceptances. Nevertheless Fidelity (8%) and M&G (2%) refused to budge, and although the stock has been de-listed they remain minority shareholders.

The battle between long-term shareholders, management and buy-out funds is a direct result of the recent three-year slump in share prices. Indeed, DAM's Ruth Keattch said, "our action will make boards think twice before recommending buy-outs. They'll maybe come and speak to the major shareholders first."

Some companies seek to de-list because lowly share valuations can have a devastating effect on their trading relationships. The annual cost of nominated advisers, Stock Exchange listing fees and public relations advisers can also be crippling, as well as an illiquid share quote and wide bid-offer spread.

Stream Group considered de-listing from AIM in May 2003, and although the company subsequently changed its mind after intense lobbying from a number of its shareholders, its share price was initially hit as shareholders took fright at the prospect of being stuck in an unlisted investment. The recovery in share price since then seems to have alleviated the situation.

Substantial Acquisition Rules (SARs)

The Substantial Acquisition Rules (SARs) are in place to restrict the pace with which a predator can acquire between 15% and 30% of a company's shares. These days we see far fewer dawn raids as the SARs restrict the acquisition of a stake to 14.9%, rather than the 29.9% under the Takeover Rules.

> A person may not, in any seven-day period, acquire 10% of the voting shares, which, if aggregated with an existing holding, would take the holding to between 15% and 30% of the company.

Essentially, a shareholder cannot acquire an aggregate stake of 15% or more in one go if it is acquired from more than one person, it is within seven calendar days and it is a 10% or greater stake. So a dawn raid would be allowed up to 14.9%, as it does not break the first condition. The same rules also apply to market makers, however the SARs are not applicable if the purchaser announces an intention to bid for the target, providing posting of the offer document is not subject to a precondition.

An announcement regarding market purchases is required to be made to the exchange and target company not later than noon the next business day. However, SARs do not require an announcement of disposals.

Tender offers

A tender offer is an invitation from a potential purchaser to the shareholders of a company to receive cash (not shares) in exchange for their holdings, and is conducted under the conditions defined by the SARs. Purchases under tender offers are limited so that the purchaser does not end up with a stake of 30%, or more, of the voting rights of the company. The details of the tender offer must appear by paid advertisement in two national newspapers.

Tender offers will lapse if less than a certain percentage of the voting capital is tendered, usually set at 1%, but in any event not higher than 5%; this prevents potential bidders testing the water without making a lasting commitment.

Fixed price or maximum price

Tender offers can be made at a fixed price or a maximum price.

- If the tender is at a **fixed price** and the number of shares tendered exceeds the shares sought, the offer will be scaled down pro-rata.
- If the offer is at a **maximum price** and oversubscribed, the strike price will be the lowest price at which the number of shares sought is met. All who tender below that price will receive that price, and those who tender at the price struck will receive that price, with the number of shares accepted decided either by ballot or on a pro-rata basis, dependent on the number of shares tendered at that price.

Tender offers are attractive as they allow accelerated market purchases not normally allowed under the SARs. Companies wanting to buy-back their own shares can also make use of them and, in these circumstances, the SARs are not applicable.

Example: JJB Sports (JJB)

On 14 January 2004, JJB Sports announced a trading statement accompanied by a tender offer for £40m worth of its own shares. Tenders could be made in whole pence at a price between 240p and 280p, or shareholders could elect to tender at the eventual strike price. Interestingly, only 7.25m shares were tendered by the close on 12 February, so the maximum price of 280p was struck, representing a return to shareholders of £20m – half the proposed amount.

Figure 2.69: JJB Sports (JJB) – tender offer

Used with permission from Bloomberg L.P.

It is interesting to note that during the period between the tender being announced and the closing date, the price rose to almost exactly the highest available under the tender, and then subsequently continued to rise until shortly before final results in early April.

Partial offers

Partial offers are conducted under the rules of the Takeover Code rather than the SARs, and are not limited to cash or the final shareholding being not more than 30%.

Panel consent is required for all partial offers and the company will be placed in an offer period, hence placing additional obligations on the board of the target. Partial offers for more than 30% of the shares will not normally be given permission if the purchaser bought shares in the target in the twelve months preceding the application.

Similarly, market purchases are not allowed during the partial offer or in the twelve months after a successful partial offer.

Partial offers where the offeror could end up with 30% or more, are conditional on approval from independent shareholders holding 50% or more. In addition, if the partial offer could result in the offeror holding between 30% and 50% of the shares, the offer must declare the precise number of shares sought, and it may not be declared unconditional unless it reaches that level.

Two examples of partial offers are:

- Halifax's partial offer for up to 60% of St James' Place Capital in April 2000; and
- GPG's partial offer for 25% of De Vere in April 2004 (GPG already had a 10% stake).

Comparison of offer types

Partial offers can be used for acquiring larger stakes, whereas tender offers are limited to 30%. Potential future bidders may prefer to acquire shares under the SARs, rather than through a tender or partial offer.

Tender offers are unlikely to be successful unless the purchaser makes a statement saying that they will not be making a bid for the company in the near future, and that commitment in itself prevents a bid for at least six months under takeover rules. If such a statement isn't forthcoming, shareholders are likely to hang onto their shares and await the bid itself. In addition, the purchaser is not permitted to offer a top-up to accepting shareholders in the event of a bid at a higher price than the tender.

Partial offers also present problems as the purchaser may make no further market purchases for twelve months after a successful partial offer.

Example: Chesterton International

An unusual example of a tender offer was made by Manchester & Metropolitan (Mark & Brian Sheppard) during the bitter battle for Chesterton International in July 2003, eventually won by Phoenix.

Despite being a recommended offer, Neil List (CEO) and Mike Backs (COO) believed that Phoenix's bid undervalued the company. To prevent Phoenix reaching 90% and exercising a compulsory acquisition of the remaining shares, M&M made a fixed price tender offer at 13.2p, closing on 6 August, for a further 19.57% of the shares. Unusually, this contained a 9.2% minimum tender condition (when its existing holding was 1.24%), ensuring that it wasn't left with a holding just below 10%. M&M managed to secure 13.1% of Chesterton, blocking a squeeze-out from Phoenix.

The regulators

The Office of Fair Trading (OFT) and the Competition Commission

The OFT is the first screen for merger decisions in the UK, referring a small minority of cases to the Competition Commission if it believes the proposed deal poses the threat of a *substantial lessening of competition*. A combined market share of around 25% is the level at which the regulators get twitchy, but around 80% of cases reviewed are deemed to offer no competition issues.

Proposed mergers or takeovers that would have a turnover in excess of £70m usually trigger an automatic basic review.

The Enterprise Act, which came into effect on 20 June 2003, gave the OFT and Competition Commission new powers, giving them independence from ministers in making merger decisions. Previously, the Commission would pass its findings to the Department of Trade and Industry for approval.

Incidentally, it may surprise some to know that cartel activity is now a criminal offence in the UK, and the OFT possesses covert bugging and surveillance powers.

The Competition Commission is now the ultimate arbiter of merger bids, conducting full investigations and ordering behavioural or structural remedies. With ministers now taken out of the process, the Competition Appeal Tribunal (CAT) has been formed to moderate the OFT's decisions. Any party wishing to challenge the OFT's decision can now take its case to the CAT, whose decision can, in turn, be appealed to a higher court on a point of law. In May 2004, the OFT gained powers to directly implement European competition rules.

The whole regulatory process is becoming more transparent with the Competition Commission now publishing provisional findings on a merger deal, giving an insight into its intentions ahead of a final decision and consulting with interested parties. The OFT also offers informal advice and confidential guidance to companies anticipating a merger. The CC is an independent non-governmental body consisting of individuals with expertise in competition matters. Any public bid automatically lapses on referral by OFT.

Stage 1

For anticipated mergers already in the public domain, the statutory voluntary pre-notification procedure using a Merger Notice can be used which provides for the OFT to consider the merger within twenty working days, with a maximum extension of ten working days. For informal submissions, the normal administrative timetable is forty working days.

Stage 2

When a merger is referred to the CC, it has twenty-four weeks, beginning on the date of the reference, to prepare and publish its report. One extension of no more than eight weeks is allowed in the event of unforseen complications. Around five to six weeks into the investigation, an 'issues letter' is usually published outlining potential problems. Provisional findings and remedies are usually published between fifteen and twenty weeks into the investigation.

Example: Safeway

The regulatory process surrounding the Morrisons bid for Safeway took nearly a year. The bid was launched on 9 January 2003, the documents being posted on 31 January and the OFT then considered the matter for ten weeks before referring all four trade bidders (including Morrisons) to the Competition Commission on 19 March. The Commission studied the bids for twenty-two weeks before submitting its report on 18 August. The DTI then took a further six weeks to consider the ruling, before publishing the report on 26 September, and referring back to the OFT to negotiate the necessary remedies, which took a further ten weeks.

The takeover clock then restarted on 8 December when the undertakings were accepted, and Morrisons had twenty-one days in which to launch a new bid – the bid being relaunched on 15 December.

The CAT first flexed its muscles in December 2003, when it quashed the OFT's decision not to refer the merger of iSoft and Torex to the Competition Commission, after representations from a rival Australian software company, IBA Health. Rather surprisingly, iSoft decided not to wait for the result of the OFT's appeal and declared its offer unconditional anyway. The stock prices had gyrated in the previous weeks as the merger looked in doubt.

Decision publication

Decisions are published on the OFT website and via RNS (usually on the hour). There can be trading opportunities around announcements that go a different way to market expectations. Also the phraseology used can be confusing. When the OFT finally released its decision on the proposed merger of iSoft and Torex at 16.00 on 24 March 2004 the following text was used:

> *The OFT has decided on the information currently available to it, that it would refer the following merger to the Competition Commission under the provisions of the Enterprise Act 2002, unless acceptable Undertakings in Lieu of A Reference can be negotiated.*

> *The completed acquisition by iSoft of Torex.*

For traders not familiar with the case, this looked like a surprise referral, but ninety minutes later iSoft confirmed that it was delighted with the decision that the OFT was clearing the merger, subject to undertakings being negotiated relating to the divestment of Torex's UK laboratory, Information Management Systems, which would be subject to a statutory consultation process. This undertaking had already been offered by iSoft to the OFT.

Figure 2.70: iSoft two day chart (IOT) – OFT confusion

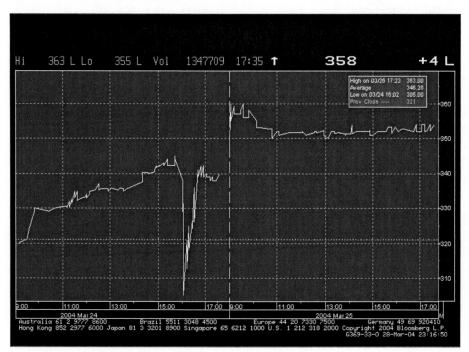

Used with permission from Bloomberg L.P.

European Commission – mergers

The EC has jurisdiction where there is a Community dimension, calculated by reference to the turnover of the companies involved, although merging parties may request the referral of a case to the Commission or to a Member State. The Commission used to have a seven-day deadline for filing of notification, but this has now been abolished. Although new EU takeover guidelines came into effect on 1 May 2004, the cross-border code is optional unfortunately, and does not outlaw poison pills, multiple share classes, or caps on voting rights.

Phase 1 (Basic)

The EC now has twenty-five working days (previously one month) to conduct an initial review and decide whether to initiate proceedings and investigate further. This period can be extended by ten working days when commitments are offered or when a Member State requests referral.

Phase 2 (In-depth investigations)

For Phase 2 cases, the basic deadline expires after a further ninety working days, extended automatically by fifteen working days if commitments are offered towards the end of the investigation. In complex cases, the deadline may be extended by a maximum of twenty additional days.

The Commission can stop the clock at any time if it feels that adequate information has not been provided.

Over 90% of mergers and acquisitions are cleared after initial review. In 2003 there were 222 merger decisions, of which 203 were made in Phase 1 (one month), with a further eleven cleared with remedies in Phase 1 (six weeks). Two clearance decisions were made in Phase 2 (five months) and a further six with remedies in Phase 2 (five months).

If companies offer concessions within the first three weeks of an investigation, the one-month deadline is extended by two weeks. If the EC decides that a further investigation is necessary, it has another four months in which to decide to adopt a decision. Although the Commission has sole jurisdiction to take decisions on mergers with a Community dimension, it may refer the case to the national authorities of a member state if there is found to be no Community dimension. The commission can block or force changes to merger terms, even if the companies involved are not part of the EU.

Rulings are made under the simplified procedure if there are no competition concerns and competitors, customers or member states have not raised any issues.

Regulatory rulings can be price-sensitive, particularly if the ruling is not as anticipated. EU rulings are published on the EU website at www.europa.eu under Press Releases in the Press Room.

Regulators can take different approaches to merger regulation. This variation in approach was largely to blame for the European regulators scuppering the Honeywell/General Electric deal in 2001.

Example: General Electric/Honeywell

In the summer of 2001, the proposed merger between General Electric and Honeywell ran into trouble with the EU and several billion dollars were estimated to have been lost by arbitrageurs. The deal had originally been announced in October 2000 and, as can be seen below, Honeywell shares jumped to 95% of the value of the share offer. The chart below represents the ratio of the Honeywell share price to the General Electric share price as a percentage. However, it became clear during 2001 that there was a serious risk the EU would block the deal, despite the US authorities having given their approval, and in fact this turned out to be the case.

Figure 2.71: GE/Honeywell – merger deal referred

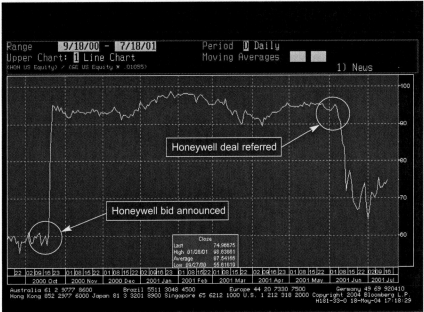

Used with permission from Bloomberg L.P.

This was the first time that a proposed merger between two US companies had been squashed solely by European regulators. This appeared to be because Mario Monti, the EU Competition Commissioner, took a fundamentally different approach to other regulators. The US concept of 'lessening of competition' makes a practice illegal if it restricts competition in some way, with no overriding business justification; whereas the EU's concept of dominance works to preserve competitors as well as consumer choice, and in this case it used its theory of bundling to express concerns that a combined GE/Honeywell would dominate some markets due to vertical integration and horizontal overlaps in closely related fields. However, the approach was somewhat discredited when the Court of First Instance later overturned a similar decision on appeal when Tetra Laval's attempted takeover of Sidel was also initially blocked under the same criteria.

European Court of Justice

The European Court of Justice is the highest court in the European Union and deals with disputes between EU governments and EU institutions, and usually hears actions brought by the Commission against member states. It also serves as an appeals court on points of law against judgements given by the Court of First Instance.

European Court of First Instance

The European Court of First Instance is the EU's lower court and has jurisdiction to hear actions brought against the Community institutions themselves. In other words it deals with all legal disputes between the EU institutions and companies or individuals. For instance, when Microsoft and the European Commission were unable to resolve their dispute in early 2004, the case was referred to the Court of First Instance.

Jurisdiction

If the proposed deal is subject to Merger Regulation, the EC generally has jurisdiction, although the member state can request that the proposed merger be referred back to it in certain circumstances. This usually involves cases of national interest or public security, certain product categories, or where the deal is expected to create a dominant position in a distinct market within the member state.

Analyst coverage can be restricted when a company is in an offer period, as the stock in question may be placed on an investment bank's *Quiet List* to prevent a conflict of interest between the corporate finance department and research department. As revised forecasts cannot be published by some research departments during this period, an opportunity may arise where there is a shortage of new research leading to catch-up when the company later comes out of the offer period.

Example: Character Group

On 11 March 2003, Character Group, the toy importer and distributor, confirmed market speculation that it had received an approach. Talks were eventually called off some six weeks later during which time the share price had risen significantly. However, there was no fall back in the share price on the news of termination of bid talks, as might be expected, because analyst upgrades which had been put on hold, were then updated and released to the market.

Figure 2.72: Character Group (CCT) – strong performance

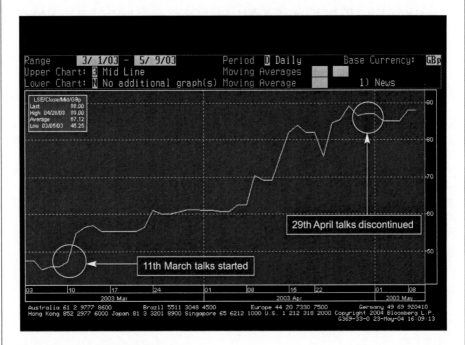

Used with permission from Bloomberg L.P.

Note: Analyst coverage can also be restricted during a regulatory investigation.

Inducement fees and break fees

Break fees are standard practice to recompense the bidding company in the event that the recommended offer lapses as a result of the board withdrawing its recommendation, or a third party trumps the original offer. They may also be payable if a bid is made after due diligence but is later not recommended. Under takeover rules they are limited to 1% of the value of the transaction, and are intended to compensate the bidder for the time and money spent on due diligence and structuring the bid.

Inducement fees are sometimes agreed to cover costs even if a bid is not forthcoming after due diligence. They were used in both the bids for Canary Wharf and Debenhams to get an offer on the table and induce an auction, and are applicable if the bidder decides not to proceed or shareholders vote against the deal. There are only a few scenarios where the fee would be applicable as, under Takeover Panel rules, there are only a few circumstances where an agreed buyer can walk away after a firm bid has been made.

Due diligence

Due diligence will be an essential stage in any takeover. Depending on the size of the company and complexity of the deal, it can take anything from a few hours to several weeks and will involve an examination of the legal, financial and operational health of a business. Normally a *data room* will be set up where accountants, lawyers and specialist consultants from the potential acquirer, will pore over such details as tenancy agreements, banking covenants, customer contracts, staff employment contracts and other liabilities. The process will also clarify potential synergies – once amusingly described by Lord Hanson (I think) as, "like the Yeti, often talked about but rarely seen" – and other benefits that may arise from the merger.

Cultural due diligence will determine the company's ethics with regard to shareholders and employees, and may throw up other non-financial, although equally important, issues that may have a key role in the integration process.

The drawbacks with hostile bids

Hostile bids can make due diligence a problem as it requires co-operation that may not always be forthcoming from the target company, meaning that the bidder may have to rely on information in the public domain. Private equity firms rarely make hostile bids, as the financing support will often be dependent on due diligence and the support of the board and shareholders. The UK Takeover Code, however, requires that all bona fide potential bidders be treated equally, so information given to the potential acquirer must also be provided to other potential bidders (friendly or otherwise). The emphasis is on bona fide, to prevent a rival getting access to commercially sensitive information when it has no intention of launching a bid. The hostile bidder may hold out the carrot of a higher offer if it is allowed to conduct due diligence than it would make if prevented from doing so.

Due diligence can be an expensive process, and a company may encourage an auction to develop by paying an inducement fee; in other words, by effectively underwriting the costs incurred by potential acquirers.

Transactions involving share swaps rather than cash, or mergers of equals (if there is such a thing), will require both parties to conduct due diligence on the other's accounts.

Transaction types

Transactions by listed companies fall into four classes, listed below, depending on the size of the deal. The comparison of size uses several parameters, known as percentage ratios, including assets, profits, turnover, consideration to market capitalisation and gross capital.

1. **Class 1**: transactions are where any of the percentage ratios listed above are 25% or more. Shareholder approval is required for a Class 1 transaction.
2. **Class 2**: transactions are when all the ratios are below 25% but one or more is above 5%.
3. **Class 3**: transactions are where all percentage ratios are less than 5%.
4. **Class 4**: Reverse takeovers (see below).

Reverse takeovers

The fourth category is a reverse takeover, where a listed company acquires an unlisted company or business where any percentage ratio is 100% or more, or there would be a fundamental change in the business, board or voting control. The company listing is automatically suspended on the announcement of a reverse takeover.

This form of takeover is typically effected when a smaller offeror company takes over a larger one, in exchange for shares in the offeror company, with the shareholders in the larger company becoming majority shareholders in the offeror company; or, alternatively, when the company being taken over is the dominant force in the combined new group.

The deal is usually friendly, and often comes about when a larger unlisted company wants to acquire a smaller listed company, sometimes only a shell, to take advantage of the smaller company's listing. The smaller company makes a share exchange offer for the larger one. If there are difficulties with minority shareholders in the smaller company, the 90% compulsory acquisition level may be more easily met by the smaller company bidding for the larger one, or by implementing the deal via a scheme of arrangement.

Risk arbitrage – analysis of a situation

As soon as a bid is announced the trader should give consideration to the following factors:

1. What is the probability that the event will complete?
2. How long will it take the deal to complete?
3. What are the chances of a competing offer?
4. What will happen if the event fails due, for instance, to regulatory intervention or because shareholders reject it as inadequate?

Probability of completion

All takeover situations can be considered to have a number of possible outcomes, each with a related probability. In a similar way to implied option volatility, the market's current assessment of the probability of a deal going through can be gauged by the price at which the asset is trading.

To take a simple example, consider a stock subject to a 400p hostile cash bid, where the bid is going to the wire. If the stock can reasonably be expected to revert to the price at which it was trading before the bid was made public (say 300p), in the event that the bid fails, all other factors being equal, there is a binary outcome to the situation, 300p or 400p. If the stock trades at 365p in the market then the market's assessment of the probability of the bid going through is:

```
(365-300) / (400-300) = 65%
```

An opportunity may exist where the trader's view on the probable outcome is different to the consensus. If there appears to be a risk-free arbitrage opportunity, either you've probably missed something or there may be a technical reason, such as difficulty in borrowing the bidder's shares to short.

Many apparent arbitrages exist purely because it is impossible to borrow the offeror's shares to sell short.

Financing

Recommended offers can comprise all cash, cash and shares, or all-share offers. There is an opportunity cost to financing a trade (the time value of money), which can be demonstrated with a simple example.

Example: Financing a cash offer

Suppose a company is subject to an agreed cash bid of 550p per share, there are no regulatory issues, and the deal is almost 100% likely to go through. The stock will not immediately trade up to 550p, as 550p cash today is worth more than 550p in, say, six weeks time, when the cash is received after tendering the shares. If interest rates are 5%, then six weeks of funding is equivalent to 3.17p.

There are also other transaction costs involved, and the tying up of capital to consider.

Therefore an arbitrageur might be prepared to pay 543p for stock now, to institutions that want to sell in the market to reinvest cash immediately, rather than wait for the cash to come through. This is particularly common in a bull market, where the institutional holders may want to reinvest the proceeds in the same sector without risking missing an uplift in prices instead of waiting for the cash to come through, and missing out on a possible rise in other stocks in the same sector in the meantime.

The arbitrageur can calculate his annualised return on the trade as:

```
550-543 = 7p
```

less financing costs (3.17p):

```
7 - 3.17 = 3.83p (over six weeks)
```

annualised:

```
(3.83 / 543) * (52 / 6) = 6% (before execution costs)
```

Many of these types of trade are conducted via contracts for difference, as the positions are highly capital intensive, yield relatively small margins of return, and stamp duty would otherwise become a significant cost.

A number of commentators attributed the rise in the share prices of AstraZeneca and GlaxoSmithKline early in April 2004, shortly after the bid by General Electric for Amersham completed, to funds maintaining their exposure to the sector by buying the remaining constituents. Although there did not appear to be any great increase in trading volumes, and it is difficult to prove through empirical data, the money flows created as a result of takeovers should always be anticipated.

As well as the re-investment of cash proceeds in other stocks in the same sector, another factor can be *flowback*. If a transaction occurs that involves a significant issue of new shares, the accepting holders may not want to retain those new shares in the offeror when they are delivered in exchange for their holding in the bid target. Where a foreign takeover is made with shares, this can create a flow of stock back onto the domestic market as soon as the new shares become available, particularly from tracking funds unable to hold the foreign stock.

Cash offers with multiple outcomes

Sometimes an offer will be announced with several potential outcomes, so that existing shareholders have the opportunity to participate in favourable outcomes such as contracts or franchises that the target company is currently involved in.

Example: First Group offer for GB Railways Group

On 16 July 2003, First Group announced a recommended cash offer for GB Railways Group. At that time GB Railways was one of three short-listed bidders for the Greater Anglia Franchise, one of five for the Northern Rail Franchise, and was awaiting the decision regarding the Wales and Borders Franchise (one of four).

The initial consideration was set at 250p cash per share, with additional deferred considerations dependent on the outcome of certain tender processes as follows:

- 200p payable on the successful outcome of Greater Anglia Franchise.
- 50p payable on the successful outcome of Northern Rail or Wales & Borders.

There were therefore four possible outcomes: 250p, 300p, 450p and 500p.

Between 16th July, when the offer was announced, and the time that the shares finally delisted after the deal went through, the share price of GB Railways traded between 285p and 330p, reflecting supply and demand and the market's current view on the likely outcomes.

Figure 2.73: GB Railways (GBR) – multiple possible outcomes

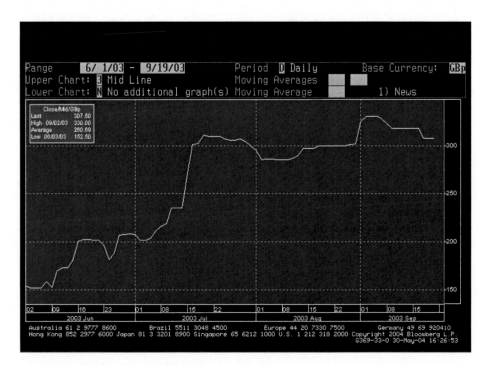

Used with permission from Bloomberg L.P.

Although the mechanics are slightly complicated by the fact that winning one franchise may influence the success of another win, a simple probability chart can be drawn up.

- The probability of winning Greater Anglia was 0.33.
- The probability of winning the Northern Rail was 0.2.
- The probability of winning Wales & Borders was 0.25.

Putting this together:

```
250p + (0.33*200p) + ((0.25 + 0.2 -(0.2*0.25))*50p) = 250+66+20 = 336p
```

The risk-adjusted fair value for GB Railways' share price was therefore 336p.

After failing to win Wales it became:

```
250p + (0.33*200p) + (0.2*50p) = 250+66+10 = 326p
```

In fact, it was announced on 22 December 2003 that GB Railways was unsuccessful in bidding for the Greater Anglia Franchise, having also being unsucessful for the Wales and Borders Franchise on 1 August 2003. First Group made it as far as one of two bidders for the Northern Rail Franchise, but failed to win that franchise too, so there was no additional payout to GB Railways' shareholders.

This is a common theme in risk arbitrage, where, not unlike option theory, the implied volatility of an option can be calculated and compared to historic volatility to ascertain relative cheapness. Similarly in a takeover situation, the market's perception of the likely outcome can be compared with the trader's calculation of the relevant probabilities to assess a trading opportunity.

Share offers

A potential bidder may offer its own shares instead of cash to its target's shareholders, which, it will argue, allows existing shareholders to benefit from becoming continuing investors in the merged entity. In addition, it may be more attractive to offer highly rated paper rather than taking on debt, or paying out of cash reserves. This can, however, be a problem for lower rated companies, where a cash offer may be essential as the additional cost of equity would be prohibitive.

Example: Lastminute.com (LMC) offer for Online Travel Corp

Take the example of Lastminute.com's recommended share offer for Online Travel Corp launched on 3 March 2004. Lastminute.com offered 0.1319 of its own shares for each Online Travel share. As LMC's shares were trading at 235p the day before the bid was announced, this valued Online Travel's shares at a see-through price of 31p (235 x 0.1319).

As can be seen from the chart, after the terms of the offer were announced the two shares move in lock step, and there is an arbitrage opportunity between the two shares. Assuming the deal goes through without interference, as this one did, Online Travel shareholders have the opportunity to tender their shares and receive new LMC shares, or to sell their shares in the market at the prevailing market price. The new shares actually became available on 13 May, shortly after the deal went wholly unconditional on 30 April, and as the offer documents were posted on 4 March, the deal took a total of ten weeks from launch to completion.

Some share exchange offers are attractive to existing shareholders who wish to maintain a going interest in the combined company, thereby not crystalising a profit or loss, as would be the case in a cash offer.

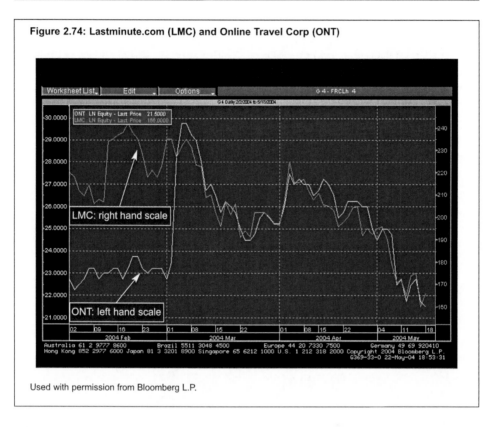

Figure 2.74: Lastminute.com (LMC) and Online Travel Corp (ONT)

Used with permission from Bloomberg L.P.

Arbitrageurs will keep the share prices of the two stocks more or less in line, although at a slight discount to Online Travel's see-through price (unless a counter bid is anticipated), allowing other shareholders an effective cash exit. Despite the bad name that arbitrageurs have, they do bring additional liquidity to the market. As can be seen from the chart it was better to sell the shares in the market at the time of the bid than hold on, due to the later underperformance of Lastminute.com. It can sometimes be difficult to anticipate how the shares of the bidder will perform. Much will depend on market conditions as well as sentiment towards the deal. If the deal is badly received the shares may suffer, whereas a good strategic logic may see an appreciation in both share prices. Existing Online Travel shareholders with a shorting facility (typically a CFD account), could short LMC shares and deliver the shares to the CFD provider against that short position when they come through – in effect selling their shares forward and locking in the current share price.

Example: Long Online Travel (ONT), short Lastminute.com

There is also an arbitrage opportunity in buying ONT shares and short-selling LMC shares; a trade that I actually executed at the time. This deal is attractive as ONT had a market capitalisation of only around £50m, and was therefore below the radar level of a lot of risk arbitrage hedge funds for whom it simply wasn't worth getting involved, as they would not be able to establish a position big enough to make it worth their while, leaving the arena to smaller players like myself.

However, I also had access to ONT stock from a seller via my broker – who would otherwise have had to take the market's bid price – and with the ability to sell LMC on SETS I could execute the arbitrage. Here's how it worked:

Prevailing market prices:

- Online Travel: 26-27p
- Lastminute: 212-213p

I am offered 70,000 ONT stock at 26.25p, so immediately short sell 9,233 LMC shares (0.1319 x 70,000) at 212p, creating a long ONT position and short LMC position, fully hedged.

My outlay is:

```
70,000 x 26.25p = £18,375
```

and my short position is of value £19,574.

This creates a locked-in profit of £1,199.

The trade described above was run for around four weeks, so I will have a financing cost, as well as commission costs. Because the long and short position are almost equal, the financing costs will simply be the difference between what you pay your CFD provider above LIBOR for long positions, and receive below LIBOR for short positions.

The kicker comes in this type of situation if a counter bid comes in from a third party, particularly if it is accompanied by a fall in the original bidder's share price, when there is a market perception that the original bidder may get entangled in an auction and end up overpaying. Unlike a cash bid, the value of the target's shares will also be linked to the bidder's share price. The short position may have to be bought back, but this is only likely to be expensive if the shares were hit hard initially by the market on scepticism over the benefits of the bid, and hence might bounce back strongly in the event that the company is saved from an unpopular acquisition by another bidder.

Cross border all-share takeovers

Cross border all-share takeovers don't happen very often, as the institutional holders in the domestic company may be unwilling or unable to accept foreign paper. There is also the currency risk as well as the risk of the acquirer's share price falling as well as the issue of flowback.

One way to compensate for this is to adopt an arrangement similar to the one that the US company General Electric did when it acquired Amersham in late 2003. A collar arrangement meant that the number of shares that GE offered in exchange for each Amersham share would increase to maintain a certain sterling value, subject to a maximum value.

The effect of arbitrage activity

Arbitrage activity can have a detrimental effect on the bidder's share price, if the size of the deal is significant in relation to the market capitalisation of the bidder. If, however, the bidder's stock is extremely liquid, and the new shares are a small proportion of the average daily volume, then a vicious circle is less likely to develop.

It could be argued that the more arbitrage activity there is during the time that the deal is going through while both stocks are quoted, the less the share overhang will be later (or flowback, in the case of a foreign share deal), as the stock has already been effectively sold forward.

Smaller company arbitrage opportunities

Many special situations that exist in smaller companies with limited liquidity can be attractive to the smaller scale trader, since he is likely to have the field to himself, as bigger players may not find it economically viable to get involved. An example would be the ONT/LMC arbitrage, already mentioned. Hedge funds rarely get involved in situations with a market capitalisation of below £100m as it is not worth their while, and they would not be able to establish a meaningful position. From an ordinary trader's point of view, the more stocks that are traded electronically the better, as those with direct market access will not necessarily have to cross the bid-offer spread.

Better liquidity and the ability to establish bigger positions will be available in the electronically traded blue chip stocks where DMA will also help in improved execution. However, other arbitrageurs will extensively research the situations and the individual will be in competition with risk arbitrage capital from elsewhere. Situations in smaller companies will be less well covered and may offer better opportunities, although a good broker who is able to source stock and deal inside the prohibitively expensive prevailing markets bid-offer spread is essential.

Example: Capital Stream offer for IDS Group

A good example of this kind of opportunity occurred in the summer of 2003 when IDS Group, the specialised computer software company, announced on 30 May a recommended cash offer of 19p per share from US company Capital Stream. This valued IDS at £11m, a 50% premium to the 12.75p price that IDS was trading at before the bid was announced. Documents were posted shortly afterwards on 31 May, with the first closing date set as 30 June.

However, on 25 June, Schroder Venture Partners announced that it was considering making an offer materially above Capital Stream's one. Schroders duly announced a cash offer at 23p per share via its Twins Acquisition vehicle. After a succession of leapfrog bids, Capital Stream eventually gave up, allowing Twins Acquisition to declare its 27p cash per share bid unconditional on 5 August, a full 42% above Capital Stream's initial offer and a 112% premium to the price of IDS Group before the offers were made. This kind of deal has all the ingredients that an arbitrageur dreams of: two competing bidders making leapfrog cash offers. The losers are the shareholders who sell too early in the marketplace, wrongly assuming that the endgame has been reached.

It ain't over until the fat lady sings.

Figure 2.75: IDS Group (IDG) – competing bidders

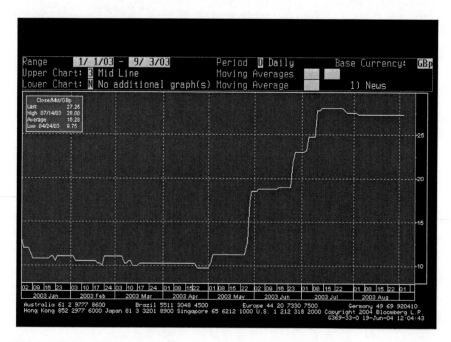

Used with permission from Bloomberg L.P.

Cash and share offers

There can be option value in cash and share offers, or where there is an all cash alternative, putting a floor under the share price. The bidder may also offer a mix and match facility, allowing shareholders to vary the proportion of shares and cash that they receive, subject to availability.

Example: Babcock International offer for Peterhouse Group

In March 2004, Babcock International offered to buy Peterhouse Group in a cash and shares deal, valuing Peterhouse at 216p a share. However, a sharp fall in the share price of Babcock meant the terms, which offered 1.1858 new Babcock shares and 64.8p cash for each Peterhouse share, had become worth less than when the deal was originally announced.

Under the mix and match facility, shareholders could elect to vary the ratio of cash and shares they received, subject to availability. With the exchange rate set at 127.5p per Babcock share under this facility, and with the shares falling back to 106p at one point, it would make sense to elect for 'max cash' unless a rise in Babcock shares was expected imminently. If the shares had performed strongly and risen above 127.5p, it would of course make sense to elect for as many shares as possible and elect for 'max shares'. Shareholders often neglect to take advantage of this extra option.

Loan note alternatives

Often a cash offer will include a loan note alternative, subject to sufficient demand.

A loan note is a document evidencing the terms on which the issuer of the loan note owes a debt to you. Interest is payable to the loan note holder until the debt is paid back. They are unsecured, unlisted and typically pay interest at 0.75% below six month LIBOR in six-month instalments in arrears. The notes can usually be redeemed at their nominal value for cash on certain dates of the year.

The capital gains tax liability is not crystallised until such time as the loan notes are cashed. They therefore offer a means of spreading capital gains over a period of time, which may be more tax efficient for certain shareholders.

Competing offers

This is where takeover situations can become extremely interesting.

History is littered with deals that everyone initially thought was a done deal, but later attracted interest from a third party; for example, BAE Systems' late entry for Alvis in June 2004. It can often be the best course of action to sit tight and not take the first offer on the table.

Particular situations to watch out for are competitive auctions, where more than one bidder is involved, and where deep-pocketed potential bidders can create price tension. There may also be strategic reasons why one bidder will not want to allow the target to fall into another's hands. Bear in mind that a target may have a different potential value to one purchaser over another. Trade buyers are likely to be able to cut costs through expected synergies, and be able to centralise costs such as amalgamating dual head offices, a saving which may not be available to a private equity buyer, who may be more interested in the cash flow of the existing business and leveraging the company up.

The opportunity often lies in taking an opposite view to the market and assessing a situation as soon as a deal is announced. Market expectations over the possible outcomes of the deal will then fluctuate as the deal evolves. If the share price immediately jumps to a premium to the offered price, it is clear that the market believes that this will not be the last word.

However, interventions can often happen, and the best opportunities develop when no-one expects a counter bid. If the stock can be bought at, or close to, the net present value of the bid (the price offered adjusted for financing), with minimal regulatory issues, then, although nine times out of ten nothing happens, the kicker comes in the tenth situation.

This strategy is capital intensive, and is akin to taking on several trades with a high probability, low risk, low reward profile, but with the option of one situation developing. It is the value of this option that a risk arbitrageur is extracting.

Trophy assets

Trophy assets are always likely to command a premium. Almost every analyst recommended shareholders accept the initial bids for the retailers Hamleys and Selfridges, but those who held on were richly rewarded when subsequent higher competing offers materialised, as the following charts demonstrate.

Figure 2.76: Selfridges (SLF) – trophy asset

Used with permission from Bloomberg L.P.

Figure 2.77: Hamleys (HYL) – trophy asset

Another situation where the market had underestimated the bidder's desire to secure an asset was the contested bid for tank maker Alvis. Here, a group of hedge funds were instrumental in inducing a counterbid from BAE Systems, trumping the agreed cash bid from General Electric of the US.

Figure 2.78: Alvis (ALV) – General Electric's offer trumped

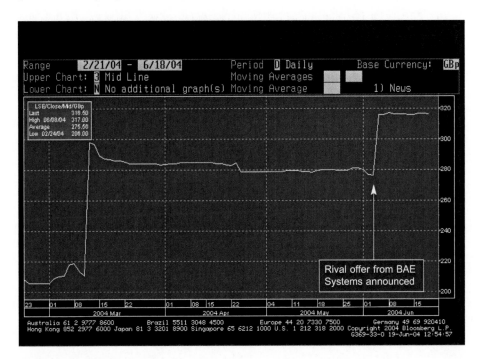

Used with permission from Bloomberg L.P.

Remember, a company is only worth what a buyer is willing to pay. Analysts often make the mistake of applying exit multiples and valuation techniques to stocks in takeover situations. Once a bid has occurred, all bets are off. The characteristics of the chart above are very common in takeover situations where sudden jumps in a share price, reflecting a development, are interspersed with long periods of low activity and turnover.

Controlled auction

Once a company has announced a strategic review (or even if it does not announce publicly that it is up for sale), a controlled auction will often ensue. Here, the universe of potential buyers is narrowed to a shortlist and serious buyers will get access to the data room. In the endgame, the ideal number of seriously interested parties is likely to be three, offering some insurance should one party drop out. The worst situation is when the buyer knows it is the only bidder.

Exclusivity

The company may announce that it has granted exclusivity to one particular bidder for a fixed period of time. One thing to be wary of is venture capitalists who often agree one price then start chopping away at it when in exclusivity.

Competitive situations – auction procedure

If a conclusion to a bid cannot be orchestrated quickly, the Takeover Panel may instigate an auction process to accelerate a result. This was the process utilised in the Debenhams bid situation in late 2003 and the competitive Hyder situation in August 2000. Under Takeover Rules, Day 46 is usually the last day that an offeror is permitted to increase its offer. As any revised offer document would need to be posted by midnight on Day 46, and prepared and printed ahead of that time, it may be inappropriate to have continual leapfrogging offers from competing bidders. To bring finality to the situation, a sealed bids procedure may be used if agreed to by all parties.

The Takeover Panel instigated an auction procedure to bring the long-running battle for Canary Wharf, between Brascan and a Morgan Stanley-led consortium, to a close by setting a timetable that both parties agreed to. Each side could revise their offer once a day between 13 April and 16 April and each party could make only one announcement per day, with the auction process concluding if no-one submitted a revised offer. Morgan Stanley finally won the auction process, although it had to change its offer to a general offer rather than a scheme of arrangement, to gain sufficient acceptances.

Sealed bids

Under the sealed bids procedure both parties submit final best bids, which can be a fixed or formula bid. In a precedent ruling during the battle for The Energy Group in 1998, the Panel decided that both types of bid were to be allowed.

Fixed bid

Here, competing bidders submit final and best offers. If there are timing issues because one offer is a general offer and the other under a scheme of arrangement, the Panel may initiate an auction process over a number of days as it did in the Canary Wharf situation, although formula bids were not allowed in that case.

Formula sealed bid (second-price auction)

Formula bids allow each bidder to bid a variable amount (up to its own stipulated maximum) over and above the other party's offer. The best offer wins but only pays the price offered by the loser, plus a percentage – this process is effectively an accelerated open auction.

Event failure

Risk arbitrageurs are the market's insurers of last resort, underwriting the risk of a deal going through in return for a premium received. Like insurance, merger arbitrage deals are best done as part of a portfolio approach with several deals in one trading book. Deals can and do fall apart, sometimes due to regulatory issues, or occasionally problems securing funding, although the Takeover Code makes it clear that funding should be watertight before launching a formal bid.

The Takeover Panel takes the launching of a formal bid extremely seriously, and it is very rare that it can be withdrawn. Even the 'material adverse change' clause can rarely be invoked, as it requires the offeror to demonstrate to the Panel that unforeseen exceptional circumstances have arisen.

In November 2001, the Takeover Panel refused WPP's request to wriggle out of its agreed deal for Tempus Group, which was pitched at 555p per share on 20 August, trumping an original agreed offer from the French company, Havas Advertising, following a collapse in share prices after the events of 11 September. As WPP had secured 93.9% acceptances by 1 October, the first closing date, the deal had gone unconditional as to acceptances.

The acceptance level is usually set at 90%, primarily because that is the level at which the compulsory provisions apply, and funding may be dependent on the bidder achieving full control. This condition can be waived down to any level, subject to a minimum of 50%, at the bidder's discretion. A bidder will usually stipulate 90% at the outset, even if the intention is to go unconditional as to acceptances at a lower level, as it grants greater flexibility and the ability to walk away if something goes horribly wrong.

This is exactly what happened when Vinci launched a hostile bid for TBI in 2001, and the 90% acceptance level was used to get out of the bid at the last moment by lapsing the offer. After the events of 11 September, the board changed its mind and accepted the offer, but Vinci only reached 83.97% acceptances to which the offer applied and promptly let the bid lapse, despite TBI claiming that it believed that there had been no material adverse effect on its business.

Acceptances

Although the number of acceptances can give a clue as to how likely the deal is to go through, there is usually little benefit in accepting a deal right away, as deadlines are almost always extended. Bear in mind that undertakings and acceptances are often conditional on the absence of a higher offer (always check the level at which these acceptances fall away, as they may indicate the level at which a rival bidder may have to pitch its offer), and letters of intent are not legally binding. Irrevocable undertakings, contrary to their impression, often cease to be binding in the event of an offer by a third party; always check the circumstances under which they cease to be binding. The Takeover Panel is tightening up the rules on letters of intent, which provide 'irrevocable' commitments, as it has been argued that the target's shareholders do not know how robust the commitment is or the identity of the accepting shareholders. The risk with making the commitments more visible is that institutions may become less willing to give a letter of intent early in an offer period, as it might antagonise the target and make it harder for the offeror to gain public support.

Tracking funds generally wait for a deal to go unconditional before tendering their shares. This can create problems for the bidder when tracking funds represent a significant proportion of the target's shareholder register. Whereas active managers can encourage a transaction by committing to letters of intent, passive holders are unhelpful to the potential bidder as their lack of action effectively makes it harder for the bidder to gain significant support ahead of formalising a deal.

An offer can generally be declared unconditional as to acceptances when 50% of the shares have been tendered, but other conditions have still to be met. Shares tendered by this time can still be returned. An offer must be declared wholly unconditional within twenty-one days of being declared unconditional as to acceptances, or within twenty-one days of the first closing date, whichever is the later. Remember that an offeror may choose to waive down a higher acceptance level as defined in the original offer document at its discretion.

When the offer is declared wholly unconditional, all shares tendered will be accepted with settlement made within fourteen days. Settlement for shares tendered after the offer is declared wholly unconditional will be made within fourteen days of tendering.

Note that if a bidder declares its offer 'final' it is not allowed to subsequently increase it unless it has specifically said that it is conditional on there being no competing offer from a third party.

Protection from siege warfare

Often the Takeover Panel will issue a 'put up or shut up' notice to a potential bidder that is stalking a company to prevent an endless siege. In this scenario the Panel will set a deadline by which the potential offeror must make an offer or walk away for a period of at least six months. The vast majority of put up or shut up notices result in no immediate formal offer being made.

Once a formal bid lapses, the offeror cannot launch a new bid within twelve months of the original offer lapsing, unless the new offer is recommended or a competing offer is made – this is to prevent the company remaining perpetually under a state of siege.

If a potential offeror withdraws an expression of interest in making a bid, they are restricted in bidding again for a period of six months. There can often be a frenzy of speculation and a share price rise leading up to the expiry of this deadline, even if the bidder has no intention of re-launching a bid. This can often present a good short-term trading opportunity.

The chart below clearly shows the market anticipating a bid for Scottish Radio Holdings from 29% holder EMAP as we approach the date from which EMAP is free to bid again after a 12-month restriction – whether or not an actual bid will transpire is another matter entirely.

Figure 2.79: Scottish Radio Holdings (SRH) – market anticipates a bid from EMAP

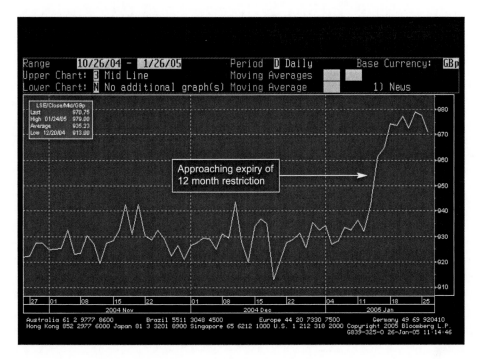

Used with permission from Bloomberg L.P.

Greenmail

Greenmail is the expression used when an unfriendly shareholder who is threatening a takeover is paid to go away. Sometimes the stock is sold back to the company or another friendly shareholder.

Offer obligations

Usually, if the potential bidder has bought shares in the target in the three months leading up to the offer period, or between the commencement of the offer period and a firm offer, the offer to shareholders should be on not less favourable terms.

A cash offer is required if 10% or more of the shares are bought by the offeror in the twelve months leading up to the offer, or during the offer period at not less than the highest price paid.

Stub equity

Stub equity allows existing shareholders access to the fortunes of the company being taken over going forward alongside the new owners. The new shares will typically be highly leveraged equity, possibly listed on AIM, which may in itself restrict some funds from holding it.

Stub equity became more popular recently to allay fears that some public to private transactions have delivered big returns over a very short period to private equity buyers. However, stub equity comes at a cost to both sides: the successful bidder will be operating in the public domain which may restrict drastic surgery, and the minority shareholders will be holding paper of an altogether different colour than before.

Accounting changes

Recent accounting changes have removed some favourable treatments for all-share bids and mergers. As it is much harder to make a hostile bid with shares rather than with hard cash, we may see an increase in hostile bids in sectors where there has traditionally been a cosy all-share merger, such as the pharmaceutical sector.

MBOs

One of the recent areas of concern has been the equal treatment of all shareholders upheld in Rule 16. There can be a conflict of interest when management, which may have a large existing stake in the business, may make an offer which is perceived to undervalue the company. The management may be confident of success because some of the large shareholders are known to them, with long-standing relationships, and will acquiesce and take a stake in the new, highly geared bidding vehicle. The takeover rules allow for an exemption for ordinary MBOs, otherwise the MBO would be difficult to implement.

To prevent this, large shareholders can be deemed to be joint offerors if they have at least 30% of the listed entity, some influence in management of the bidding vehicle, and no special terms like a guaranteed exit.

In addition, Rule 16 stipulates that no side deals are allowed. The Takeover Panel ruled in July 2004 that Enterprise London could not increase its offer for Dynamic Commercial Finance (DCF) because 29% shareholder Unicorn sold its stake to Enterprise with an agreement that Enterprise would make up the difference if it succeeded in gaining control of DCF at a higher price. This was a clear breach of Rule 16.

Triple net asset value (property assets)

Triple net asset value has become an increasingly popular valuation benchmark for properties being taken private, since the takeover of MEPC by GE Capital and Hermes in 2000 first used the measure to justify its offer price. Whereas net asset value is the gross valuation of the properties less the book value of the debt, triple NAV takes into account deferred tax and capital gains tax that would be paid if the portfolio was liquidated, and the redemption value of debt, assuming it was repaid.

This is a valid measure if the costs were incurred by the bidder, but often the portfolio is not liquidated, the debt is left in place, and costs associated with paying back the debt and replacing it with new debt is not encountered. Triple NAV does not reflect potential future pipelines of development and is a static valuation, so cannot factor in where valuations are forecast to rise. Therefore it is not necessarily an appropriate measure to apply at all stages of the property cycle, particularly if the company is not going to be broken up and sold off as it doesn't necessarily account for future potential upside. It doesn't seem consistent for potential bidders to use triple NAV when they won't later incur some of the costs that are taken into its account for its calculation.

Online M&A resources

One of the best websites to keep an eye on the latest reports regarding takeover situations is the Intelligence Headlines at Mergermarket.

Reference

Mergermarket: www.mergermarket.com

Appendices

- Glossary

- Directory of online stockbrokers

- Directory of CFD brokers

- Directory of spread betting firms

- Trading resources

- Stock codes

- Trade codes

- Market Maker codes

- Stock indices – UK

- Stock indices – International

- Company profile of the FTSE 100 Index

- Sector profile of the FTSE 100 Index

- FTSE 100 Quarterly Reviews

- Derivatives dealing comparison Table

- Cash shells

- Shell companies

- UK ADRs

Glossary

accelerated initial public offering (AIPO)

In an AIPO the broker forms a new company to acquire the assets and then invites a small number of institutions to bid for shares in the new vehicle, rather than carrying out a more usual book building exercise. The acquisition vehicle is then floated on AIM. In effect, companies pre-sell their shares to institutions. The process was pioneered by Collins Stewart when it floated Northumbrian Water on AIM in 2003.

alpha

The outperformance of an asset against a benchmark that can be attributed to a factor, such as a fund manager's added value, rather than to the general market or sector performance.

auction call process

Before continuous trading commences at 08.00 there is a pre-market auction between 07.50 and 08.00 which is known as the 'auction call process'.

backwardation

A backwardation occurs when a bid is higher than an offer.

beta

Beta is a measure of the sensitivity of a share to movements in the general market.

If a company's share has a beta of 1, it tends to rise and fall in line with the market. A beta of less than one, say 0.8, would imply that if the benchmark index fell 10%, the stock would only fall 8%. Defensive stocks tend to have low betas, occasionally negative, whereas growth stocks tend to have higher betas.

book building

A bank will often use a 'book building' exercise to gauge market sentiment for a placing, rather than attempting to estimate the right risk price itself by offering the shares at a fixed price.

callable bonds

Callable bonds are repackaged bonds issued by investment banks, generally yielding more than the underlying, with an embedded option giving the issuer the right of repurchase if triggered by certain events.

cash market

The normal share trading market, as distinct from derivatives markets such as CFDs, options or futures.

choice

When the bid and the offer are the same price.

chinesing the spread

Buying shares and shorting an associated instrument, in other words the reverse of the normal approach. For example, shorting a convertible bond against buying the underlying shares.

close period

There is often confusion over the closed period, which is commonly assumed to be the two months leading up to the publication of the interim or final results (if the company reports on a half-yearly basis). However, the closed period can be shorter if the time between the close of the financial year and the publication of results is shorter, and it is this period that counts as the closed period. If a company reports quarterly (common practice in the US), the closed period is one month, or the period from financial year-end until publication if shorter. Directors are prohibited from dealing during the closed period.

committed principals

Where less liquid stocks, traded on SEATS Plus, have less than two market makers, the market makers are called committed principals.

concert party

Where an agreement exists between two parties to acquire and act collectively in regard to their shareholdings. Usually referred to in the context of takeovers and disclosure requirements.

convertible arbitrage

Buying the convertible and selling short the underlying stock to take advantage of a relative mis-pricing. The reverse trading strategy can also be applied if the convertible is deemed to be overvalued in comparison to the underlying (see *chinesing the spread*).

correlation

The likelihood of two shares moving in the same direction at the same time. A correlation of +1 implies that two stocks would always move in the same direction, although not necessarily by the same percentage. A correlation of -1 would imply that two stocks always move in the opposite direction.

CREST

The settlement organisation for UK shares.

CREST Sponsored Membership

Shareholders unwilling to lose the benefits of directly holding share certificates, but wanting to benefit from the quicker settlement and other advantages of CREST, can elect to have a CREST Sponsored Membership.

cross-over credit

When a company moves from junk to investment grade, or the reverse.

dead cat bounce

Where a stock rallies upwards on low volumes after a sharp fall, encouraging buyers and giving the impression of a rally, before the price resumes its slide southwards.

dealer in front

A market maker declares 'dealer in front' to a broker if he is currently quoting that stock to another member firm, or has executed a trade and has not had a reasonable opportunity to change his price.

distressed securities arbitrage

Buying or shorting securities in companies that are typically encountering severe financial or trading difficulties, in the anticipation of a likely positive outcome or restructuring not reflected in the current share price.

equity hedge (long/short equity)

Combining long and short holdings. Overall, portfolios may be net long or net short, depending on market conditions.

equity market neutral

Long and short positions but net exposure will be zero.

event-driven arbitrage

Special situations, spin-offs, recapitalisations, corporate actions and share buy-backs. Based around predicting the outcome of a situation.

exchange for physical

A transaction whereby an investment bank undertakes to exchange for a client, say, FTSE 100 futures contracts for FTSE 100 Index component stocks.

front month contract

The futures contract (in a calendar series) that is the closest to expiring.

Global Master Securities Lending Agreement (GMSLA)

Stock lending and borrowing is governed by standardised legal agreements that have evolved over the years, but the industry is moving towards the Global Master Securities Lending Agreement (GMSLA) which standardises issues such as the treatment of corporate actions, defaults and non-delivery, under which the signing parties are legally bound.

greenmail

The term used when an unfriendly shareholder, who is threatening a takeover, is paid to go away. Sometimes the stock is sold back to the company or another friendly shareholder.

greenshoe option

A term often used in the context of IPOs: when the underwriter of an IPO is granted an option to sell additional shares if demand warrants it, or buy additional shares back to provide stabilisation for a limited period after trading commences. The name comes from The Green Shoe Company, which was the first to use this type of option. It can give the issuer an opportunity for price arbitrage during the stabilisation period.

grey market

Often an IPO stock will trade on a when issued basis (in the 'grey market') for a period of time before unconditional dealings commence.

historic volatility

A measure of the historic price changes of a security over a specific period of time. Defined as the standard deviation of the continuously compounded returns on the security. One standard deviation either side of a share price trend represents a band inside which the share price would be expected to remain 66% of the time.

iceberg orders

A way of disguising bigger orders by submitting only part of a large order, which is automatically reloaded when the first part is executed. Member firms were executing these orders for some time, but there was always a risk of missing further execution between execution of the first order and subsequent re-loading of another order, however quick the firm's computer driven system was. The London Stock Exchange introduced the iceberg feature to bring this functionality onto the actual order book itself, rather than having to be programmed into the firm's connectivity with the SETS system. Effectively, the functionality is now available additionally at the Exchange level rather than just at the firm level. Iceberg orders are colloquially known as re-loaders.

implied volatility

Implied volatility can be calculated for an option and represents what the market thinks future volatility will be for the underlying stock or index.

indicative offer

Where a company expresses an interest in bidding for another company, without a full commitment to make a bid.

inter-dealer brokers (IDBs)

Market makers are able to deal between themselves anonymously using 'inter-dealer brokers'. For years market makers had four different IDB screens on their desks, but the introduction of SETS and SETSmm has reduced demand and now only Cantor Fitzgerald handles the majority of screen-based inter-market deals.

Level 2

A Level 2 screen indicates the depth of the market by displaying all the bids below (and including) the best bid, and all the offers above (and including) the best offer.

macro arbitrage

Correctly anticipating price movements in global markets using a top-down global approach to identify extreme price mis-valuations in stocks, foreign exchange, commodities and interest rates.

mandatory quote period

Market makers are obliged to offer continuous buy and sell prices during the mandatory quote period (between 08.00 and 16.30).

market order

An order without a specific price attached, which will be executed at the best prevailing price, maximising the chance of execution.

member firms, broker-dealers and market makers

Throughout the book there are references to *broker-dealers* and *market makers*. Both are member firms of the London Stock Exchange, but the latter have an obligation to make continuous two-way prices in the stocks that they are registered in.

Nominated Adviser (Nomad)

All companies listed on AIM must have a Nominated Adviser, which will usually be the company's broker. This is in place of the Main Market's system of suitability criteria and regulations.

nominee accounts

Stockbrokers have increasingly encouraged clients to use 'nominee accounts', where shares are held centrally in the electronic settlement service called CREST, which are cheaper and faster to use. There are around five million retail shareholders in the UK who hold their shares in dematerialised form in nominee accounts.

Normal Market Size (NMS)

When shares are traded on the London Stock Exchange, the market makers have to quote a bid price and offer price at which they will deal. But the prices they quote, which are disseminated to brokers via the SEAQ system, only have to be honoured up to a certain size of order. The Normal Market Size defines what that figure is for each company.

Portfolio System for Institutional Trading (POSIT)

POSIT is an Electronic Communications Network (ECN) for institutions bringing together buyers and sellers in an anonymous environment.

Primary Information Providers (PIPs)

The regulatory news providers (since the London Stock Exchange monopoly was ended in April 2002) are now called 'Primary Information Providers' (PIPs). The principle PIPs are: RNS Newswire (London Stock Exchange), PR Newswire, Waymaker Wire News and Business Wire. PIPs in turn issue regulatory announcements to Secondary Information Providers (SIPs), like Bloomberg, Reuters, Thomson Financial and Investegate.

reduced size market makers

Some market makers can register as 'reduced size market makers', which means that they can display prices in a size below NMS.

Regulatory News Service (RNS)

A regulated service which ensures that price-sensitive information from listed and AIM companies, and certain other bodies, is disseminated to all RNS subscribers at the same time. The London Stock Exchange used to have a monopoly on RNS releases, but this monopoly was ended on 15 April 2002. The regulatory news providers are now known as 'Primary Information Providers' (PIPs), and all listed companies are contracted with at least one PIP service to comply with the obligations regarding the release of regulatory news under the Listing Rules.

relative value arbitrage

Taking a simultaneous long and short position in two securities that are historically correlated, e.g. pairs trading.

Retail Service Provider (RSP) network

The RSP network allows automatic instantaneous execution of smaller orders, normally under the Normal Market Size (NMS), thus removing the manual process of phoning a market maker. BZW, Merrill Lynch and Winterflood originally developed the RSP system to release market makers from having to deal with multiple small orders.

reverse takeovers

Reverse takeovers (or back door listing), are often structured so as to allow a much bigger business with an easy access to a stock market quotation.

risk arbitrage

A strategy often employed by hedge funds that anticipates the successful outcome of a takeover, merger, MBO or corporate action.

RSP Gateway

Recently developed by the London Stock Exchange in an attempt to co-ordinate the matrix of RSPs.

Rule 9 waivers

Rule 9 waivers are so called because, normally under Rule 9 of the Takeover Code, once a party has increased its stake above 30% in a company it is obliged to make an offer for the whole company.

Schatz

Colloquial term for the two-year German government bond future.

shell companies

Shell companies have little or no underlying business activities, usually consisting of just cash and, more importantly, a stock market quote. Shell companies are interesting as they provide an alternative route for a company wanting a listing on one of the exchanges. Instead of an expensive IPO, a company can simply buy an already listed shell company, and reverse into it.

short selling

The selling of a stock one doesn't currently own, in the anticipation of a fall in the share price. Subsequently the position can be bought back, hopefully at a lower price, and the difference can be pocketed.

spoofing

Large orders that are placed on the order book, but miraculously disappear as soon as they are in danger of actually trading.

touch

The prevailing best bid and best offer prices (usually displayed in the yellow strip of a Level 2 screen). Also referred to as 'Level 1'.

tree shaking

Where market makers shuffle a share price back on little or no volume after a sharp rise, to induce profit takers to sell stock, allowing them to close short positions at more favourable prices.

UKLA Official List

The Main Market of the London Stock Exchange.

volatility

A measure of a security's propensity to go up and down in price. A volatile share is one which has a tendency to move violently through a great share price range. Mathematically, this is expressed as the standard deviation from the average performance. Generally speaking, the higher the volatility of a share, the higher the price of option/warrants on the share will be.

volume weighted average price (VWAP)

The calculation of current VWAP for any particular stock is: the total value traded during the day so far divided by the number of shares traded. In other words, for each trade, multiply the number of shares (shape) by the price at which it was traded, then add them all together and divide by the total number of shares traded. This gives an average price, weighted towards where the majority of the shares traded. VWAP has become one of the primary benchmark measures of trade execution, partly because of the greater awareness among institutional investors of the importance of trading costs.

whopper

Colloquial term for a worked principal agreement (WPA) trade.

witching

In the UK a day is designated as 'triple witching' when index futures and options, and stock options all expire on that same day. The US now has 'quadruple witching' on days where index futures and options, and stock futures and options all expire on the same day.

worked principal agreement (WPA)

An agreement by a member firm to act as principal to trade a SETS stock at some point in the future. The trade size must be at least eight times NMS and, once a WPA has been entered into, the dealer must attempt to improve either on the price or size agreed. The trade is colloquially known as a 'whopper'.

Directory of online stockbrokers

Barclays Stockbrokers	www.stockbrokers.barclays.co.uk
Comdirect	www.comdirect.co.uk
E*Trade	www.etrade.co.uk
FasTrade (Charles Stanley)	www.fastrade.co.uk
Halifax Sharebuilder	www.halifax.co.uk/sharedealing
Hargreaves Lansdown	www.h-l.co.uk
iDealing	www.idealing.com
Interactive Investor	www.iii.co.uk
Saga Share direct	www.saga.co.uk
Selftrade:	www.selftrade.co.uk
TD Waterhouse	www.tdwaterhouse.co.uk

Directory of CFD brokers

Berkeley Futures	www.bfl.co.uk
Cantor Index	www.cantorindex.co.uk
City Index	www.cityindex.co.uk
Deal4free	www.deal4free.com
E*Trade	www.etrade.co.uk
GNI touch	www.gnitouch.com
Hargreave Hale	www.hargreave-hale.co.uk
Hargreaves Lansdown	www.h-l.co.uk
Hichens Harrison & Co	www.hichens.co.uk
iDealing.com	www.idealing.com
IFX Markets	www.ifx.co.uk
IG Markets	www.igmarkets.com
Man Financial	www.manfinancial.com
Onewaybet.com	www.onewaybet.com
Refco	www.refco.com
Sucden	www.sucden.co.uk
TwoWayTrade	www.twowaytrade.com

Directory of spread betting firms

Cantor Index	www.cantorindex.co.uk
Capital Spreads	www.capitalspreads.com
City Index	www.cityindex.co.uk
Deal4free	www.deal4free.com
Finspreads	www.finspreads.com
iDealing.com	www.idealing.com
IG Index	www.igindex.co.uk
Spreadex	www.spreadex.com
TradIndex.co	www.tradindex.com

Trading resources

Trading platforms

As an advocate of direct access trading, the key platforms for trading that stand out for me are:

- E*Trade Professional: www.etrade.co.uk
- GNI Touch: www.gnitouch.com
- IG Markets: www.igmarkets.com

An in-depth review of the three platforms and their features can be found at:
www.investorschronicle.co.uk/content/archive/2004/Tools/tools_20040305_1.html

Professional information providers

- Bloomberg Professional: www.bloomberg.co.uk
  $1,700 per month

- Reuters: www.reuters.co.uk
  Reuters Trader web-based £450 p/m
  Reuters 3000Xtra £750 p/m

- Knowledge Technology Solutions (KTS): www.ktsplc.com
  QuoteTerminal £90 p/m
  MarketTerminal £150 to £200 p/m

  Features:
  AFX and Dow Jones news feeds, broker forecast
  Links to 120 markets
  No trading functions

- Proquote: www.proquote.net
  Owned by London Stock Exchange
  Web-based, European and UK coverage

  Proquote Clearview
  £1,260 per annum + exchange fees + VAT (Level 1)
  £1,890 + exchange fees + VAT (dedicated Level 2)
  No trading facility although Proquote Trader offers direct market access to member firms only.

Key UK websites

- Breakingviews: www.breakingviews.com

- Citywire: www.citywire.co.uk
  Shrewd investors, secret buying and directors' dealings analysis.

- Digital Look: www.digitallook.com

- Hemscott: www.hemscott.com

- MergerMarket: www.mergermarket.com

- Motley Fool: www.fool.co.uk
  In particular Paul Scott's Paulypilot board, one of the hidden gems of the internet.

- News Review – www.news-review.co.uk
  Excellent website including the Weekend City Press Review, a weekly email sent out on a Sunday evening comprehensively detailing the weekend's press coverage. The 16-page pdf document is indexed by company and newspaper. A subscription is around £750 per year.

Best charting websites

- ADVFN: www.advfn.com

- BigCharts: www.bigcharts.com

- MoneyAM: www.moneyam.com

- StockCharts: www.stockcharts.com (US stocks only)

UK daytraders' websites

- ADVFN: www.advfn.com
  Level 2, M-codes, breakouts, biggest movers, highest volume, momentum, most SEAQ traders frequent this site.

- MoneyAM: www.moneyam.com
  Mainly SETs traders, similar features to ADVFN, daily market round-up email.

- T2W: www.trade2win.com
  UK trading community.

Other trading related websites

- applied derivatives.com: www.appliederivatives.com

- erivativesreview: www.erivativesreview.com

- ItPaysDividends: www.itpaysdividends.co.uk

- Sharelockholmes: www.sharelockholmes.co.uk

- t1ps: www.t1ps.com
  A stable of websites run by tipster Tom Winnifrith, including a fortnightly Evilcast from veteran bear raider Simon Cawkwell. A sister site also worth a look is www.uk-analyst.com.

- UK Stock Challenge: www.stockchallenge.co.uk

- Investegate: www.investegate.co.uk
  Regulatory announcements

Hedge fund sites

- HedgeFund Intelligence: www.hedgefundintelligence.com

- HedgeFund.net: www.hedgefund.net

- HedgeWorld: www.hedgeworld.com

US sites

- Briefing.com: www.briefing.com

- First Call: www.firstcall.com (Thomson Financial)

- Institutional Investor: www.institutionalinvestor.com

Annual reports

There is a free annual reports service offered by WILink plc, a subsidiary (believe it or not) of the old Knutsford shell company. The group specialises in investor relations and the provision of investment information services and is chaired by Nigel Wray.

Further details can be found at www.wilink.com where reports can be downloaded.

Magazines

- *Investors Chronicle* (every Friday)

- *Shares* (every Thursday)

- *Traders'* (monthly)

Stock codes

This page describes the common codes associated with securities.

EPIC

Some time ago, the London Stock Exchange devised a system of code names for listed companies. These codes provide a short and unambiguous way to reference stocks.

For example, the code for Marks & Spencer is MKS. This code is easier to use than wondering whether one should call the company Marks & Spencer, Marks and Spencer or Marks & Spencer plc.

These codes were called *EPIC* codes, after the name of the Stock Exchange's central computer (Electronic Price Information Computer) prior to 1996. Codes are standardised now and comprise of three characters (e.g. NMS), with a fourth character indicating a secondary stock (e.g. NMSW, for New Media Spark warrants). Some securities still have four characters, a leftover from the old system (e.g. BOOT for Boots, BARC for Barclays).

TIDM

A search today of the London Stock Exchange website will be in vain for any mention of EPIC codes. That's because after the introduction of the Sequence trading platform, EPIC codes were renamed *Tradeable Instrument Display Mnemonics* (TIDMs), or *Mnemonics* for short. So, strictly, we should now be calling them TIDMs or Mnemonics – but almost everyone still refers to them as EPIC codes.

Reference

London Stock Exchange: www.londonstockexchange.com

Yahoo Finance: finance.yahoo.co.uk

SEDOL

SEDOL stands for *Stock Exchange Daily Official List Number*, and are seven-digit security identifiers assigned by the London Stock Exchange. They are only assigned to UK-listed securities.

CIN

CIN stands for *CUSIP International Number*, where CUSIP is the *Committee on Uniform Securities Identification Procedures*. CIN codes are the international extension of CUSIP codes used for Canadian and US securities. The codes are ten-character: the first character is always a letter, which represents the country of issue; the next six characters are numbers which represent the issuer; followed by two digits representing the security; the final digit is the check digit.

ISIN

ISIN stands for *International Securities Identification Number*, and are twelve-digit alphanumeric identifiers assigned by the International Standards Organisation (ISO) in order to provide standardisation of international securities. The first two letters represent the country code; the next nine characters usually use some other code, such as CUSIP in the United States or SEDOL in Great Britain with leading spaces padded with 0. The final digit is the check digit.

Reference

Corporate Information: www.corporateinformation.com/defext.asp

A good description of international security codes and company suffixes (e.g. 'PLC' in the UK).

Source: The UK Stock Market Almanac 2005

Trade codes

The UK market uses several different trade codes associated with each trade. Different vendors use different trade codes; for instance, Reuters uses O for a non-protected portfolio trade, whereas Bloomberg uses N. I have used the London Stock Exchange's official codes; the most important trade codes are as follows:

Code	Trade code description
AT	*Automatic Trade* A normal order book trade conducted electronically on SETS or SETSmm.
O	*Ordinary trade* A standard trade, dealt for normal settlement made through a market maker. Most SEAQ trades will be O trades and O trades in SETS stocks indicate a trade executed with a market maker 'off-book' or 'in-house'. Trade publication may be delayed for larger orders to give market makers an opportunity to unwind the trade.
B	*Broker to Broker* A transaction between two member firms, neither of which is a market maker nor designated fund manager. An example would be a large line of stock sold by one broker to another, or a trade executed on the POSIT system by a member firm. It means a market maker hasn't taken one side of the bargain, so market impact is unlikely unless it is executed outside the bid-offer spread. Also used when a broker dealer deals with another broker dealer, which is not a member firm. B codes do not apply to order book securities.
X	*Cross at the same price* Usually an agency order crossed directly between buyer and seller. Can also be a put through or riskless principal transaction with two non-members.
N	*Non protected portfolio* Both N and P trades relate to portfolio trades, i.e. baskets of stocks. The N code signifies that the client took the risk and it is a fully disclosed portfolio transaction, i.e the basket was executed on an agency basis. A program trade that is dealt with at prices prevailing at a certain time.
P	*Protected portfolio* The P code signifies that the trade is on a principal basis and the market maker has guaranteed execution with the possibility of improvement. It is common to see a stream of trades, particularly P trades, booked through the market after the market close as the order has been worked throughout the day. Also used to report transactions resulting from a worked principal agreement to effect a portfolio transaction including order book securities.

VW	Volume Weighted Average Price The transaction was effected with reference to the volume weighted average price over a given period.
M	Market maker to Market maker A transaction between two market makers registered in the security. Trades done between market makers via an IDB will also print as M trades. M trades publish immediately as there is no risk position to protect.
T	Single Protected Transaction Here a large order is left with a market maker to work which might otherwise disrupt the price. For example, the client may want to buy 20K shares but only 10K are available so the client leaves the order with the market maker to work, on the understanding that he will commit to a guaranteed minimum. The market maker will buy the stock over a period in bits and pieces and then book the trade at the end. The London Stock Exchange is notified automatically when the trade is taken on and afterwards when it is booked out but not disclosed to the marketplace until afterwards. Can occur for SEAQ and SEAT stocks.
K	Block trade Applicable to SEAQ stocks. Publication is delayed by five business days or until 90% of the order has been unwound. If the NMS of the stock is below 2,000, the trade must be fifty times NMS to qualify. If the NMS is 2,000 or above, it must be at least seventy-five times NMS to qualify. The block trade facility is not available for transactions in bid situations, SETS stocks or in conjunction with a worked principal agreement or protected trade.
WT	Worked Principal Trade Also known as a 'Whopper'. Reporting a trade from a worked principal agreement which is individual and not part of a portfolio. The market maker is given an order to fill as best they can over a period of time.
O	Overnight A transaction that took place outside of the normal reporting period of 07.15 to 17.15.
C	Bargain condition indicator A trade subject to bargain conditions such as special cum-dividend, ex-dividend, bonus, rights or cash settlement.
L	Late trade This will be appended to the trade if publication was delayed or an amendment has been made to the trade. A trade that is six times NMS does not have to be reported for an hour after execution and would be a late trade. Also if the bargain were amended, for instance for the settlement date, that would also be a late trade.

LC	*Late Trade Correction* Used when reporting a correction submitted more than three days after publication of the original trade report. Alternatively if the transaction has not been published, a correction more than three days after the original trade report was submitted.
CT	*Contra Trade* Used to publish a contra trade. A contra trade cancels an earlier erroneous trade on the order book or in a SEAQ crossing.
PC	*Post Contra* Used to report a contra trade on the order book when the date of the contra trade is not the same as the trade date.
ST	*SEAQ Cross* This is the code used for a transaction occurring in a SEAQ cross.
UT	*Uncrossing Trade* The price that the auction uncrosses at. Usually, but not always, the same at the official close.
OC	*Official Close* Usually the same as the uncrossing price, unless there has been insufficient volume in the closing auction.

Market maker codes

Every market maker has a three- or four-character code that is assigned by the London Stock Exchange. These codes are displayed on a Level 2 screen and also the yellow strip when a market maker is on the bid or offer.

Code	Market maker	Code	Market maker
ABNV	ABN AMRO Equities	HSBC	HSBC Securities
ALTI	Altium Capital	INV.	Investec Investment Bank
ARBT	Arbuthnot Securities	JEFF	Jefferies International
BARD	Robert W. Baird	JPMS	JP Morgan Securities
BEST	Bear, Stearns International	KBC	KBC Peel Hunt
BGWL	Bridgewell Securities	KLWT	Dresdner Kleinwort Wasserstein
CANA	Canaccord Capital	LEDR	LCF Edmond de Rothschild
CAZR	Cazenove	LEHM	Lehman Brothers International
CITI	Citigroup Global Markets	MLSB	Merrill Lynch International
CNKS	Cenkos Securities	MOST	Morgan Stanley International
CODE	Code Securities	NMRA	Nomura International
CSCS	Collins Stewart	NUMS	Numis Securities
CSFB	Credit Suisse	PIPR	Piper Jaffray
DAVY	J.&.E Davy	PMUR	Panmure Gordon
DEUT	Deutsche Bank A G	SCAP	Shore Capital Stockbrokers
ETRA	E*Trade Securities	SEYP	Seymour Pierce Ltd
EVO	Evolution	TEAM	Teather & Greenwood
GOOD	Goodbody Stockbrokers	UBS.	UBS
GSCO	Goldman Sachs International	WDBM	Williams de Broe
HOOD	Hoodless Brennan & Partners	WINS	Winterflood Securities

Stock indices – UK

FT Ordinary Share Index (FT 30)

The FT 30 Index was first calculated in 1935 by the *Financial Times* newspaper. The Index started at a base level of 100, and calculated from a subjective collection of thirty major companies, which in the early years were concentrated in the industrial and retailing sectors.

For a long time the Index was the best known performance measure of the UK stock market, but it became less representative of the whole market and was also price-weighted (like the DJIA), and not market capitalisation-weighted. Although the Index was calculated every hour, the increasing sophistication of the market needed an index calculated every minute, and so the FT 30 has been usurped by the FTSE 100.

FTSE 100

Today, the FTSE 100 Index (sometimes called the 'footsie') is the most well-known index tracking the performance of the UK market. The Index comprises 100 of the top capitalised stocks listed on the London Stock Exchange, and represents approximately 80% of the total market (by capitalisation). It is market-capitalisation-weighted, and the composition of the Index is reviewed every three months. The FTSE 100 is commonly used as the basis for investment funds and derivatives, and was first calculated on 3 January 1984 with a base value of 1000.

The FTSE 100 Index, and all the FTSE indices, are calculated by FTSE International, a joint venture between the *Financial Times* newspaper and the London Stock Exchange.

FTSE 250

Similar in construction to the FTSE 100, except it comprises the next 250 highest capitalised stocks listed on the London Stock Exchange after the top 100. Sometimes referred to as the index of 'mid-capitalised' stocks, this index comprises approximately 18% of the total market capitalisation.

FTSE 350

Similar in construction to the FTSE 100, but including all the companies from the FTSE 100 and FTSE 250 Indices.

FTSE Small Cap

Comprised of companies with a market capitalisation below those in the FTSE 250, but above a fixed limit. This lower limit is reviewed every December. In December 2003 the lower limit was set to approximately £56m. Consequently the FTSE Small Cap Index does not have a fixed number of constituents. In mid-2004, there were approximately 338 companies in the Index, which represented about 2% of the total market by capitalisation.

FTSE All-Share

The FTSE All-Share is the aggregation of the FTSE 100, FTSE 250 and FTSE Small Cap Indices. Effectively all those London Stock Exchange listed companies with a market-capitalisation above the lower limit for inclusion in the FTSE Small Cap Index. In mid-2004, there were approximately 688 companies in the Index. The FTSE All-Share is the standard benchmark for measuring the performance of the broader UK market.

FTSE Fledgling

This Index comprises the smallest companies that do not meet the minimum size requirement of the FTSE Small Cap Index.

FTSE TMT

Reflects the performance of companies in the Technology, Media and Telecommunications sectors.

FTSE techMARK All-Share

An index of all companies included in the London Stock Exchange's techMARK sector.

FTSE techMARK 100

The top 100 companies of the FTSE techMARK All-Share, under £4bn by full market capitalisation.

Source: The UK Stock Market Almanac 2005

Stock indices – International

Dow Jones Industrial Average Index (DJIA)

The DJIA is the oldest continuing stock index of the US market, and is now the most famous stock index in the world. Created in 1896, it originally comprised of just twelve stocks, but over the years the Index expanded and today it includes thirty stocks. The index is weighted by price, which is unusual for a stock index. It is calculated simply by summing the prices of the thirty stocks and dividing by the *divisor*. Originally the divisor was 30, but this has been adjusted periodically to reflect capital changes such as stock splits, and is currently about 0.2. This means that companies with high stock prices have the greatest influence in the index – not those with large market values. Only one company has remained in the Index since the beginning: General Electric.

Standard & Poor's 500 (S&P 500)

This is the main benchmark index for the performance of the US market. The Index is weighted by market value, and constituents are chosen based upon their market size, liquidity and sector. The Index was created in 1957, although values for it have been back-calculated several decades.

NASDAQ 100

This Index tracks the performance of the 100 largest stocks listed on the NASDAQ exchange, and is calculated using a modified capitalisation-weighting method ("modified" so that large companies like Microsoft don't overwhelm the Index). NASDAQ companies tend to be smaller and younger than those listed on the NYSE, and although there is no attempt to select technology stocks, it is regarded as the tech stock index. The Index can be traded as there's an ETF associated with it (the most actively traded ETF in the US). The ETF has the symbol QQQ, and is sometimes referred to as the 'Qs' or 'Qubes'.

Nikkei 225

The Nikkei 225 Index is owned by the *Nihon Keizai Shimbun* ('Nikkei') newspaper. It was first calculated in 1949 (when it was known as the Nikkei-Dow Index) and is the most widely watched stock index in Japan. It is a price-weighted index of 225 top-rated Japanese companies listed in the First Section of the Tokyo Stock Exchange. The calculation method is therefore similar to that of the Dow Jones Industrial Average (upon which it was modelled).

TOPIX

The TOPIX Index is calculated by the Tokyo Stock Exchange. Unlike the Nikkei 255, TOPIX is a market-capitalisation-weighted index. The Index is calculated from all members of the First Section of the Tokyo SE, which is about 1,500 companies. For these reasons, TOPIX is preferred over the Nikkei 225 as a benchmark for Japanese equity portfolios.

Hang Seng

The Hang Seng Index was first calculated in 1964. Today it has thirty-three constituents representing some 70% of the total Hong Kong market by capitalisation.

CAC 40

The CAC 40 Index is the main benchmark for Euronext Paris (what used to be the Paris Bourse). The index contains forty stocks selected among the top 100 by market capitalisation and the most active stocks listed on Euronext Paris. The base value was 1000 on 31 December 1987.

DAX

The DAX 30 Index is published by the Frankfurt Stock Exchange, and is the main real-time German share index. It contains thirty stocks from the leading German stock markets. The DAX is a total return index (which is uncommon), whereby it measures not only the price appreciation of its constituents but also the return provided by the dividends paid.

Source: The UK Stock Market Almanac 2005

Company profile of the FTSE 100 Index

No.	Name	EPIC	Turnover (£m)	Profit (£m)	Profit (%)	Capital margin (%)	Weighting (%)	Cum -weighting (%)
1	BP PLC	BP.	130,314	9,194	7.1	109,469	9.79	9.79
2	HSBC Holdings PLC	HSBA		7,181		97,620	8.73	18.52
3	Vodafone Group PLC	VOD	33,559	-5,047	-15.0	84,770	7.58	26.09
4	GlaxoSmithKline PLC	GSK	21,441	6,329	29.5	67,984	6.08	32.17
5	Royal Bank of Scotland Group (The) PLC	RBS		6,159		50,044	4.47	36.65
6	AstraZeneca PLC	AZN	10,561	2,354	22.3	43,752	3.91	40.56
7	Shell Transport and Trading Co PLC	SHEL	45,213	4,971	11.0	40,318	3.60	44.16
8	Barclays PLC	BARC		3,845		34,128	3.05	47.22
9	HBOS PLC	HBOS		3,766		27,257	2.44	49.65
10	Lloyds TSB Group PLC	LLOY		4,348		24,146	2.16	51.81
11	Diageo PLC	DGE	9,440	654	6.9	21,249	1.90	53.71
12	Tesco PLC	TSCO	30,814	1,600	5.2	20,796	1.86	55.57
13	Anglo American PLC	AAL	10,443	1,498	14.3	18,859	1.69	57.26
14	British American Tobacco PLC	BATS	10,570	1,567	14.8	18,191	1.63	58.88
15	BT Group PLC	BT.A	18,519	1,948	10.5	15,704	1.40	60.29
16	Rio Tinto PLC	RIO	5,171	1,173	22.7	14,731	1.32	61.60
17	National Grid Transco PLC	NGT	9,033	1,362	15.1	14,430	1.29	62.89
18	Unilever PLC	ULVR	30,150	3,205	10.6	14,193	1.27	64.16
19	BHP Billiton PLC	BLT	12,661	2,499	19.7	13,007	1.16	65.33
20	BG Group PLC	BG.	3,587	1,290	36.0	12,366	1.11	66.43
21	Aviva PLC	AV.		1,390		12,349	1.10	67.54
22	Standard Chartered PLC	STAN		864		11,316	1.01	68.55
23	Centrica PLC	CNA	17,931	778	4.3	10,466	0.94	69.48
24	Reckitt Benckiser PLC	RB.	3,713	660	17.8	10,181	0.91	70.39
25	Cadbury Schweppes PLC	CBRY	6,441	564	8.8	9,525	0.85	71.25
26	British Sky Broadcasting Group PLC	BSY	3,656	480	13.1	9,342	0.84	72.08
27	Prudential PLC	PRU		350		9,244	0.83	72.91

28	Abbey National PLC	ANL		-686		9,013	0.81	73.71
29	Imperial Tobacco Group PLC	IMT	3,200	656	20.5	8,998	0.80	74.52
30	GUS PLC	GUS	7,548	692	9.2	8,667	0.77	75.29
31	Marks & Spencer Group PLC	MKS	8,302	782	9.4	8,110	0.73	76.02
32	mmO2 PLC	OOM	5,694	95	1.7	7,959	0.71	76.73
33	Scottish Power PLC	SPW	5,797	792	13.7	7,578	0.68	77.41
34	SABMiller PLC	SAB	6,880	757	11.0	7,122	0.64	78.04
35	Compass Group PLC	CPG	11,286	358	3.2	6,846	0.61	78.66
36	Legal & General Group PLC	LGEN		469		6,782	0.61	79.26
37	Kingfisher PLC	KGF	8,799	427	4.8	6,587	0.59	79.85
38	BAE SYSTEMS PLC	BA.	8,387	233	2.8	6,388	0.57	80.42
39	Reed Elsevier PLC	REL	2,605	267	10.2	6,367	0.57	80.99
40	Scottish & Southern Energy PLC	SSE	5,124	607	11.9	6,341	0.57	81.56
41	WPP Group PLC	WPP	18,621	350	1.9	6,053	0.54	82.10
42	BAA PLC	BAA	1,970	539	27.4	6,019	0.54	82.64
43	Carnival PLC	CCL	1,629	153	9.4	5,748	0.51	83.15
44	Land Securities Group PLC	LAND	1,286	373	29.0	5,619	0.50	83.65
45	Boots Group PLC	BOOT	5,325	581	10.9	5,306	0.47	84.13
46	Xstrata PLC	XTA	1,951	199	10.2	5,270	0.47	84.60
47	Wolseley PLC	WOS	8,221	426	5.2	5,079	0.45	85.05
48	Allied Domecq PLC	ALLD	3,410	483	14.2	5,059	0.45	85.51
49	Morrison (Wm) Supermarkets PLC	MRW	4,944	320	6.5	5,033	0.45	85.96
50	Pearson PLC	PSON	4,048	152	3.8	5,015	0.45	86.40
51	Associated British Foods PLC	ABF	4,909	457	9.3	4,984	0.45	86.85
52	Smith & Nephew PLC	SN.	1,179	230	19.5	4,812	0.43	87.28
53	Reuters Group PLC	RTR	3,197	49	1.5	4,780	0.43	87.71
54	Sainsbury (J) PLC	SBRY	17,141	610	3.6	4,676	0.42	88.13
55	BOC Group (The) PLC	BOC	3,718	352	9.5	4,433	0.40	88.52
56	ITV PLC	ITV	2,078	39	1.9	4,325	0.39	88.91
57	Gallaher Group PLC	GLH	3,641	379	10.4	4,293	0.38	89.29
58	Hilton Group PLC	HG.	8,931	171	1.9	4,261	0.38	89.67

59	Man Group PLC	EMG		435		4,225	0.38	90.05
60	Old Mutual PLC	OML		443		4,202	0.38	90.43
61	Alliance & Leicester PLC	AL.		525		4,136	0.37	90.80
62	Rolls-Royce Group PLC	RR.	5,645	180	3.2	4,030	0.36	91.16
63	InterContinental Hotels IHG Group PLC		3,483	36	1.0	4,029	0.36	91.52
64	Smiths Group PLC	SMIN	3,056	217	7.1	3,993	0.36	91.87
65	Next PLC	NXT	2,516	353	14.0	3,970	0.35	92.23
66	British Land Co PLC	BLND	498	186	37.4	3,885	0.35	92.58
67	Scottish & Newcastle PLC	SCTN	3,594	100	2.8	3,585	0.32	92.90
68	3i Group PLC	III		0		3,565	0.32	93.22
69	Dixons Group PLC	DXNS	6,492	366	5.6	3,086	0.28	93.49
70	United Utilities PLC	UU.	2,060	338	16.4	3,085	0.28	93.77
71	Northern Rock PLC	NRK		387		3,052	0.27	94.04
72	Severn Trent PLC	SVT	2,015	254	12.6	2,999	0.27	94.31
73	Hanson PLC	HNS	3,619	137	3.8	2,828	0.25	94.56
74	Rentokil Initial PLC	RTO	2,366	397	16.8	2,724	0.24	94.80
75	Liberty International PLC	LII	362	110	30.4	2,713	0.24	95.05
76	Daily Mail and General Trust PLC	DMGT	1,933	108	5.6	2,650	0.24	95.28
77	Cable and Wireless PLC	CW.	3,671	-224	-6.1	2,634	0.24	95.52
78	Imperial Chemical Industries PLC	ICI	5,849	85	1.5	2,609	0.23	95.75
79	Friends Provident PLC	FP.		260		2,584	0.23	95.98
80	British Airways PLC	BAY	7,560	230	3.0	2,521	0.23	96.21
81	AMVESCAP PLC	AVZ	1,158	36	3.1	2,514	0.22	96.43
82	Shire Pharmaceuticals Group PLC	SHP	761	-298	-39.2	2,424	0.22	96.65
83	REXAM PLC	REX	3,112	5	0.2	2,419	0.22	96.87
84	Alliance UniChem PLC	AUN	8,799	196	2.2	2,409	0.22	97.08
85	Yell Group PLC	YELL	1,187	-44	-3.7	2,342	0.21	97.29
86	Whitbread PLC	WTB	1,788	212	11.8	2,325	0.21	97.50
87	William Hill PLC	WMH	5,946	171	2.9	2,214	0.20	97.70
88	Capita Group (The) PLC	CPI	1,081	94	8.7	2,163	0.19	97.89
89	Sage Group (The) PLC	SGE	560	151	27.0	2,128	0.19	98.08

90	Hays PLC	HAS	2,498	-477	-19.1	2,118	0.19	98.27
91	Exel PLC	EXL	4,987	149	3.0	2,107	0.19	98.46
92	Royal & Sun Alliance Insurance Group PLC	RSA		-146		2,095	0.19	98.65
93	Tomkins PLC	TOMK	3,150	132	4.2	2,032	0.18	98.83
94	Johnson Matthey PLC	JMAT	4,493	178	4.0	2,031	0.18	99.01
95	Antofagasta PLC	ANTO	607	202	33.2	2,016	0.18	99.19
96	Bunzl PLC	BNZL	2,728	195	7.1	1,950	0.17	99.36
97	EMAP PLC	EMA	1,050	144	13.7	1,916	0.17	99.54
98	Enterprise Inns PLC	ETI	481	173	36.0	1,887	0.17	99.70
99	Bradford & Bingley PLC	BB.		263		1,865	0.17	99.87
100	Schroders PLC	SDR	428	66	15.3	1,448	0.13	100.00

Note: Figures as of September 2004

Sector profile of the FTSE 100 Index

The table below displays the sector weightings in the FTSE 100 Index.

Sector	Capitalisation weighting (%)	No. companies
Banks	23.48	10
Oil & Gas	14.50	3
Pharmaceuticals	10.42	4
Telecommunications Services	9.93	4
Mining	4.82	5
Media & Entertainment	3.83	9
Beverages	3.31	4
General Retails	3.19	6
Life Assurance	3.14	5
Tobacco	2.81	3
Utilities, Other	2.77	4
Food & Drug Retailers	2.73	3
Food Producers & Processors	2.57	3
Leisure & Hotels	1.83	6
Support Services	1.63	6
Aerospace & Defence	1.29	3
Electricity	1.24	2
Real Estate	1.09	3
Transport	0.95	3
Personal Care & Household Goods	0.91	1
Chemicals	0.81	3
Speciality & Other Finance	0.73	3
Construction & Building Materials	0.71	2
Investment Companies	0.62	1
Health	0.43	1
Software & Computer Services	0.19	1
Insurance	0.19	1
Engineering & Machinery	0.18	1

Note: Figures as of September 2004

FTSE 100 quarterly reviews

A table of companies entering and exiting the FTSE 100 Index since January 2001, as a result of the quarterly reviews.

Company	In	Out
Alliance UniChem	Sep 02	
ARM Holdings		Jun 02
Autonomy Corporation		Mar 01
Brambles Industries		Dec 02
British Airways	Dec 02, Dec 03	Sep 02, Mar 03
British Land Co	Sep 01	
Bunzl	Jun 02	
Cable & Wireless	Mar 03	Dec 02
Canary Wharf		Apr 03
Capita Group	Jun 04	Jun 03
Carlton Communications		Sep 01
Celltech Group		Mar 02
CMG		Sep 01
Colt Telecom Group		Sep 01
Corus Group	Mar 02	Dec 02
Electrocomponents		Jun 02
Emap	Oct 02	
EMI Group		Sep 02
Energis		Sep 01
Enterprise Inns	Mar 04	
Enterprise Oil	Sep 01	
Exel		Mar 01
Foreign & Colonial Investment Trust	Mar 03	Mar 04
Friends Provident	Sep 01	
GKN		Dec 01
Hays	Dec 03	Jun 03
Innogy Holdings	Sep 01	

InterContinental Hotels Group (demerger of Six Continents)	Apr 03	
International Power		Sep 02
Invensys		Mar 03
Johnson Matthey	Jun 02	
Kelda	Mar 03	Sep 03
Lattice (following merger between National Grid and Lattice)		Oct 02
Liberty International	Dec 02	
Logica		Jun 02
Man Group	Sep 01	
Marconi		Sep 01
Misys		Sep 01
Mitchells & Butlers (demerger of Six Continents)	Apr 03	Dec 03
Northern Rock	Sep 01	
P & O Princess Cruises	Dec 01	
Provident Financial	Mar 03	Dec 03
Rexam	Sep 02	
Rolls-Royce	Jun 03	Mar 03
Royal & Sun Alliance	Jun 03	Mar 03
Scottish and Newcastle	Mar 01	
Sema	Mar 01	
Severn Trent	Sep 01	
Spirent		Sep 01
Telewest Communications		Sep 01
Tomkins	Sep 02	
Whitbread	Dec 02	
Wolseley	Sep 01	
Xstrata	Jun 02	
Yell Group	Sep 03	

Source: FTSE International

Derivatives dealing comparison table

Question	Futures	Spread Betting	CFDS	ETFs	Options	Covered Warrants
New broker required?	Yes (but can probably use to deal in options)	Yes (but same broker may deal in CFDs)	Yes (but same broker may do spread bets)	No, trade through your existing broker	Yes, but many option brokers trade futures too	Not necessarily
Minimum account size?	Probably	Low	Varies but generally higher than for spread betting	Not applicable	Not necessarily	No
Dealing specifics?	Buy/sell, contract, delivery month	Buy/sell, product, expiry, stake size	Buy/sell, stock/index	Buy/sell, product	Buy or write, stock, put or call, strike, expiry, style	Buy to open, sell to close a specific warrant
Minimum trade size?	£2 per index point x margin; 1000 x stock price x margin	Yes, but far from onerous	Varies but some have no minimum	No	One contract = 1000 shares or £10 per index point	No, can deal in any size
Margin % needed?	Varies with volatility of underlying. 5-30%	Varies with volatility of underlying – more than futures	Varies but can be less than futures	Not applicable, you have to put up 100%	Not applicable – pay 100% of premium	Not applicable – pay 100% of premium
Spreads?	Tight in index futures, less tight in stock futures	Varies with product and firm – less on dailies	Deal at 'cash' market price	Varies – often possible to deal inside the 'touch'	Varies – often wide on low priced options	Relatively narrow, capped by exchange
Commission?	Varies but usually £10 per lot down to £4	No	Commonly 0.25% of consideration; some charge zero	Yes, as for shares	Yes, often flat rate plus exchange levy	As for shares – often flat rate per trade
Stamp duty?	No	No	No	No	No	No
CGT on gains?	Yes	No	Yes	Yes, as for shares	Yes	Yes

Source: 'The Investor's Toolbox', by Peter Temple

Cash shells

Cash shells as at 07/02/05. Main market members in bold.

Name	Code	Cash (£m)	Market cap.
Abraxus Investments	AXU	1.6	1.55
Advanced Visual Comms	ACV	0.08	0.23
Amberley	AMB	2.3	4.3
Assoc. Brit. Engr	**ASBE**	**1.1**	**0.83**
Azure Holdings	AZH	0.0	0.27
Base Group	BS.	0.15	1.27
Capital Management & Inv.	CMIP	4	34
Capricorn Resources	CIR	0.306	3.3
Fortfield Investments	FIV	0.075	0.68
FTV	FTG	0.38	0.79
Future Internet	FTI	0.56	0.76
Highway Capital	**HWC**	**0.66**	**0.91**
IAF	**IAF**	**0.34**	**2.58**
JAB Holdings (OL)	JBH	0.25	1.42
Judges Capital	JDG	0.60	2.20
Legendary Investments	LEG	1.50	1.41
Leisure Ventures	LSV	0.0	0.18
Maisha	MSA	0.5	0.43
Mark Kingsley	MKP	2.7	1.92
Melrose	MRO	12	14.7
Meon Capital	MC.	1.0	3.3
Mid-States	**MST**	**7.5**	**7.9**
Mosaique	MQE	0.07	0.75
Netcentric Systems	NCS	0.1	0.35
Nettec (OL)	**NTC**	**10.6**	**9.6**
Optimisa	OPS	0.26	1.3
Quintessentaily English	QES	0.24	0.92
RAM Investment Group	**RAM**	**0.0**	**4.1**
RII	RIN	0.12	1.3

Safeland	SVO	2.6	4.34
Silentpoint	SLP	1.2	2.36
Streetnames	STM	1.5	2.44
Tom Hoskins	TMH	0.27	0.2
World Trade Systems	**WTS**	**0.09**	**0.57**
West 175	WEP	0.23	0.16
Zyzygy	ZYZ	0.7	3.36

This list is not comprehensive, and cash balances are approximate and subject to change.

Shell companies

Shell companies have little or no underlying business activities, usually consisting of cash and, more importantly, a stock market quote. Shell companies are interesting as they provide an alternative route for a company wanting a listing on one of the exchanges. Instead of an expensive IPO, a company can simply buy an already listed shell company, and reverse into it.

Reverse takeovers (or *back door listings* as Australians accurately describe them), are often structured so as to allow a much bigger business easy access to a stock market quotation. The operation is conducted by the shell company buying the bigger company for shares, such that the large number issued effectively make the shareholders of the target company the effective majority owners of the combined company.

Any peripheral businesses are usually sold off and a change of name is a common feature. By my calculation there are over fifty shell companies listed on the UK market, mostly on AIM, but not all these companies will be suitable as a cheap listing vehicle. Issues to be considered are outstanding litigation or pension liabilities, and the sheer number of small shareholders who all have to be mailed with reports and accounts. Also, big controlling shareholders, like a long-standing family interest, can be a nuisance and make some cash shells unattractive.

On the plus side, there may be historical revenue, or capital tax losses that could be utilised to offset against future profits.

The personalities currently involved with the shell company, or brought on board at the time of a reverse takeover, may also influence shareholders' perception of the company's prospects. Probably the best known of all is Michael Edelson, the Shellmeister, having brought to market around eighteen shells so far.

UK ADRs

Below is a list of UK companies that have American Depositary Receipts (ADRs) that trade in the US.

Company name	Ticker	CUSIP	Ratio	Exchange	Sector
10 GROUP PLC	TENPY	880244 10 8	1 : 1500	OTC	HOLDING & INVESTMENT COMPANIES
3DM WORLDWIDE PLC	TDMWY	885547 10 9	1 : 10	OTC	CHEMICALS
4IMPRINT GROUP PLC	FOREY	35104M 10 2	1 : 2	OTC	COMMERCIAL & INDUSTRIAL SERVICES
ABBEY NATIONAL PLC	ANBPRB	002920 70 0	1 : 1	NYSE	BANKS
ABBEY NATIONAL PLC	ABYNY	002920 10 6	1 : 2	OTC	BANKS
ACAMBIS PLC	ACAM	004286 10 0	1 : 2	NASDAQ	PHARMACEUTICALS
ALLIED DOMECQ PLC	AED	019121 20 1	1 : 4	NYSE	BEVERAGES
AMARIN CORP PLC	AMRN	023111 10 7	1 : 1	NASDAQ	PHARMACEUTICALS
AMVESCAP PLC	AVZ	03235E 10 0	1 : 2	NYSE	FINANCIAL SERVICES
ANGLO AMERICAN PLC	AAUK	03485P 10 2	1 : 1	NASDAQ	MINING
ANTOFAGASTA PLC	ANFGY	037189 10 7	1 : 2	OTC	MINING
APPLIED OPTICAL TECHNOLOGIES PLC	AXOPY	03822M 10 1	1 : 10	OTC	COMMERCIAL & INDUSTRIAL SERVICES
ARCOPLATE HOLDINGS PLC	APHUY	03965Q 10 9	1 : 1	OTC	TEXTILES
ARM HOLDINGS PLC	ARMHY	042068 10 6	1 : 3	NASDAQ	SEMICONDUCTORS
ASSOCIATED BRITISH FOODS PLC	ASBFY	045519 40 2	1 : 1	OTC	FOOD PRODUCTS & SERVICES
ASTRAZENECA PLC	AZN	046353 10 8	1 : 1	NYSE	PHARMACEUTICALS

ATLANTIC CASPIAN RESOURCES PLC	ALCRY	048277 10 7	1 : 0.001	OTC	OIL & GAS
BAA PLC	BAAPY	05518L 20 6	1 : 1	OTC	ENGINEERING & CONSTRUCTION
BAE SYSTEMS PLC	BAESY	05523R 10 7	1 : 4	OTC	AEROSPACE
BARCLAYS PLC	BCS	06738E 20 4	1 : 4	NYSE	BANKS
BENFIELD GROUP LTD	BFLDY	081841 10 8	1 : 2	OTC	INSURANCE
BERKELEY TECHNOLOGY LTD	BKLYY	8437M 10 7	1 : 10	OTC	FINANCIAL SERVICES
BESPAK PLC	BPAKY	086342 10 2	1 : 1	OTC	HEALTHCARE PRODUCTS & SERVICES
BG GROUP PLC	BRG	055434 20 3	1 : 5	NYSE	OIL & GAS
BHP BILLITON PLC	BBL	05545E 20 9	1 : 2	NYSE	MINING
BIOPROGRESS PLC	BPRG	090657 10 7	1 : 10	NASDAQ	PHARMACEUTICALS
BOC GROUP PLC	BOX	055617 60 9	1 : 2	NYSE	CHEMICALS
BOM HOLDINGS		055919 20 3	1 : 1	OTC	HOLDING & INVESTMENT COMPANIES
BOOTS GROUP PLC	BOOYY	099482 10 1	1 : 2	OTC	RETAIL SERVICES
BP PLC	BP	055622 10 4	1 : 6	NYSE	OIL & GAS
BRITISH AIRWAYS PLC	BAB	110419 30 6	1 : 10	NYSE	AIRLINES
BRITISH AMERICAN TOBACCO PLC	BTI	110448 10 7	1 : 2	AMEX	AGRICULTURE
BRITISH ENERGY PLC	BGYNY	110793 40 3	1 : 75	OTC	ELECTRIC UTILITY
BRITISH LAND CO PLC	BTLCY	110828 10 0	1 : 1	OTC	REAL ESTATE
BRITISH SKY BROADCASTING PLC	BSY	111013 10 8	1 : 4	NYSE	MEDIA

BT GROUP PLC	BTY	05577E 10 1	1 : 10	NYSE	TELECOMMUNICATIONS
BUNZL PLC	BNL	120738 30 7	1 : 5	NYSE	COMMERCIAL & INDUSTRIAL SERVICES
CABLE & WIRELESS PLC	CWP	126830 20 7	1 : 3	NYSE	TELECOMMUNICATIONS
CADBURY SCHWEPPES PLC	CSG	127209 30 2	1 : 4	NYSE	FOOD PRODUCTS & SERVICES
CAMBRIDGE ANTIBODY TECHNOLOGY GROUP PLC	CATG	132148 10 7	1 : 1	NASDAQ	BIOTECHNOLOGY
CARADON PLC		140910 10 0	1 : 1	OTC	HOLDING & INVESTMENT COMPANIES
CARNIVAL PLC	CUK	14365C 10 3	1 : 1	NYSE	ENTERTAINMENT
CATALYST MEDIA GROUP PLC	CLYMY	14887E 10 8	1 : 10	OTC	ELECTRONICS
CATER BARNARD PLC	CRBDY	14911M 10 0	1 : 50	OTC	FINANCIAL SERVICES
CATLIN GROUP LTD	CNGRY	149188 10 4	1 : 2	OTC	INSURANCE
CENTRICA PLC	CPYYY	15639K 30 0	1 : 10	OTC	GAS PRODUCTION & SERVICES
CHARTERHALL PLC	CTHAY	161905 20 3	1 : 1	OTC	HOLDING & INVESTMENT COMPANIES
CHLORIDE GROUP	CDGPY	170262 20 8	1 : 5	OTC	ELECTRICAL MANUFACTURING
COLT TELECOM GROUP PLC	COLT	196877 10 4	1 : 4	NASDAQ	TELECOMMUNICATIONS
COMPASS GROUP PLC	CMPGY	20449X 20 3	1 : 1	OTC	FOOD PRODUCTS & SERVICES
COOKSON GROUP PLC	CKSNY	216379 10 7	1 : 5	OTC	MANUFACTURING
CORPORATE SERVICES GROUP PLC	CPSVY	220036 30 5	1 : 5	OTC	COMMERCIAL & INDUSTRIAL SERVICES

CORUS GROUP PLC	CGA	22087M 10 1	1 : 10	NYSE	METAL PRODUCTION & DISTRIBUTION
DANKA BUSINESS SYSTEMS PLC	DANKY	236277 10 9	1 : 4	NASDAQ	OFFICE EQUIPMENT
DIAGEO PLC	DEO	25243Q 20 5	1 : 4	NYSE	BEVERAGES
DISPLAY.IT HOLDINGS PLC	DYITY	25469N 10 0	1 : 1	OTC	INTERNET PRODUCTS & SERVICES
DIXONS GROUP PLC	DXNGY	255875 20 5	1 : 3	OTC	RETAIL SERVICES
EBOOKERS PLC	EBKR	278725 10 6	1 : 2	NASDAQ	INTERNET PRODUCTS & SERVICES
EIDOS PLC	EIDSY	282485 10 1	1 : 1	NASDAQ	SOFTWARE
EMI GROUP PLC	EMIPY	268694 20 5	1 : 2	OTC	ENTERTAINMENT
ENERGIS PLC	ENGSY	29266H 10 0	1 : 5	OTC	TELECOMMUNICATIONS
ENODIS PLC	ENO	293491 10 6	1 : 4	NYSE	HOLDING & INVESTMENT COMPANIES
EUROTUNNEL PLC	ETNLY	298799 30 5	1 : 2	OTC	TRANSPORTATION
FRIENDS PROVIDENT PLC	FRDPY	35851M 10 7	1 : 10	OTC	INSURANCE
FUTUREMEDIA PLC	FMDAY	360912 10 9	1 : 1	NASDAQ	INTERNET PRODUCTS & SERVICES
GALLAHER GROUP PLC	GLH	363595 10 9	1 : 4	NYSE	AGRICULTURE
GENEMEDIX PLC	GNMXY	36870R 10 1	1 : 1	OTC	BIOTECHNOLOGY
GKN PLC	GKNLY	361755 60 6	1 : 1	OTC	AUTO PARTS & EQUIPMENT
GLAXO-SMITHKLINE PLC	GSK	37733W 10 5	1 : 2	NYSE	PHARMACEUTICALS
GOLDSHORE HOLDINGS PLC	GPPHY	381485 10 1	1 : 10	OTC	ADVERTISING
GRANGER TELECOM HOLDING PLC		387169 10 5	1 : 4	144A/REGS	TELECOMMUNICATIONS

GRESHAM HOTEL GROUP PLC	RYHOY	783500 20 0	1 : 2	OTC	HOTELS & MOTELS
GRIFFIN GROUP PLC	GGPFY	398227 10 8	1 : 50	OTC	FINANCIAL SERVICES
GUS PLC	GUSSY	40330M 10 8	1 : 1	OTC	RETAIL SERVICES
HANSON PLC	HAN	411349 10 3	1 : 5	NYSE	BUILDING PRODUCTS & MATERIALS
HBOS PLC	HBOOY	42205M 10 6	1 : 3	OTC	BANKS
HILTON GROUP PLC	HLTGY	43283M 10 9	1 : 2	OTC	ENTERTAINMENT
HSBC EUROPEAN ABSOLUTE LTD		44328N 20 1	1 : 10	144A/REGS	FINANCIAL SERVICES
HSBC HOLDINGS PLC	HBC	404280 40 6	1 : 5	NYSE	BANKS
IMPERIAL CHEMICAL INDUSTRIES PLC	ICI	452704 50 5	1 : 4	NYSE	CHEMICALS
IMPERIAL TOBACCO GROUP PLC	ITY	453142 10 1	1 : 2	NYSE	AGRICULTURE
INDEPENDENT ENERGY HLDGS PLC	INYYQ	45384X 10 8	1 : 1	OTC	ELECTRIC UTILITY
INSIGNIA SOLUTIONS INC	INSG	45766J 10 7	1 : 1	NASDAQ	SOFTWARE
INTER-CONTINENTAL HOTELS GROUP PLC	IHG	458573 10 2	1 : 1	NYSE	HOTELS & MOTELS
INTERNATIONAL POWER PLC		46018W 10 2	1 : 10	144A/REGS	ELECTRIC UTILITY
INTERNATIONAL POWER PLC	IPR	46018M 10 4	1 : 10	NYSE	ELECTRIC UTILITY
INVENSYS PLC	IVNSY	461204 10 9	1 : 2	OTC	MANUFACTURING

IS HIMALAYAN FUND NV		46419V 10 9	1 : 10	144A/REGS	FINANCIAL SERVICES
J SAINSBURY PLC	JSAIY	466249 20 8	1 : 4	OTC	FOOD PRODUCTS & SERVICES
J.D. WETHERSPOON PLC	JDWPY	472146 10 9	1 : 5	OTC	RETAIL SERVICES
JKX OIL & GAS PLC	JKXOY	47758M 10 6	1 : 25	OTC	OIL & GAS
JOHNSON MATTHEY PLC	JMPLY	479142 30 9	1 : 2	OTC	CHEMICALS
KEYWORLD INVESTMENTS PLC	KYYYY	493724 10 8	1 : 500	OTC	ENTERTAINMENT
KIDDE PLC	KIDPY	493793 10 3	1 : 10	OTC	COMMERCIAL & INDUSTRIAL SERVICES
KINGFISHER PLC	KGFHY	495724 40 3	1 : 2	OTC	RETAIL SERVICES
LAURA ASHLEY HOLDINGS PLC	LARAY	518581 20 2	1 : 5	OTC	RETAIL SERVICES
LEGAL & GENERAL GROUP PLC	LGGNY	52463H 10 3	1 : 5	OTC	INSURANCE
LIBERTY INTERNATIONAL PLC	LBYIY	530616 10 1	1 : 1	OTC	REAL ESTATE
LLOYDS TSB GROUP PLC	LYG	539439 10 9	1 : 4	NYSE	BANKS
LONDON FINANCE AND INVESTMENT GROUP PLC	LFVGY	541814 20 8	1 : 1	OTC	FINANCIAL SERVICES
LONMIN PLC	LNMIY	54336Q 20 3	1 : 1	OTC	MINING
M 2003 PLC	MTWOY	553793 10 0	1 : 2	OTC	TELECOMMUNICATIONS
MARCONI CORP PLC	MRCIY	56630M 10 1	1 : 2	NASDAQ	TELECOMMUNICATIONS
MARKS & SPENCER GROUP PLC	MAKSY	570912 10 5	1 : 6	OTC	RETAIL SERVICES

MATCHNET PLC		576660 10 4	1 : 1	144A/REGS	INTERNET PRODUCTS & SERVICES
MITCHELLS & BUTLERS PLC	MLB	60668M 20 7	1 : 1	NYSE	RETAIL SERVICES
MMO2 PLC	OOM	55309W 10 1	1 : 10	NYSE	TELECOMMUNICATIONS
NATIONAL GRID TRANSCO PLC	NGG	636274 10 2	1 : 5	NYSE	ELECTRIC UTILITY
NDS GROUP PLC	NNDS	628891 10 3	1 : 1	NASDAQ	INTERNET PRODUCTS & SERVICES
NOVAR PLC	NVARY	66987Q 10 0	1 : 1	OTC	MANUFACTURING
OLD MUTUAL PLC		680031 10 1	1 : 10	44A/REGS	INSURANCE
PEARSON PLC	PSO	705015 10 5	1 : 1	NYSE	MEDIA
PENINSULAR AND ORIENTAL STEAM NAVIGATION CO /THE	POSRY	707190 40 1	1 : 2	OTC	TRANSPORTATION
PETER HAMBRO MINING PLC	POGNY	71602M 10 4	1 : 2	OTC	MINING
PHYTOPHARM PLC	PHYOY	71942W 10 1	1 : 2	OTC	PHARMACEUTICALS
PLANESTATION GROUP PLC	PGPFY	72702M 10 1	1 : 50	OTC	REAL ESTATE
PREMIER FARNELL PLC	PFP	74050U 10 7	1 : 2	NYSE	ELECTRONICS
PREMIER FARNELL PLC	PFPPR	74050U 20 6	1 : 1	NYSE	ELECTRONICS
PREMIER OIL PLC	PMOIY	740536 10 7	1 : 1	OTC	OIL & GAS
PRESTBURY HOLDINGS PLC	PBRYY	74111X 10 8	1 : 10	OTC	FINANCIAL SERVICES
PRO-MARKET GLOBAL PLC	PMKGY	74267N 10 2	1 : 20	OTC	COMMERCIAL & INDUSTRIAL SERVICES
PROTHERICS PLC	POTUY	743707 10 1	1 : 4	OTC	BIOTECHNOLOGY
PROVALIS PLC	PVLS	74372Q 20 6	1 : 30	NASDAQ	PHARMACEUTICALS
PRUDENTIAL PLC	PUK	74435K 20 4	1 : 2	NYSE	INSURANCE
QXL RICARDO PLC	QXLRY	74912W 50 7	1 : 250	OTC	INTERNET PRODUCTS & SERVICES

RANK GROUP PLC	RANKY	753037 10 0	1 : 2	NASDAQ	COMMERCIAL & INDUSTRIAL SERVICES
REDBUS INTERHOUSE PLC	RDBIY	757253 10 9	1 : 5	OTC	TELECOMMUNICATIONS
REED ELSEVIER PLC	RUK	758205 10 8	1 : 4	NYSE	MEDIA
RENTOKIL INITIAL PLC	RTOKY	760125 10 4	1 : 5	OTC	COMMERCIAL & INDUSTRIAL SERVICES
REUTERS GROUP PLC	RTRSY	76132M 10 2	1 : 6	NASDAQ	MEDIA
REXAM PLC	REXMY	761655 40 6	1 : 5	NASDAQ	PACKAGING & CONTAINERS
RIO TINTO PLC	RTP	767204 10 0	1 : 4	NYSE	MINING
ROLLS-ROYCE GROUP PLC	RYCEY	775781 20 6	1 : 5	OTC	AEROSPACE
ROVER GROUP PLC		779360 20 5	1 : 1	OTC	RETAIL SERVICES
ROYAL & SUN ALLIANCE INSURANCE GROUP	RSA	78004V 20 2	1 : 5	NYSE	INSURANCE
ROYAL BANK OF SCOTLAND GROUP PLC	RBSPRM	780097 79 6	1 : 1	NYSE	BANKS
ROYAL BANK OF SCOTLAND GROUP PLC	RBSPRL	780097 78 8	1 : 1	NYSE	BANKS
ROYAL BANK OF SCOTLAND GROUP PLC	RBSPRD	780097 60 6	1 : 1	NYSE	BANKS
ROYAL BANK OF SCOTLAND GROUP PLC	RBSPRG	780097 88 7	1 : 1	NYSE	BANKS
ROYAL BANK OF SCOTLAND GROUP PLC		780097 AG 6	1 : 1000	OTC	BANKS

ROYAL BANK OF SCOTLAND GROUP PLC		780097 AF 8	1 : 1000	OTC	BANKS
ROYAL BANK OF SCOTLAND GROUP PLC	RBSPRE	780097 70 5	1 : 1	NYSE	BANKS
ROYAL BANK OF SCOTLAND GROUP PLC	RBSPRF	780097 80 4	1 : 1	NYSE	BANKS
ROYAL BANK OF SCOTLAND GROUP PLC	RBSPRK	780097 82 0	1 : 1	NYSE	BANKS
ROYAL BANK OF SCOTLAND GROUP PLC	RBSPRJ	780097 85 3	1 : 1	NYSE	BANKS
ROYAL BANK OF SCOTLAND GROUP PLC	RBSPRI	780097 86 1	1 : 1	NYSE	BANKS
ROYAL BANK OF SCOTLAND GROUP PLC		780097 AE 1	1 : 1000	OTC	BANKS
ROYAL BANK OF SCOTLAND GROUP PLC	RBSPRH	780097 87 9	1 : 1	NYSE	BANKS
SABMILLER PLC		78572M 20 4	1 : 1	44A/REGS	BEVERAGES
SABMILLER PLC	SBMRY	78572M 10 5	1 : 1	OTC	BEVERAGES
SAGE GROUP PLC	SGPYY	78663S 10 2	1 : 4	OTC	SOFTWARE
SCHRODER VENTURES INTERNATIONAL INVESTMENT TRUST PLC		80809M 10 6	1 : 1	144A/REGS	FINANCIAL SERVICES
SCOTTISH & SOUTHERN ENERGY PLC	SSEZY	81012K 30 9	1 : 1	OTC	ELECTRIC UTILITY

SCOTTISH POWER PLC	SPI	81013T 70 5	1 : 4	NYSE	ELECTRIC UTILITY
SENETEK PLC	SNTKY	817209 30 7	1 : 1	OTC	HEALTHCARE PRODUCTS & SERVICES
SHELL TRANSPORT & TRADING CO PLC	SC	822703 60 9	1 : 6	NYSE	OIL & GAS
SHIRE PHARMACEUTICALS	SHPGY	82481R 10 6	1 : 3	NASDAQ	PHARMACEUTICALS
SIGNET GROUP PLC	SIG	82668L 87 2	1 : 10	NYSE	RETAIL SERVICES
SKYEPHARMA PLC	SKYE	830808 10 1	1 : 10	NASDAQ	PHARMACEUTICALS
SMITH & NEPHEW PLC	SNN	83175M 20 5	1 : 5	NYSE	HEALTHCARE PRODUCTS & SERVICES
SOPHEON PLC	SOPEY	83577P 10 3	1 : 10	OTC	COMPUTERS
SOUTHWEST RESOURCES PLC		845219 40 1	1 : 5	OTC	MINING
SPIRENT PLC	SPM	84856M 20 9	1 : 4	NYSE	TELECOMMUNICATIONS
SURFCONTROL PLC		868763 20 2	1 : 3	OTC	SOFTWARE
SURFCONTROL PLC		868763 10 3	1 : 3	144A/REGS	SOFTWARE
TATE & LYLE PLC	TATYY	876570 60 7	1 : 4	OTC	FOOD PRODUCTS & SERVICES
TAYLOR NELSON SOFRES PLC	TYNLY	877255 10 9	1 : 15	OTC	ADVERTISING
TESCO PLC	TSCDY	881575 30 2	1 : 3	OTC	FOOD PRODUCTS & SERVICES
THUS GROUP PLC	THSGY	886286 10 3	1 : 200	OTC	TELECOMMUNICATIONS
TOMKINS PLC	TKS	890030 20 8	1 : 4	NYSE	HOLDING & INVESTMENT COMPANIES
TPN HOLDINGS PLC	TPNHY	872958 10 3	1 : 1	OTC	HOLDING & INVESTMENT COMPANIES
TRINITY MIRROR PLC	TNMRY	89653Q 10 5	1 : 2	OTC	MEDIA
TULLOW OIL PLC	TUWLY	899415 10 3	1 : 10	OTC	OIL & GAS

UNICORN SERVICES PLC	UCRSY	904913 10 0	1 : 10	OTC	COMPUTERS
UNILEVER PLC	UL	904767 70 4	1 : 4	NYSE	FOOD PRODUCTS & SERVICES
UNITED KINGDOM OF GREAT BRITIAN & NORTHERN IRELAND	GBNIY	390254 20 9	1 : 20	OTC	FINANCIAL SERVICES
UNITED UTILITIES PLC	UU	91311Q 10 5	1 : 2	NYSE	WATER PRODUCTS & SERVICES
VEOS PLC	VEOSY	92334M 10 5	1 : 25	OTC	HEALTHCARE PRODUCTS & SERVICES
VERNALIS PLC	VNLS	92431M 10 7	1 : 2	NASDAQ	PHARMACEUTICALS
VI GROUP PLC	GVIP	92554H 10 9	1 : 20	OTC	SOFTWARE
VIRGIN EXPRESS HOLDINGS PLC	VIRGY	92765K 20 6	1 : 1	OTC	AIRLINES
VODAFONE GROUP PLC	VOD	92857W 10 0	1 : 10	NYSE	TELECOMMUNICATIONS
WARNER CHILCOTT PLC	WCRX	93443W 10 9	1 : 4	NASDAQ	PHARMACEUTICALS
WELLINGTON UNDERWRITING PLC		94966A 10 2	1 : 10	144A/REGS	INSURANCE
WEMBLEY PLC	WMBYY	950468 20 7	1 : 4	OTC	ENTERTAINMENT
WOLSELEY PLC	WOS	97786P 10 0	1 : 2	NYSE	DISTRIBUTION & TRADING SERVICES
WPP GROUP PLC	WPPGY	929309 30 0	1 : 5	NASDAQ	ADVERTISING
XENOVA GROUP PLC	XNVA	984111 30 2	1 : 10	NASDAQ	BIOTECHNOLOGY

Source: www.adr.com

Index